In this exhilarating descripti⟨ Earth, Radu Cinamar present⟨ the Inner Earth through the process of feeling and the effects that will develop from such an experience. To enhance the reader's understanding of this very guarded subject, *Inside the Earth — The Second Tunnel* includes multiple illustrations that include depictions of Inner Earth geography.

Familiar characters from the Transylvania Series also reappear, including the enigmatic Tibetan lama, Repa Sundhi, also known as Dr. Xien, who states:

> "If someone had a device or machine that could start up and go everywhere they want, especially towards the center of the Earth, the machine would be blocked and stop at a certain point because of the frequency of vibration to be found there. Just how far you can go with such a machine can be limited by reason of your own consciousness which can in and of itself restrict the dimensional range of such a device or the extent to which it can penetrate other realms. This applies to both human beings as well as material objects. Your ability to access such a region is determined by what your own individual frequency of consciousness can or will allow you to experience."

Inside the Earth — The Second Tunnel **is not only the** story of an exciting adventure, it is an opportunity for initiation as you explore the frequencies of your own inner nature.

❋

INSIDE THE EARTH
THE SECOND TUNNEL

By Radu Cinamar
Edited by Peter Moon

SkyBooks

NEW YORK

Cover art by Creative Circle Inc.
Typography by Creative Circle Inc.
Published by: Sky Books
           Box 769
           Westbury, New York 11590
           email: skybooks@yahoo.com
           website: www.timetraveleducationcenter.com
           www.skybooksusa.com
           www.digitalmontauk.com

Library of Congress Cataloging-in-Publication Data

Cinamar, Radu / Moon, Peter
      The Inner Earth — The Second Tunnel
      240 pages
      ISBN 978-1-937859-20-6
1. Body, Mind, Spirit: Occultism 2. Body, Mind, Spirit: General
Library of Congress Control Number

This book is dedicated to General Obadea

OTHER TITLES FROM
SKY BOOKS

by Preston Nichols and Peter Moon
The Montauk Project: Experiments in Time
Montauk Revisited: Adventures in Synchronicity
Pyramids of Montauk: Explorations in Consciousness
Encounter in the Pleiades: An Inside Look at UFOs
The Music of Time

by Peter Moon
The Black Sun: Montauk's Nazi-Tibetan Connection
Synchronicity and the Seventh Seal
The Montauk Book of the Dead
The Montauk Book of the Living
Spandau Mystery
The White Bat — The Alchemy of Writing

by Joseph Matheny with Peter Moon
Ong's Hat: The Beginning

by Stewart Swerdlow
Montauk: The Alien Connection
The Healer's Handbook: A Journey Into Hyperspace

by Alexandra Bruce
The Philadelphia Experiment Murder:
Parallel Universes and the Physics of Insanity

by Wade Gordon
The Brookhaven Connection

by Radu Cinamar with Peter Moon
Tranyslvanian Sunrise
Tranyslvanian Moonrise
Mystery of Egypt — The First Tunnel
The Secret Parchment

CONTENTS

INTRODUCTION — by Peter Moon............9

EDITOR'S NOTE — by Sorin Hurmuz............17

PRELUDE — by Radu Cinamar............19

CHAPTER ONE — A Powerful Shock............29

CHAPTER TWO — The Great Controversy............73

CHAPTER THREE — Tomassis, the Ancient Root.......111

CHAPTER FOUR — Apellos, the Crystal City............139

CHAPTER FIVE — The Guardian............167

CHAPTER SIX — The Magic Portal in Yosemite.......187

CHAPTER SEVEN — The Center of the Planet and the
Sublime World of Shamhala....209

EPILOGUE — by Peter Moon............233

LEFT PROFILE OF THE ROMANIAN SPHINX

This is the sphinx beneath which, according to Radu Cinamar, there is a chamber built some 50,000 years ago which contains technology that is far more advanced that our current human technology.

RIGHT PROFILE OF THE ROMANIAN SPHINX

This is the same rock as the above sphinx but the photograph is from the other side. Behind the "cat's whiskers" is the shape of a woman with long hair which is more pronounced in color. It is not graffiti but seems to be crafted by nature. There are many rock formations in this part of the world that appear to have been designed by superior beings who utilized the elements of nature to create mysterious art work.

INTRODUCTION

For those of you who have picked up this book without any prior knowledge of the circumstances surrounding Radu Cinamar and his previous work, I will lay out a background and summary. During the Cold War, there was a natural alliance between the two communist nations of Romania and the People's Republic of China. Trying to keep up with the West in regards to the most advanced and esoteric methods of reconnaissance and espionage, the Romanians sought out the help of the Chinese as they did not really trust the Russians. As part of a cultural exchange program whereby Chinese students were able to participate in educational programs in Romania, the Chinese government sent the Romanians an expert in parapsychology who would set up a secret department that would deal with all abnormal occurrences. These were referred to as "K events," but in pop culture terms of today, these might now be termed as "X-File" events. Known as Department Zero, this special unit was only known to the head of state and the head of security. Besides housing and caring for paranormal subjects, Department Zero also trained them. The expert in parapsychology who set up this unique department is known to us as Dr. Xien, and he was introduced to us in the first book of this series, *Transylvanian Sunrise*.* Although Dr. Xien is an intriguing character, we do not learn too much about him in that book. We do know that he was called in after the birth of another very interesting character who also turns out to be one of the progenitors of the *Transylvania Series*. His name is Cezar Brad, and he is born with an umbilical cord that is so thick, the doctors have to use an ordinary saw to sever it. As this is an anomaly, Cezar comes under the scrutiny and eventual tutelage of Department Zero and forms a close personal relationship with Dr. Xien from a very young age. Cezar is trained in a host of spiritual and psychic disciplines that would rival the best your imagination might offer.

As fate would clearly demonstrate, Dr. Xien was grooming Cezar to serve as a steward and guardian for what is arguably considered the greatest archeological discovery in the history of Mankind: a secret and previously inaccessible chamber beneath the Romanian Sphinx containing futuristic holographic technology that was put together some 50,000 years ago.

---

* The book you are reading now, *Inside the Earth — The Second Tunnel*, is the fifth in a series of books by Radu Cinamar which are collectively, along with Peter Moon's *The White Bat*, known as the *Transylvania Series*. The previous works include *Transylvanian Sunrise*, *Transylvanian Moonrise*, *Mystery of Egypt — The First Tunnel*, and *The Secret Parchment — Five Tibetan Initiation Techniques*.

In what could be termed a virtual Noah's Ark that far exceeds the thinking and experiential capacity of those who lived in biblical times (or even in our own times for that matter), this chamber includes technology whereby one can place their hand on a table and see their own DNA rendered in three-dimensional holograms. Other devices on the table enable one to see the DNA of alien species from other planets with accompanying star renderings so that one can see where they actually originate from. By placing two hands on different parts of the table, one can also "mix" the DNA of two species so as to see how they might look if hybridized. As the tables themselves are six feet high, the creatures who built them were gigantic compared to humans of today.

This remarkable chamber also includes a "projection hall" whereby one can see a holographic rendition of the history of Earth that is particularly tailored to the individuality of whomever might be viewing it. This history, however, abruptly cuts off in about the Fifth Century A.D., perhaps because it requires some sort of software update. One of the more intriguing aspects of the Projection Hall is that it also contains three mysterious tunnels that lead into the bowels of the Earth and similar facilities in Iraq, Mongolia, Tibet and also beneath the Giza Plateau in Egypt.

Although Cezar, through the tutelage of Dr. Xien, was set up by fate to be the overseer of this remarkable archeological discovery, it was not his role to write the story of what was found and its implications. As these events were unfolding, Cezar handpicked Radu Cinamar to write these volumes. Serving as a mentor to Radu, Cezar gave him a rapid fire education in all of the political machinations going on behind this discovery while also introducing him to the world of psychic phenomena and esoteric studies. We learn about this in the first volume, *Transylvanian Sunrise*, but we are not told exactly why Cezar picked Radu. What I can tell you from what I have learned thus far is that Cezar is a remarkably adept individual, and he knew precisely what he was doing. His psychic sensibilities are quite formidable and proved to be accurate in this case. Radu got the job done, and with the release of this book, he now has five volumes in English.

You might think that this discovery was a wonderful opportunity to enlighten Mankind and take advantage of all that this newly discovered technology has to offer for the benefit of humanity at large. Many, if not most, of the Romanians in the government who were privy to the discovery viewed it that way. Circumstances, however, dictated otherwise.

Cezar informed Radu that the actual discovery of this secret and previously unknown chamber took place when the Pentagon discovered it via the use of ground penetrating radar that operated through satellites. It is understandable that the Americans would use all technology at their disposal for reconnaissance purposes as well as to scrutinize all geographical anomalies and resources on the planet. Right or wrong, this is the purpose of the Department of Defense. What was most challenging about this intelligence, however, was that Masonic interests in the Pentagon funneled this information to a leader in Italian Freemasonry, a Signore Massini, who represents a hidden global elite that wanted access to and control of this chamber for themselves. Accordingly, Massini approached Cezar who was then the head of Department Zero and sought his cooperation. Cezar, who did not trust Massini, was forced to cooperate to a certain extent due to political circumstances. Thus, the evil interests of an Italian Freemason forged an unprecedented alliance between Romania and America with the former suddenly being admitted to NATO. The specifics of these political intrigues are detailed in the book *Transylvanian Sunrise* which is primarily the story of Cezar's life and his involvement with the uncovering of these amazing artifacts.

While the enigmatic and mysterious Dr. Xien set the stage for Cezar to uncover this secret chamber through rigorous training and education, he is a distant memory when the discovery is made and seemingly completely uninvolved in any tangible way with the political machinations and evil intrigues which allowed it to even take place. Dr. Xien, however, is an interested party and a definite progenitor of the information revealed in these books, and this comes into clear view in the second book of the series, *Transylvanian Moonrise — A Secret Initiation in the Mysterious Land of the Gods*.

Transylvanian Moonrise begins with an editor's note from the Romanian editor, Sorin Hurmuz, who includes numerous excerpts from the Romanian press that not only corroborate Cezar's story as told by Radu but give insights into why it is credible. Above and beyond these facts, it might interest you to know that a key area near the Romanian Sphinx is blacked out on Google Earth. Besides that, Americans were seen en masse during the time of the excavations that were taking place near the Romanian Sphinx in 2003. I have also spoken to several well-placed people in Romania who believe the general story to have merit. Exactly what has taken place and all of the details are still largely a mystery, but Radu's books offer us the only clues. In addition to that, they are remarkable stories and teaching devices which integrate the mundane aspects of politics with some of the most esoteric concepts of occultism as well as the cutting edge of technology.

Radu's narrative in *Transylvanian Moonrise* begins with a mysterious man named Elinor trying to contact the enigmatic author through his publisher, Sorin Hurmuz, who has generally been instructed to stonewall any people wishing to meet with Radu. In fact, Sorin has never met with Radu and only communicates with him by special courier or with a prearranged phone card. When it is eventually discovered that Elinor is speaking on behalf of a Tibetan lama, both Sorin and Radu change their tune and a meeting is eventually arranged. This meeting is filled with a panoply of metaphysical revelations which present an entirely new paradigm by which to view the events described in *Transylvanian Sunrise*. After an amazing indoctrination into the ancient art of alchemy and the prospects of immortality, Radu meets the lama who reveals himself to be none other than Dr. Xien and explains that he once served in the royal court at Lhasa under the name of Repa Sundhi at the time of the Chinese invasion of Tibet. Escaping that purge, he somehow ended up in the employ of the Chinese government and adopted a different identity as Dr. Xien.

Repa Sundhi has a very specific agenda for this meeting with Radu and it has to do with what is the focal point of the fourth book in the *Transylvania Series: The Secret Parchment — Five Tibetan Initiation Techniques* (more on that later). In *Transylvanian Moonrise*, Radu learns that the lama wants to take him to the Apuseni Mountains of Transylvania. Once there, a mysterious but well-described space-translation takes place that literally transports them (as well as Elinor, who remains in their company) to certain rarefied high peaks of Tibet which are inaccessible to humans by normal transportation means. Radu is escorted into a cave where he meets another progenitor of the *Transylvania Series*. Her name is Machandi and she is a blue goddess and tantric dakini who not only educates and initiates Radu but gives him an ancient manuscript which is to be translated from ancient Tibetan and published, first in the Romanian language. Having finally been translated into English, it is the centerpiece of *The Secret Parchment*.

While *Transylvanian Moonrise* refers to the characters in *Transylvanian Sunrise* and the lama is included in the dramatic events that take place, the two books are astonishingly different and offer complementary views of the overall scenario from completely different perspectives. The third book in the series, *Mystery of Egypt — The First Tunnel*, is no exception. Radu is recruited to join Department Zero on a journey with Cezar into the mysterious "First Tunnel" in the Projection Hall of the Bucegi complex. This leads to a hidden chamber beneath the Giza Plateau in Egypt. What they find there is no less astonishing than what has already been offered in the first two books. The purpose of the mission is to recover neatly organized slate-like tablets that are in fact a type of ancient "DVD" that project holographic "memories" of the history of the world. The tablets do not require a projector and are so numerous that they can only hope to return a portion of them to their home base, after which they will be sent to America for detailed study. Even though they cannot recover everything in one mission, what they do retrieve would take a team of viewers a considerable amount of time to view.

There is also an occult chamber containing a device consisting primarily of huge crystals that facilitates the projection of one's consciousness back into time. It is not a physical time travel device. It should be noted that it requires a certain amount of psychic and esoteric development to be able to withstand the rigors of projecting oneself into time, even if the physical body is not being utilized. We also learn that this device is bioresonant in that it is tuned to the physiological, mental and emotional conditions of the subject as well as their own past experiences. In other words, you would have different experiences than would I and so on.

Another intriguing aspect of the time device is that there is a certain amount of censorship present. When Cezar attempts to project his consciousness into time in order to see who created the device, he encounters blockages. While it is informative and useful in certain respects, it contains mysteries which it does not want penetrated, at least at this particular time. All of this gives rise to interesting speculation.

These censorship issues further fuel the controversy Cezar ignites by relaying his initial experience in the time device whereupon he returns to the time of Jesus in the First Century. Radu also recounts what he saw in his original experiences in the Projection Hall (beneath the Romanian Sphinx) when he witnessed events surrounding the crucifixion of Christ. This account contains UFOs wreaking havoc amidst a virtually insurmountable thunder storm while a fearing populace scrambles to save their own lives. It leaves us with a hornets nest of information, the result of which has been more than a few questioning the veracity of the authors. I should add, however, that most of the reading audience thus far has not blinked at the accounts given. They have enjoyed the book and are not judgmental about the authors. What is perhaps the most relevant aspect of this experience, however, is the fact that the device which facilitates it is bioresonant. Whether the events presented are indeed real in a conventional sense, they are certainly events that the collective consciousness has wrestled with for thousands of years.

What happens in *Mystery of Egypt*, however, is superceded by what occurs in the fourth volume, *The Secret Parchment*. Radu finds himself in the middle of the political and conspiratorial intrigue that is swirling around the effort to control the holographic chamber beneath the Romanian Sphinx. Accordingly, Radu is sent to the United States to attend a remote viewing program in the Pentagon, all in an effort to defuse the rising political tensions. As the conspiratorial intrigues escalate into a full scale political and esoteric war, there is an intervention by superior spiritual forces, one of which includes Radu being recalled to Romania in order to meet with Repa Sundhi to facilitate the translation of the ancient Tibetan manuscript or "secret parchment" which had been given to him by Machandi as described in *Transylvanian Moonrise*. While the parchment presents five invaluable techniques for spiritual advancement (these are not the same as the already known yoga exercises known as the "Five Tibetans"), its very presence in the world has ignited a series of quantum events, extending from a bizarre structure emerging from the snow in Antarctica, serving an antenna function, which is at the crossroads between signals to Jupiter's moon Europa as well as Mount McKinley, and Transylvania. As incredible as the discovery of this extraterrestrial connection is, it only escalates the attempt to undermine the structure of Romania's Department Zero when the Americans learn that the signal to Transylvania reveals a passage way of solid gold tunnels, extending miles into the underground, leading to ancient hieroglyphics, embedded in gold, indicating the locale as the nexus of the Inner Earth where "all the worlds unite." Not too far from the nexus, accessible through more passageways of pure gold, is an incredible room of golden thrones with panels of yet more hieroglyphics and a mysterious portal that appears to be a direct conduit to outer space; and, presumably, an outer space of another universe. These discoveries were made by a certain Professor Constantine who, upon reporting them and taking a team from the government to investigate, was whisked away and never heard from again. Although the investigators were killed, Professor Constantine was able to make a summary report to Cezar Brad; and the file for such was deemed to be the highest state secret of the country of Romania. Even so, Department Zero was unable to find any access to these passageways and, despite considerable effort, no further discoveries were made. Although Machandi's secret parchment is translated and we are treated to its specific wisdom, *The Secret Parchment — Five Tibetan Initiation Techniques* leaves us with a very great mystery that is left dangling.

I also contribute to the book by revealing my own adventures in the area and learning of the ancient legends and how these fit into the scheme of Radu's adventures. It turns out that Professor Constantine was indeed a real character who disappeared, and I am even shown where he once lived. There is also a Valley of the Golden Thrones, and it is in this region that I make one of the most remarkable discoveries that I have ever stumbled upon.

Although it has not been mentioned in any of the previous books, I was led to a cave by a Romanian archeologist in 2014. Known as Cioclovina Cave, it is the site of one of the greatest archeological finds in Romania which indicate a civilization did indeed occupy caverns within the inner earth and in the vicinity mentioned by Radu. Cioclovina Cave represents a sort of grand central cave station with some seven other caves interlinking with it, representing at least seven kilometers of tunnels.

While the aforementioned findings concerning Cioclovina Cave are of great relevance with regard to Radu's claims, there is an even more startling confirmation from Dr. David Anderson, my scientist friend who originally brought me to Romania in 2008. In an interview conducted by myself in 2015, he revealed for the first time that Cioclovina Cave was the site of the largest discharge of space-time motive force ever recorded. Space-time motive force is a term Dr. Anderson coined to signify an energy that is released as a result of time dilation that occurs in the process of frame-dragging. If you are further interested in this aspect and would like a full explanation, you can watch the video series *Time Travel Theory Explained* at my website *www.timetraveleducationcenter.com*. This function is also explained in the appendix of the book *Transylvanian Moonrise*.

What all of this means in layman's terms is that Dr. Anderson's findings indicate that this area was the site of heavy duty time travel experiments. He was completely surprised that I happened to come across this very area by happenstance during my adventures in Romania. Note that this area was never a targeted area of interest for me. I had an off day and was brought there by an archeologist I knew at his instigation. He had no idea of the time experiments or the like. The archeologist, by the way, told me that the stories I relayed to him about Radu's books, which he had not read at that point, correlated with many stories he had heard about the area.

While there are many so-called "side tunnels" or supplementary threads of great interest that involve Dr. Anderson and my other associates in Romania, I am getting off subject. Radu is very well aware of Dr. Anderson and mention's him in the prelude to this new book. It is quite possible that all of these different threads might coalesce into a single homogeneous thread some day; but for now, we will get to the subject at hand: *Inside the Earth — The Second Tunnel*. And just so you understand, the Second Tunnel refers to one of a series of three tunnels in the projection room located within the chamber beneath the Romanian Sphinx. The First Tunnel, named in the title of the third book in the series, *Mystery of Egypt — The First Tunnel*, leads to a chamber beneath the Giza Plateau. The Second Tunnel, the subject of this book, leads to underground cities and installations. The Third Tunnel leads to Tibet with an offshoot branch to the Carpathians (near Buzau, Romania) and then towards Iraq; and from there to Mongolia and the Gobi Plateau.

As you have now been either oriented or reoriented to the subject and hand, you are now prepared to read Radu's most recent work: *Inside the Earth — The Second Tunnel*. Radu was silent for eight years after completing *The Secret Parchment* and, as I said earlier, a very great mystery was left dangling. This hiatus is now at end, and you can begin unfolding this great mystery as you turn the page.

Peter Moon
Long Island
September 27, 2017

INSIDE THE EARTH

EDITOR'S NOTE

We have a saying in Romania (*Nu aduce anul, ce aduce ceasul!*) that does not translate so smoothly into English. Perhaps the best English translation reads as follows: "What the year has not brought us can surprisingly manifest in a sudden single moment." Such was it that in the month of February 2017 when, after so many years of stillness and not hearing anything from Radu, that all of a sudden, in just one moment, everything changed. Finally, he reappeared, ready to give answers to all of the many readers that have continually asked me about Radu's return, his work, and anything else you might imagine.

In life, there are moments that will cause you to think in a rather profound manner. For example, Einstein said, "There are two ways of living your life: as if no miracles would exist or that everything would be a miracle."

Maybe it is too much to say that Radu's return would be like a miracle for us, but it is indeed a very big surprise for all of the readers of the Transylvania series; and this is especially so because this volume contains a lot of information that represents gold for us. Radu will answer a lot of questions. He will also have a lot of propositions and opinions, but besides that, he will be able to better explain some mysteries that until now we would find unresolvable.

In a few lines, Radu informed me that this is the exact right moment for him to continue the revelations concerning the projection room in the Bucegi Mountains, also mentioning that this series of volumes will not stop here and that what he will publish in the future will bring amazing elements about the past and future of Mankind to the attention of both his readers as well as the scientific community.

Everything that Radu has ever sent to us over the years has been read with great intensity and emotion and we have discovered a lot of magic inside of the previous four volumes. We did, however, find it necessary to suggest a few minor changes to the text in this book. The reason for this is that certain information, if released indiscriminately, could have negative consequences on our publishing company as well as the Ministry of Internal Affairs. Radu immediately accepted these minor modifications and is gladly thanked for his understanding and prompt response.

This new volume, *Inside the Earth - The Second Tunnel,* represents a foundation for a new paradigm with regard to us understanding our own planet. At the same time, it offers an esoteric as well as a physical way to access the worlds of mystery inside the earth. No matter how we decide to view this book; and no matter how we interpret it, our concept about Terra, the Earth, has to be reevaluated.

PRELUDE

After publishing the fourth volume of the *Transylvania Series, The Secret Parchment - Five Tibetan Initiation Techniques,* I considered that whatever I had discovered and told in the original series of four books was enough. There was no intention of a deeper presentation on my behalf, and this was especially so by reason of the fact that my new position inside of Department Zero included much greater responsibility and would take up most of my time.

When I explained my point of view to Cezar, he agreed with me in a certain way, but he also said that the entire world needs to know this information and this includes the fact of the reality that exists beyond routine appearances. For this reason, he said that I should keep the idea before me of continuing the series and telling the world what I have discovered. At that time, however, I was way too enthusiastic about the course of events that had taken place inside of my own life and consequently did not pay attention to Cezar's advice. It was only after a few years that I came to realize the necessity of coming back to my writing in order to let the world know about my knowledge and experience. In fact, I consider it a must.

I should also add that a major factor with regard to my decision to resume writing has a lot to do with my readers. My editor, Sorin Hurmuz, let me know that after seven years of stillness and quietness on my part, there were many questions with regard to whether there would ever be another appearance of mine. Accordingly, this volume will give you many answers, and I hope that it will delight all of my readers in a special way. I must, however, mention a few things first.

For a few years now, different websites and blogs have appeared that were either using my name or the subjects that I have written about. Although such activities are the result of people having been inspired by my books to bring certain facts, mysteries and suppositions to the public's attention, I am not a party to such websites; and I should add that they really have nothing or little to do with what I have written about in the previous volumes. I do, however, appreciate this fact as being a positive one as the enthusiasm of the those posting these articles and information can definitely open new horizons to those that are interested in these topics. My only caveat is that you should be very careful in discerning the information that is presented.

It is an entirely different matter, however, with regard to the Facebook pages that use my name and definitely give the impression that I am the one behind it. While it is every human being's freedom to name their blog, website or social media sites however they want, I want to adopt a very radical position by stating very clearly and directly to all of my readers that I do not have nor did I ever have any connection to such sites or the people behind them nor the information that is presented. In fact, I cannot put it more clearly that I do not have anything to do with anything that is being said in the virtual space of mass media with regards to my own individual self or the subjects I have written about in the earlier volumes. This includes everything that has been said in this direction by way of postings, analysis, forums, personal opinions or articles that have sought to bring the topics of my books into discussion. The only way that I have chosen to make myself well known is through the four volumes that were sent to and published by DAKSHA Publishing Company (of Bucharest) that owns my rights for the volumes that have already appeared as well as for the ones that will appear in the future.

It is a very different point of discussion, however, when it comes to Mr. Peter Moon, the director of the publishing company Sky Books of New York, who has made a very elegant, adept, persistent and fundamental contribution to the primary subject of my written volumes. A very correct human being with a lot of integrity, he is very well prepared in the domain of esotericism, and I thank him for the effort of coming to Romania several times in order to inform himself in the best way that he could through all of the connections that he has taken the opportunity to create.

One of the significant portals of awareness opened by Peter Moon is the association he has managed to forge with Dr. David Anderson, a physicist who very well understands the necessity of shielding certain information almost totally. This is by reason of his position as a scientific consultant and sub-contractor for the Pentagon as well as every government agency of the USA that he has worked for. The subject of the volume that is presented here can be an excellent study for David.

I should also add that opinions about my own personal identity that are expressed in online websites or any other means of mass media are sometimes very funny when they are attempting to assimilate me in any possible way with another Romanian writer that has achieved considerable notoriety by publishing fiction books. For me, this presents a very big question mark. How can someone make this type of affirmation that has nothing to do with logic nor the education of a certain person?

For example, a comparative analysis can be easily done with regard to style, content, and the way he treats a subject as opposed to myself. So, because I want things to be as clear as possible, I strongly confirm here that, under any circumstances, I am not that person nor am I a group or organization that would have written the previous four volumes.

While there have been some factors having to do with politics or the secret services that have kind of pressured me to make known everything that I know, there have also been opposite forces and occult energies that have threatened me against communicating what I know or have seen. A lot of intrigues and interests swirl around the subject of this book, and the most difficult situation is that one is not allowed to say anything or almost nothing about what occurs. You will understand better if I explain a little about Department Zero.

Even though Department Zero is independent and very well integrated when it comes to state matters, it is still required to use a tremendous amount of diplomacy. General Obadea and Cezar had to engage is a considerable amount of intervention just so the first four volumes could be released to the public. Unfortunately, General Obadea is no longer here. In May 2011, he died because of a brain stroke. While I do not wish to speculate about that, I do want to remind everyone that the General was one of the deepest patrons of my country (Romania) and even though his influence was very hidden, it was very decisive in key moments for the state. General Obadea's death also represented a very important moment for the Department. In the beginning of 2012, the Department was in great danger of being dissolved and assimilated within another structure from inside the services. The position of Cezar Brad, however, and his strong influence and extraordinary ability in solving very delicate situations has made it possible to maintain the continuity of the Department. This not only enhanced his relationships with diplomatic factions and the secret services, it has earned him a lot of respect that has led to him being admired at a very high level. This includes foreign diplomatic channels as well as their own secret services.

As a result of new circumstances and necessities, the structure and operations of Department Zero have been rethought. As a natural course of events, the position of General Obadea has been taken over by Cezar; and in Cezar's place came Lieutenant Nicoara.

Prior to the restructuring of Department Zero, I had been in charge of the section for "unconventional" training or what some might translate as being "paranormal" training. Moreover, in 2014, I was handed the task of funding and conducting, inside of the Department, a special directive concerning collaboration with foreign secret services regarding "sensitive" information known as "limit operations." This refers to all of the "K type" phenomena that occurs both on the ground and in space but especially for such that has a connection with the Projection Room in Bucegi as well as the three tunnels within. Cezar's decision to entrust me to set up this section had to do with the experience I had gained in my relationships with certain American intelligence agencies. This was a result of all of the training I had undergone ten years ago in addition to numerous trips that I took afterwards to the United States or other locations, all of them having to do with "limit operations." Utilizing the knowledge of diplomacy that I had already gained allowed me to develop some relationships and useful bonds with the members of different services in the West.

The most significant benefit of these promotions was my own increase in authority which now gives me free and direct access to the Projection Room. We are not talking about a level of governmental security here but rather one of internal security, a special clearance that is exclusively authorized by Department Zero in liaison with a section from the Pentagon. This type of very special agreement was established in 2005 with the purpose of reducing, almost completely, any political interference. For example, the U.S. Defense Department and a specific Committee from the Romanian Parliament put pressure on to significantly extend the list of those who could be admitted to the Projection Room. They even attempted to actualize a certain control over the secret complex inside of the Bucegi Mountains.

At that particular time, both Colonel Obadea and Cezar realized it would be very difficult for them to handle the flow of forces and interests that were already targeting access to the secret complex in Bucegi. This is why, with all of the relationships and interventions, they first requested and then arranged for a reunion of both Romanian and American sides where the political participation was minimal: a representative from the defense departments of both countries. I do not want it to be misunderstood that this case was or is about a "military industrial complex," but rather a militarily secured complex. This had the purpose of keeping a certain balance of interests, all of which is very sensitive when it comes to the Bucegi location.

Previous discussions and arrangements implied and fostered a lot of tension. Delays were requested and even certain undercover threats were taking place from both sides. Eventually, however, both the military and political factions agreed upon the negotiations with the subject of "plausible denial" being addressed. For us, this was a diplomatic way of avoiding any "contribution" from the political sphere, the influences and interests of which are complicated. If these interests would have succeeded in gaining power or control of the Bucegi complex in one way or the other, things could easily have escalated out of control, especially in the context of today's geopolitical climate. Accordingly, an exclusive military type of control has been decided upon. Things are actually even more complicated concerning these matters, but I will stop here.

Free access to the Projection Room signified "a big breath of oxygen" for me. The death of General Obadea left an empty space in myself, and it also represented a big loss to the Department. Due to high external pressures that were aiming to take control of both Department Zero and the Bucegi complex, it was difficult to maintain smooth running of the Base for any length of time. But due to Cezar's personality, calmness and maturity, as well as the loyalty of other remarkable people inside or the Department, it was possible for Department Zero to continue its activity. Issues were brought up or created on both side of the Romanian and American Secret Services as well as the defense departments of both countries. To a certain extent, the situation was reminiscent of the previously mentioned circumstances from 2005; but now it was easier to solve due to the immeasurable experience that had been gained as well as the discoveries that have taken place.

From the American side, General Roddey had important and influential words to say; and this had to do, to a great extent, with his very close connection and friendship to General Obadea. At the bilateral meeting that took place in 2012, Admiral Ken Hudson, a special delegate of the Pentagon, made a surprisingly beneficial intervention that came along with what appeared to be a special mandate. Later on, Cezar confessed to me that the harmful influence of an important occult lodge had been removed from the organizational structure and this neutralized a lot of tensions and bilateral disagreements even though there were still some left to be solved.

Everything calmed down. Department Zero continued its activity with its structure improved and its funding increased. Our partnership with the Americans was prosperous even if it were only to be viewed from the perspective of the very advanced technology that they have furnished to guarantee security in the area of Bucegi. If I were to make a comparison of what I saw in 2003, when I was first introduced to the place, the exterior is currently unrecognizable. The landscape in the immediate area surrounding the entrance in the mountain was slightly modified in order to allow continuous surveillance and efficient control while two other areas have been put under holographic projection. Everything is now controlled from the inside of the mountain that was specially designed next to the entrance in the Great Gallery. To a certain extent, the inclination of the Americans was to reproduce their own base structure from Cheyenne Mountain. The technology they have brought in and applied at the external location in Bucegi, however, is much more advanced than what I noticed at Cheyenne Mountain.

Even though I was accompanied by Cezar inside of the Projection Room many times until 2014, I was then given free and individual access. The nature of this new function I have allows me to establish the list of people who are going to be next to visit the Room, who will accompany them and also the period of time assigned to the visit. The protocol is very strict and pretty complicated because, besides the required military staff, there are teams of scientists who periodically visit the location. Even though these teams are never larger than three people, document analysis shows that the place has been visited over the years by dozens of scientist from all over the world.

In the thirteen years that have passed by since the discovery in the Bucegi Mountains, only nine scientists have actually penetrated the inside of the Projection Room and studied what is found there. The rest of the teams referred to only studied material or data provided to the laboratory that was subsequently built inside of the mountain and next to the entrance inside the location or to another detached lab in the capital.

Many readers might imagine that the Great Gallery and the Projection Room represent some sort of a "museum" in which the flow of people is continuous and pretty intense. In this case, assessing the truth of the matter requires correctly understanding the nature of the discovery that has been made. This discovery represents a series of characteristics and phenomena that are often bewildering to the psychic and the mental state of the ordinary human being. I think the most appropriate rendering of what happens to someone after penetrating the Great Gallery can be made by using the phrase: "an unexpected transformation of behavior and thought." Once you get into the Projection Room, the mind strives to be isolated from memories or secondary thoughts. In a way that can hardly be described, the mind is kind of "suspended" and "quiet." The thoughts are rare and they blend with a kind of very deep emotion, almost having a sacred character. In the beginning, when I visited the place for the first time, I thought this sensation was being generated by the extraordinary greatness of the construction and the space there, by reason of the very advanced technology and the unique situation. In the years that followed, however, I figured out that the phenomena continually and identically repeats itself. In other words, it is not due to some subjective tendencies but is a consequence of the very special vibration that exists in that place.

The general impression is one of "another world." This is not only because of the specifics of the technology and the objects from inside but, above all, through an "intuitive knowledge" that appears and modifies the nature of one's thoughts and actions. The meditative and relaxation impulse is emphasized along with a feeling for noble and elevated things as well as for everything that is good, beautiful and imbued by a soul-uplifting aspiration.

We quickly realized that access to this special place can only be offered to a certain category of people who first require proper mental and physical training. Even the personnel assigned to routine periodic tasks either had to be chosen from a collection of superior officers or they had to take special training courses. Without proper psycho-mental training, any penetration inside of the Room will come with the risk of some bizarre manifestations that might occur subsequently. Cezar told me that these aspects were understood only after noticing the strange behavior of some soldiers who had been present immediately after the discovery of the complex inside of the mountain. Those people seemed disconnected from reality and did not recover completely until a few weeks later. Their motor functions were also affected. Hardly moving, the body became rigid with the eyes gazing at a single point even though audible and visual stimuli were present. This is the reason why the question of establishing a training program and proper testing for the people who penetrate that area was specifically raised. With the foundation of the counterintelligence section inside of the department that I lead, I was able to review the protocol and make it suitable for current needs.

This topic has always been one of the most sensitive subjects in our discussions with our partners from other states. They seem not to understand the fact that the Projection Room represents more than a simple physical hole inside of the mountain, even being very technology laden itself. Indeed, we can talk about another concept and vision, about a huge difference of technology, but that particular space is also a "crossing" and this aspect seems to be inconceivable to modern science. We quickly came to the conclusion that, in order to correctly understand what the underground complex from the Bucegi Mountains means, it is necessary to abandon most of the principles and the materialistic way that most modern scientists think with. A proof in this sense is that, by 2010, the scientists involved in studying the Bucegi location could not provide any clues to the various aspects and question marks presented by this secret location.

It was discovered that the most important aspect is that, once penetrating into the Great Gallery, and especially inside of the Projection Room, the frequency of vibration of the biological being changes. This is the key to understanding all of the apparently weird processes that happen with the psychic and mental aspects of people, as well as the often strange perceptions that interfere when penetrating the three tunnels that extend from the Projection Room. I do not want to get ahead of myself at this point because this is one of the main subjects I will be addressing in this volume.

The experience I had during the first expedition that I was part of profoundly affected me. This was my adventure described in the book *Mystery of Egypt — The First Tunnel*. This was not only the result of the unique discovery concerning the Occult Room beneath the Giza Plateau in Egypt but also because of the specific states of consciousness I experienced during the journey through that First Tunnel. I thought that the expeditions through the other two tunnels would be similar with the one from the First Tunnel, but reality turned out to be completely different. By the end of 2014, I found this out from Cezar's stories. Only after having been assigned to lead the special section within the Department did I have the possibility and extraordinary experience of going on expeditions through the other two tunnels.

Up to that time, Cezar has made several trips, especially through the Second Tunnel towards the Inner Earth; and he was sometimes gone for periods lasting several months. I tried to fill Cezar's absence in my life with proper training in the field of esotericism and paranormal; and after my integration into the Department's structure, I dedicated myself to the organization, training and achievement of necessary experience in this very difficult and slippery domain of the secret services.

From the conversations I had with Cezar, I fully understood the importance of personal training representing an essential ingredient for success when it comes to future expeditions. He told me that in regards to the tunnel towards the Inner Earth (the Second Tunnel) and the one towards Iraq (the Third Tunnel), things were different and a certain interior preparation was required that was more intense than that which was needed in preparation for accessing the Bucegi complex. Cezar's words made me even more curious, but I patiently waited and tried to stay elevated by following his directions, continuing the training within the Base and also the stages of special preparation from the remote-viewing program in the Unites States.

After General Obadea's death, however, the situation became difficult and the time periods of Cezar's absence were very burdensome. In a certain sense, his role tended to become that of an "ambassador" to the inside of the planet, and during one of the discussions I had with him, in between two trips, he told me that the issue of him remaining within the Inner Earth had been raised. The General's death changed the course of things and Cezar returned, fully conscious that, in his absence, the General's work of a life time and also all the secrets of the Department would have been learned, controlled and exploited in very dangerous and selfish ways.

During that very tension filled period of time, my reunion with Elinor was like a ray of light. At the end of 2012, he surprisingly returned to the country for a few days; and, for me, this was like a water fountain in the middle of the desert. His look was changeless, and he seemed even a little bit younger than when I last saw him. Elinor appeared in his unmistakable way, entering naturally and debonair in the room of his mansion where the library is situated. I visited there in one of the few free moments that I allowed myself after going to work in the Department. Most of my time was spent within the Alpha Base or on other trips within the country or abroad, all on Department business. Either it was a remarkable synchronicity or Elinor simply knew that I was in his mansion at that time. No matter what the answer might be, his presence was a wonderful surprise and the next couple of days were a delight as we engaged in discussions and shared complex information with each other. He confessed to me that, generally speaking, his visits happen once every six to seven years. People like him or Dr. Xien have a special statute and their missions usually take place over very long periods of time. But, while Doctor Xien is acting through governmental connections, Elinor is part of an "invisible" category of human beings that are strongly "hunted" by certain occult societies; and, first and foremost, by the "Organization." This is why his presence has to be incognito and his residences across the world remain unknown.

Since 2013, Cezar remained within the Base for most of the time. It was like a return to the good times when I was spending hours a day talking to him, carefully taking notes on what he was saying to me, asking and clarifying different aspects. My time as a novitiate had now long since ended and I was now experienced. We mainly discussed his amazing trips to the Inner Earth, about those mysterious worlds and the phenomena that characterizes them, about the implications of this type of knowledge, and many other options and plans that would possibly have a beneficial result for the country.

I think that the fall of 2014 was the most beautiful time I have lived so far. If someone thinks that fairy tale moments cannot exist in a dream landscape inside of a top secret militarized base, then he is certainly wrong. It was the unspoken happiness of the freedom of knowledge that came once I had been assigned to my new position. There were also Cezar's amazing descriptions through which he revealed to me an incredible world in an incredible place. There was also the extraordinary mysteries of the history of Mankind and the temporal library that can be reached through the Third Tunnel.

During one of those remarkable evenings, in the light of a sublime and calm sunset, Cezar told me that we would soon leave on a new expedition. My dream for years was now becoming a reality. I was going to penetrate the Inner Earth for the first time, to discover mysteries that would remain unknown and not understood for the majority of people. I already knew that the situation concerning the Second Tunnel was more complicated than the one regarding the tunnel towards Egypt and even more confusing with regards to the capacity of the common man to understand. I was already informed about some of these aspects, but the one who was going to clarify these matters for me was Doctor Xien who announced his arrival at the Base during that period. I had received the notification of his coming from the Chinese services. Doctor Xien was going to be accompanied by his assistant, the enigmatic and thrilling Shin Li.

The discussions, explanations and the main events that followed represents the content of this volume and refer to the journeys that Cezar and myself took together to the Inner Earth in November and December of 2014.

Radu Cinamar
January 10th, 2017

CHAPTER ONE

A POWERFUL SHOCK

WHAT THE JOURNEY TO THE
CENTER OF THE PLANET REALLY MEANS

The new expedition which I was about to undertake into the Inner Earth came with one more surprise when Cezar told me that we were the only two people who would be taking the journey. Even so, this idea was not really something too new because I already knew that the majority of trips through the Second Tunnel, especially in between 2008-2012, were taken by him only. Cezar had avoided giving me information on this subject because he considered it to be very sensitive. The only person he would talk to in this regards was General Obadea. From some allusions that he made to me, however, I figured out that something major was being prepared and that he had succeeded in establishing some very important connections during his previous expeditions.

With the limited knowledge I had at the time, I could only imagine that, one way or another, Cezar had penetrated the mythical realm of Shambhala. What I have found out in the years that followed, however, which is based upon my own personal experience as well as the explanations I was given, offers a very complex perspective of the subject that cannot be judged simplistically. Accordingly, I will not be referring to the main studies that have already appeared on this theme, starting with the writings of Ossendovski, Roerich, Bernard nor to the various articles which portrays diverse aspects and strange facts about the empty interior of the Earth. All of these works transmit something, but none of these descriptions show the overall picture nor the correct understanding of what truly exists in the inland of our planet.

THE FULL EARTH AND THE EMPTY INNER EARTH

Scientists themselves state, and they state it properly, that it is not possible for them to collect, let alone study, material samples from depths of thousands of kilometers beneath the earth; and, consequently, they can only make theories based on indirect measurements that are not absolutely precise. On the other hand, the stories and the books that have been published on this subject describe the subject of the empty inland of the Earth in very general terms without any details or conclusions, also being imprecise.

We can, however, make a clear distinction between two ideas or major concepts. First, contemporary science says that the planet is "full" with a certain solid stratified composition. On the other hand, there is a segment of the population who believes that, in reality, the interior of the planet is empty. Consequent to these contrary views, the latter ones are categorized by the scientific community and the mass-media as being supporters of conspiracy theories. It is not clear at all, however, what these so-called conspiracies are actually directed towards and who the so-called conspiracy theorists are against, but the common and rough front of materialistic science and state interests have succeeded in making the subject appear to be ridiculous.

The credibility of a subject decreases once it is made to look like a joke as opposed to a starting point for a debatable discussion. In the same vein, we can just as well consider modern science's theory about the internal structure of our planet as being a conspiracy because it is not supported with either dates and concrete measurements but only with approximations, interpolation and hypotheses. That is why rejecting the idea that the Earth is empty on the inside does not represent a fair attitude, especially when there are elements that can sustain it. Some of these elements are even famous, such as the mysterious operation High Jump in 1947 when Admiral Byrd of the American Navy led a vast military expedition into the area of Antarctica. Byrd also made odd and mysterious declarations about the interior of the Earth. No matter how much Admiral Byrd or the expedition is discredited or ignored, the facts are still facts and they remained registered.

The idea of the planet being empty on the inside represents a taboo subject to all of the armies and the secret services of the world. It is considered a top state secret that can only be compared with the secrets concerning extraterrestrial civilizations due to the ideological, economic and military impact such revelations might stir up. In this regard, the policy of denying, slighting or ignoring such uncomfortable ideas, even though they point to the truth, are considered to be the most appropriate. When it comes to the great powers of the world, and the United States of America in particular, the idea of the Earth being empty on the inside is most definitely viewed as an occult subject. And if things might be clear to insiders on the subject of UFOs and extraterrestrial civilizations, even if such has not been revealed to the public, there is almost nothing known about the interior of the Earth. This ignorance, as well as the incapacity to control the phenomena that comes with penetrating the center of the planet or knowing what is there has given shivers to the military and political leaders over the past decades.

In such cases, it is the uncertainty factor that bothers them the most. Apparently, none of the military and political leaders of the world know what exactly exists inside of the planet. They do not know what to expect, but on a particularly very high level of security, some of the information agencies know very well certain inside "access areas," the ones from the South and North Poles being the most important. Although the United States, Canada and Russia have special monitoring and study programs, they have no possibility of controlling the phenomena they encounter nor do they understand it. Penetrating the inside of the Earth has always represented a technological and conceptual struggle for Mankind.

ENIGMATIC PHENOMENA

When the secret complex from the Bucegi Mountains was discovered, it represented an unexpected leap forward which seemed to offer an extraordinary opportunity to clarify the situation with regard to the interior of our planet. We convinced ourselves pretty quickly, however, that things were far from being that simple. There were tensions and misunderstandings from the very start, primarily because the location was in Romania and Americans could not control it directly.

On the other hand, there are just a few who understand that penetrating the Inner Earth has nothing to do with either armament, military strategy or with funding. One of the important aspects is the fact that not just anyone can move through the Second Tunnel towards the empty interior of the planet, thus dramatically reducing the number who either could or did undertake expeditions through this tunnel. Moreover, while not everyone resists such expeditions, something undetermined seems to block the access to human beings. They suddenly feel a general state of sickness, nausea and manifest panic attacks.

It should also be pointed out that even intense individual training does not assure unconditional success in these matters because, in a strange way, such people have neither the potential nor possibility of penetrating the tunnel or inner region of the planet beyond a certain area.

These unusual situations triggered certain frustrations, but we realized quite quickly that we had to deal with phenomena that we could not control through will, weapons or technology. What was clearly highlighted for both the Americans and ourselves was the fact that access to the Inner Earth is not an open ground and that the phenomena accompanying a ride through the Second Tunnel exceeds the capacity of contemporary science's ability to understand.

As far as I am concerned, I had the opportunity to be given valuable explanations from both Dr. Xien and from Cezar, both of whom clarified my understanding of the inside structure of our planet. In a simple and direct way, Dr. Xien pointed out the main scientific and esoteric elements in order for me to have a clear vision on this subject. Before that remarkable discussion, I had, to a certain extent, done my own research by consulting the main references on the currently extant data about the internal structure of the Earth.

THE MODERN SCIENTIFIC CONCEPT
ABOUT THE INSIDE OF OUR PLANET

Basically, scientists think that the Earth is solid and rigid on the inside and have extended this conclusion to apply to all telluric bodies of the cosmos. They reason that if our planet is empty inside, then all of the other solid planets should be the same. This means that all telluric planets are either full and solid on the inside or empty on the inside. Following this concept, it is not reasonable to either think or assume that some of the planets are full and others are empty because, as has been noticed when planetary masses are compared, their densities appear to be similar. This is why scientists have concluded that telluric planets form and structure themselves in a similar way, meaning that they are either full or empty on the inside.

Unfortunately, they have chosen the version of the Earth being solid and rigid on the inside, raising many issues that have remained unsolved. Although the internal structure of the planet has been elaborated upon by science, all of it is based upon assumptions and extrapolations of results derived from various measurements. These often provide strange or even contradictory factors that cannot be understood.

The currently accepted scientific concept is that there is a solid sphere in the center of the Earth that is mainly composed of iron and nickel, both being metals with powerful magnetic properties. This solid metal sphere would represent, in a scientist's view, the core or the internal nucleus of the Earth. It is surrounded by a thick magma layer which represents the so-called outer nucleus of the Earth. The scientists affirm that, because of the rotational movement of the planet and through the intense dynamism between the internal and external core, all of which is solid, thermal energy is emanated towards the surface which generates the magnetic field of the Earth.

Going further, science tells us that this ensemble in the center of the planet, composed from the internal and external nucleus, is surrounded by a thick mantle in a semi-solid state (viscous matter, meaning magma of different types), surrounded by what we call the Earth's crust on the exterior, the latter considered to be solid.

In reality, nothing is clear for physicists and geologists regarding the internal structure of the planet. There is considerable contradictory data and results that cannot stand up to an unseen scientific model.

For example, what is the real source of the magnetic field of our planet? How is it truly created? In this regard, like the theories about the internal structure of the Earth, it is only assumptions that are made, all based upon sustaining certain concepts and approximations, all of them relying upon a hypothetical model which researchers created in spite of the fact that they have no idea about what is really going on inside of our planet.

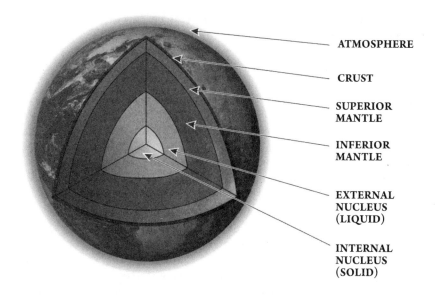

ATMOSPHERE

CRUST

SUPERIOR
MANTLE

INFERIOR
MANTLE

EXTERNAL
NUCLEUS
(LIQUID)

INTERNAL
NUCLEUS
(SOLID)

**THE BASIC STRUCTURE OF THE INSIDE OF
OUR PLANET IN THE SCIENTIFIC VISION**

Their entire vision is purely materialistic. Even so, nobody has scientifically surveyed an actual "vertical cross section" of the planet in order to establish the truth of the theory of its internal structure. Although scientists have not been able to penetrate more than twelve kilometers into the Earth with current technology, they publish convinced opinions on what exists in the nucleus of Terra, over 6,300 kilometers depth.

THE DELUSORY VISION OF THE "EXTERIOR" AND "INTERIOR"

From this point on, you will read the explanations of Dr. Xien. I met with him and Shin Li in the protocol room inside Alpha Base, sitting comfortably around the oval table in the middle of the room. The purpose of the meeting was to serve as a training seminar for the journey through the Second Tunnel that I was about to make with Cezar.

As it seemed natural to me, I started the conversation by commenting on the fact that modern science does not conceive of the idea of an empty interior of the planet. Just as soon, however, Dr. Xien started a discussion which confused me.

"Everything scientists believe about the interior of the Earth being full and rigid represents an illusion based upon their own conceptual limitations.

This also applies to everything that other researchers say who are attempting to explain the existence of a cavity in the middle. Both see the Earth based upon measurement units which are being used in current science. They analyze the data they have based upon the level of understanding they have reached. What they consider the "answer" to be with regard to the inside of the Earth does not represent the real state of things. It is more of a state of mind adapted to the scientist's ability to understand and conceive with regard to the current moment, based upon the existing devices of measurement. This is how their level of consciousness is, representing the limited extent to which they have been able to penetrate the mystery of the planet."

Thinking for a moment that Dr. Xien was mocking me, I was looking for the reason why he would do such thing. I soon got over it though. After all, this was only a reaction of self-importance from my side.

"Okay. Then what is the truth?" I asked him. "It is my understanding that neither one nor the other are right. So, is there an empty interior of the Earth?"

"There is certainly a very special reality in the heart of the planet," replied Dr. Xien, "but it is not 'inside' — it only exists. When scientists say a planet has a higher or a lower volume, this is nothing more than a quantitative appearance, without any quality aspect of that celestial body. Therefore, basically speaking, there is no 'interior' or 'exterior' because these terms belong to a limited language only. This language is due to the incorrect understanding scientists have about space."

I have to admit the fact that I was stunned. Until that moment, I thought I was mastering certain knowledge about physics, but what I heard from Dr. Xien stunned my mind, making me wonder if whatever I knew had any grain of truth in it. I could not question the wisdom of the Doctor, thus there was nothing left for me but to try and better understand what he was telling me.

"If we draw a circle on a piece of paper, our concepts make us think there is an 'interior' and an 'exterior' with reference to that circle", he continued explaining to me. "However, this observation is only in relation to that piece of paper, which is bi-dimensional. If we were to actually be bi-dimensional beings and live on the piece of paper, the circle we drew would then indeed be a limitation for us, meaning it would 'split' that reality into what we call 'interior' and 'exterior.' But, if we look at this matter from the point of view of someone who lives in the tridimensional world, humanity for example, the circle does not actually delimit anything. For us, the 'interior' and 'exterior' on the paper is irrelevant. Now, move the example on the paper from the bi-dimensional plane to a superior plane such as, for example, to a tridimensional plane. You do not have a circle anymore but a sphere which delimits a so-called 'interior' and 'exterior.' However, for a being that lives in four dimensions, the sphere from the tridimensional plane does not limit a 'closed' volume at all.

For that being, it would be like the circle drawn on the piece of paper was for us. Everything is an apparency and our limitations makes us consider that there is a so-called 'empty space' inside the Earth."

Dr. Xien's logic was perfect and I started to realize that our discussion clearly had a greater depth than I could yet understand. I realized that my own concepts and ideas about the world did not fit in.

What I was hearing did not mean that my own ideas were necessarily incorrect, but it was more likely there was an underlying difficulty with regards to my being able to understand and process the information. Dr. Xien continued explaining.

"To go on a trip from somewhere on the surface of the Earth to the world 'inside,' it is not enough to calculate the distance from here to there. You must change the measurement (units) in order to understand how you should travel that distance. The way you travel assures you that you can reach what you generally call 'the interior of Earth' from here. That is because there is clearly no real and material 'empty hole' inside the Earth, but rather a mysterious world in a superior level of existence that exists in the area of the so-called 'interior' of the planet."

I was starting to see the logical chain of the subject.

"Do you mean that the distance between a spot from the surface and another from the center of the Earth is appearance?" I asked, looking to better understand his point of view.

"Yes, that is what I mean. After all, what does 'distance' mean to you?"

I thought for a while, trying to properly choose my words.

"A measure or a quantity of space that I can pass to, from one spot to another," I responded.

"Indeed, it is a measure, but it is a measure that does not reflect reality in itself; rather, it is just your way of seeing space between two spots. But, if you change perspective, then your concept about space becomes irrelevant. Because of your perspective, a small or a big distance only represents a way of saying that you can or cannot reach from one place to another. In fact, you then add another measure in order to define distance, and this new measure is time. How would you express the distance from Earth to the Sun? You could say it is distance in kilometers, but you are not measuring with an instrument such as a meter. Instead, you say that it takes eight minutes at the speed of light to travel that distance because you are conscious that you cannot walk that distance. The time needed to go by foot from Earth to the Sun, supposing you could do it, would represent a time that cannot be measured by you. So, in this way, you have solved the problem."

"What solution?" I asked, not understanding what he meant. "This only changes the reference system of measurement. Time is being referenced instead of space."

"That's right. You are using the measurement reference that corresponds to your understanding as well as the degree to which your consciousness has opened. When you measure something, whether it is big or small, you do so in correspondence with the capacity of your own consciousness or awareness."

I could not understand too well what it was that he was trying to say.

"The system of measurement does not matter!" I insisted. "Everybody knows that the distance to the Sun is huge!"

"Does the eagle know? It is a being. Just as you do, it does estimate distances, especially when it hunts; but he does it in his own way, based upon the instinct and the experience it has acquired. What would humans have said about this distance in the year 1200? What would an autistic say? What about an imbecile?"

I had to admit that the subject was more delicate than I had imagined. It was not so difficult to be understand, and I realized that I had to be more careful. I agreed that things were clearer now.

Dr. Xien returned me to our discussion.

"When you see or analyze the situation inside the Earth, you just feel like something is there because you cannot otherwise explain the situation, nor can you give yourself answers. You think that if you dig far enough you will first get to sand, then break stones, reach water, then lava and other such geological layers. Man cannot imagine much about it other than what he already knows, all of which is based upon what science tells and teaches him. This is valid as much for a beggar as for an intellectual..."

"Who seeks out an acceptable theory for what might be found inside the Earth?" I added, anticipating what he was about to say and glad that I could finally see the connection to the subject discussed from the start.

"Exactly. People imagine that there must be 'something' in the center of the planet that is tangible and material because that is the way they have been mentally prepared to know and understand. As their experience takes place on the surface of a spherical planet and is associated with its exterior, they automatically think that there must be a corresponding 'interior' of the planet. So, it is a conceptual problem."

Concentrating upon the things I was now learning, I was surprised but also fascinated by the simple and eloquent way Dr. Xien could explain a truth that is available to everyone but remains systematically ignored.

"Some scientists are asking themselves if that solid, iron and nickel ball really exists inside of Earth," he continued. "Others wonder if there are people living there inside. None of them are observing that their view is partial and limited because they are imagining that there is a world functioning based upon the same material laws as those existing on the surface. Yet, if they were to start digging to the center of the Earth, going deeper and deeper, they would undoubtedly have to change their perspective as well as their system of measurement".

I stood thinking for a few seconds. Dr. Xien had a direct, fast and intelligent way of presenting things that did not allow for interruptions nor meaningless mental "escapes." You had to maintain your focus of attention, especially when the subject was important. Processing and assimilating his information had to happen in real time, otherwise you risked losing the coherence of the explanations.

"You mean a mental and perceptive accustomization appears?" I asked.

"A mental automatism, a thinking reflex? People have a tendency to judge things, even when they do not know them, using a model of what they already know. This means that, relating to the inside of the Earth, they only calculate the distance from the surface to the center, always ignoring the qualitative perspective of this 'distance'."

Dr. Xien showed his approval by nodding his head.

"Yes, this is the process. Everyone habitually relates to their environment based upon the way they were taught and how they have viewed things over their entire life. That is why scientists imagine that the core of the Earth is an incandescent metal sphere — because this way they have a 'solution' that is based upon apparent effects: gravity and the electromagnetic field of the planet. Spreading this knowledge further, many people take for granted what they are told and repeat the same thing. Even so, what they are imagining does not exist. Nevertheless, they have the sensation and feeling of the existence of a solid nucleus of the planet, all based upon their mental programming that is a result of the knowledge and experience they have acquired up to that point. Due to the limitations of their 3-D perception, they believe the planet to be just a sphere filled with physical matter. Then, they observe particular characteristics of the planet and create models approximating scientific observations. In this way, they conceive of a 3-D mathematical model of the Earth that prevents a correct understanding of what our planet really is. In other words, scientists strongly believe in what actually does not exist."

Although I felt that I had a clue of his ideas and explanation, I thought how difficult it could be for others to think this way. Even though I had seen and gone through a lot of amazing experiences up to this point in my life, it was still challenging for me to adapt to this new system of thought presented by Dr. Xien. All of a sudden, I was discovering a new perspective surrounding reality, one that I had never considered and one which had no 'virus' of illusion. I wondered how many people could actually understand such things, let alone want to look deeper into these aspects. Making efforts to adapt myself to these new ideas in 'real time' was not very difficult, but they still hit powerfully the deeply rooted concepts inside my mind.

THE MAGNETIC FIELD OF THE PLANET:
ENIGMAS AND INTERPRETATIONS

Feeling that I still did not quite have a perfectly clear understanding, I asked Dr. Xien another question.

"Tell me then, how would you pose the question concerning the case of the Inner Earth? What is really there?"

"Currently, it is said that there is a solid metal core, cooling slowly by sending heat continuously to the surface; but as I have already said, this idea only represents an interpretation of scientists that is blindly embraced by the rest of the population."

"Okay, but there are measurements, there are some effects, some results that were pointed out," I said, pretty confused. "These scientists are talking according to some evidence!"

The concepts and opposition were creating a tough conflict inside my mind. They were, I felt, a manifestation of my strong mental prejudices. Feeling as if I had my "feet in the air," I was struggling, but I tried to encourage myself.

"It cannot be — something is not right! It is impossible for the geologists and physicists to be this wrong. They must have used certain technology to in some way determine the existence of the inner metallic sphere or, at least, they must have extrapolated their results in order to arrive at this admissible conclusion. There must be an explication somewhere that unites both their observations and what you are explaining to me now."

Dr. Xien answered me with a lot of calm.

"You cannot unite something false with something true. It is like the illusion created in a show of magic. The magician shows you an a trick and you believe it comes out of what you have observed and recognized up to that point, but the explanation behind it is totally different. What you have seen and recognized in your mind is but an illusion. What he does is real. Such researchers are like spectators to such a show. They see some effects and construe a result according to what they see and with what they measure, but the reality is different."

"All right, what is it then?" I asked impatiently.

"In the case of the nucleus from the center of the Earth, you need to start from the idea that researchers obviously do not know that there is a solid iron and nickel sphere. They just suspect it. They think something along the lines of "if the Earth has a magnetic field, then what could generate it? It obviously cannot be produced by the crust. Nor does the lava have enough force to generate a field so intense. What is it then? For such a magnetic field to be able to exist inside the center of the Earth, it must be an iron and nickel sphere, surrounded by lava, and this tandem manifests a strong movement creating magnetic field!'"

"Yes, it is a logical conclusion although I admit it is just a theoretical one."

"As you say, it is just a theory of their own interpretation. They cannot otherwise explain the existence of such a strong magnetic field of the planet. Scientists cannot understand what it is and how this magnetic field has been generated in any other way other than through what they have already learned from the current laws and theories in physics."

"Do you mean that they are wrong and that they make incorrect studies?" I asked, surprised.

"Not necessarily. I actually said that they construe in a limited way what they observe based upon what they have so far known as being reality. No matter the 'simulations' they see on the computer or their other ways of extrapolating, they end up suiting themselves with the result that they wish for and that they assume exists. They then become satisfied that their ideas have been verified. The truth is that what they think of the nucleus of the Earth represents the only logical theory that could have been arrived at, based upon the extant knowledge of science, and that this gives the answer to the presence of the Earth's magnetic field. This, however, is not sufficient."

I had been looking towards the doctor's assistant, Shin Li, for a while. She was sitting still on the chair with her arms elegantly propped on the table, like a statuesque and alluring beauty. I was thinking that, to me, she was an intangible mystery and, somehow, I was regretting that Dr. Xien was not revealing this fascinating unknown as well.

At that very moment, the following words suddenly appeared in my mind: "Do not disperse your attention. Go deeper into the mystery."

As I fathomed these words, I witnessed that Shin Li was looking right at me as if her eyes were born from ancestral water, sending me this strong telepathic message. Shying away, I was unsure of myself as I noticed what appeared to be an amused nuance, a fine irony that mitigated her intense gaze. I preferred, however, to get back to the discussion with Dr. Xien and focus on that. Although only a few seconds had passed, Shin Li was manifesting the extraordinary capacity that she sometimes demonstrated, of creating the sensation that space and time are expanding. This was not the first time that I had dealt with such a thing while in her vicinity.

"Still," I said, continuing my conversation with Dr. Xien, "there must be something generating this magnetic field of the planet, isn't there?"

I had already asked the obvious question that I was prepared to ask. Scientists have made their observations and determinations, interpreting seismic waves. All of these are based upon something. You cannot simply say that their words are just in vain.

Dr. Xien smiled again, but it could barely be seen. Intuitively, I then understood that I was not the only one who knew about the telepathic transmission of Shin Li's. But, due to his level of knowledge, he answered me as if nothing in particular had made a significant or surprising impact upon him.

"There is a sort of triangular dance that occurs between the electric field, the magnetic field and their concentration in what we label to be 'matter.' It is a triangle of recurrent transformations where these three different types of manifestations must be in balance with one another.

I was following Dr. Xien's hand drawing as he explained the general outline of this process. After a while, I took the paper and folded it carefully, knowing that I would refer to it later on when I would be writing about these things. The two sketches from below represent his paper drawing.

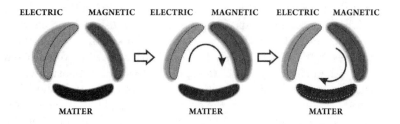

CONVERSION OF ELECTRIC FIELD - MAGNETIC FIELD - MATTER

"Matter 'gives birth' to a ripple, a manifesting wave that comes apart in three components: mass, space and time," Dr. Xien continued explaining. "This means a condensation of electric and magnetic energy because mass corresponds to condensed matter; space corresponds to the electric field; and time corresponds to the magnetic field. In fact, the magnetic field of the Earth is nothing other than the 'wave' of the our planet's physical presence in the Universe. It is the 'echo' of our planet's material presence in the space and time of the Universe."

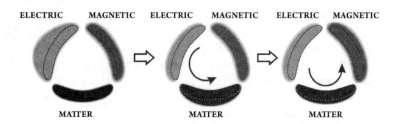

CONVERSION OF ELECTRIC FIELD - MATTER - MAGNETIC FIELD

MAGNETIC FIELD OF EARTH AND ITS MAGNETIC POLES

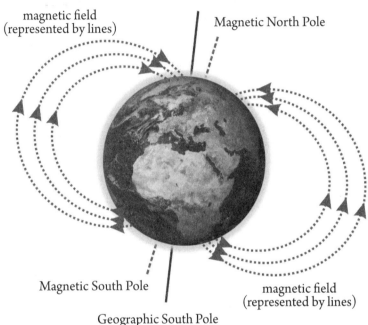

Axis of Rotation
Geographic North Pole

magnetic field
(represented by lines)

Magnetic North Pole

Magnetic South Pole

Geographic South Pole

magnetic field
(represented by lines)

THE "CORE" OF THE PLANET

Things began to clarify more and more. Still, some things seemed not to correlate, so I continued with another question.

"If matter appears as you say, it means there also exists a core in the planet. What could make me think there is not? I think scientists relay this in their theory."

"A planet does not represent just a sphere of amorphous matter in cosmic space, even if it is solid or gaseous. Nothing born or appearing in the universe is random nor senseless. There is a superior source for everything, and this includes the making of an object or a shape that appears, even when it seems to have no soul or life in the material world. It does not just come from 'nothingness' or some so-called chaotic or 'hazardous' forces as science suggests."

41

Dr. Xien stopped for a few seconds. Then, undoubtedly under the impulse of a sudden inspiration, he continued talking, filled with feeling and sensitivity.

"Take the example of a human being. There is a cause, a starting source. After conception occurs, the embryo appears and then develops more. Follow the steps: birth, gradual growth, teaching, and parental care. Those who conceived and gave birth to the child are still a source of inspiration and development as a moral and emotional center. The intention and life knowledge that is planted by the parents inside of the child remains and develops gradually. The initial information is kept within the child like an unseen but always present source. It is the heritage of the parent transferred to the child."

Seeing that I did not succeed in fully understanding what he wanted to say, Dr. Xien offered me another example.

"Consider that a sculpted statue is a real work of art by reason of the refinement and beauty it was created with. It is in a state of perfection you can almost see, even if the constituent matter it was created with is amorphic."

Having a vague impression that Dr. Xien was making an allusion to my daydreaming in the direction of the mysterious Shin Li, I became more attentive.

"Do not let yourself be guided by the concepts that others have wanted you to believe in in terms of beauty and harmony because they taught you in a certain way that was based upon their own perception which, in turn, is subject to their level of ignorance. You have to perceive the shape and exterior features of an object like a marble structure just as much as you pay attention to that which is generating it. Although the physical characteristics might be unidentifiable, it is filled with the spirit of its creator. He is the source, impregnating the work with the breath of life and his magnetic energy; and you can almost see this magnetism even after thousands of years. A prime example is the statue of Aphrodite and its creator, Fidious."

Finally, I was no longer having doubts about Dr. Xien's ironic strategy. My eyes stared above the table without saying anything.

So subtly would he combine esoteric aspects and precious teaching with his fine humor and the clear perception of what is happening around him. In the presence of such beings, you feel somehow naked, as if you cannot hide anything from them. What is interesting, however, is that you do not even want to hide things from them. The tendencies are contrary . On the one hand is the egotistical process of hiding yourself. On the other hand is the superior intuition of evolution and the correct understanding of what you actually are. Long ago, I adopted the second way which, by the way, Cezar has been an eminent proponent of. Now, Dr. Xien and Shin Li were looking to prepare me for another meaningful jump in my evolution.

The subject presented was very interesting, but I intervened, wishing to clarify a specific aspect. In the cases of both a sculpture and a human being, we have a consciousness and even a visible source of that which created them. But, I did not see what the source would be in the case of a planet. Where is it? As you can see, that could be a problem. The answer was shocking, even if Dr. Xien expressed it without blinking.

"The source is in the center of the planet. That is the beginning of that which forms and maintains the core. In a way, scientists feel something about this, but their mistake is that they want to solve the problem only from the viewpoint of the material aspect. These are the fundamental limitations of scientific thinking and knowledge on the Earth right now. It is a blockage because, for now, science does not conceive of a superior level than material reality. It is all attributable to some rusty materialistic concepts. Not even quantum physics has been able to break through such conceptual numbness.

"How would you explain to scientists that most of their thinking fabric is faulty with regard to the way they conceive matter as well as the entire universe? An unacademic mind with no diplomas or honorific titles could understand aspects of the world's structure and its manifest nature. The scientific intelligence blocked in dogmas and prejudices is meaningless when compared to spiritual and esoteric knowledge in the real sense of intellectual flexibility. Then, quite naturally, comes the wisdom derived from the direct experience of different levels of reality.

"One of these factors refers to celestial bodies such as planets and stars. Are they only matter?"

"Not all," I replied quickly. "Cezar has already spoken to me about their subtle structure, about the way they should be looked at and understood as living beings because, in the end, that is what they really are: big souls manifesting. But, in our discussions, he has not detailed their inner structure or core.

"Yes, there is a stage based upon levels of manifestation. A human be-ing is on a certain level. A planet or a star is on another evolutionary level. The thing they have in common, the human as much as the planet, is their tendency towards evolution no matter what shape or place they have in this dimensional scale.   So what is the function of the core of a planet? What is it actually? It is the heart of the planet. Its purpose for living, just as in the case of a human, cannot function without a heart. It is the center of your being but the subtle fundamental is the soul. Let us say that a doctor's hand could touch a patient's heart, but he cannot touch their soul because it is a subtle reality superior to that of the heart. It is, however, his being, just on a higher level of understanding closer to the universal source. It is the very same in the case of the nucleus of a planet which is the center of its subtle being. Just as it is with your heart having the capacity to be in touch with the supreme reality throughout which you can touch infinity. That is the nature of the nucleus of a planet which contains a reality offering the same type of fulfillment and amazing evolution for the being that the planet is. The difference here is that things are not what contemporary science imagines them to be."

"But, what is it? If I were to go from the surface to the interior of the planet, further and further, what would I see?"

"It would be like a spiritual journey on an evolutionary road. On any planet, no matter its evolutionary level on the surface, if you were to be able to go inside, you would discover that the reality on the inside is much more evolved. You cannot go to the center of a planet just by travelling at the material level. Even if you look at things symbolically, they have meaning. It is like coming back home, a returning to the source which is the spiritual core. It is always the center, the source, the discontinuous spot generating all the rest. Apparently, it is nothing; but still, it represents everything for the planet. You are then closer to the essence of that planet.

SIMULATION: TRAVELLING TO THE CORE OF THE PLANET

I felt my entire being filled with interest and impatience because what I was finding out had an enigmatic response in my soul, impelling me to find out more information in a more detailed way. It was the sweetness of an effervescent intuition telling me that all the information was not given to me by accident and that I was ready to live such an experience soon. Indeed, it happed faster than I would have expected it to. Still, I will return to Dr. Xien's essential explanations. I proposed a unique situation.

"Let us assume that the technological conditions are accomplished in order to dig a tunnel large enough to send a capsule with a human crew. Let us say that the angles of descending are adjusted so that the travel occurs under normal conditions. The tunnel follows this direction throughout the center of the Earth. What would the scientists and crew encounter? "

"For a while, they would see solid matter, earth, rocks, then lava. Let's say they would have the means to pass through the lava. Here, things become more complicated. It is like when you go to the sun by space ship. In order to resist, it is necessary to have a ship equipped with a very strong magnetic field so that you can get closer to the star without getting crushed by the very strong forces and radiation emitted. Also, let's say that on her way to the center of the Earth, the crew of the ship has everything necessary to break through the massive bed of lava and to resist the energetic field it emits. The members of the crew would then begin to cross that lava deposit, but the further they go, the more they will have to protect themselves in order to resist the pressure, the temperature and the massive radiation. Technologically speaking, they would have to create such an intense magnetic field that they would actually transform themselves, including their biological matter, all of this resulting in a very changed perception."

"What do you mean?" I asked, a little puzzled.

"It is as if you have taken a man from 1600 and put him to work on a computer. In order for you to do so, you have to start teaching him how, but in that moment that he will know how to work the computer, he will then have reached an advanced knowledge level than the one that his original world has. His understanding has changed, and this inevitably facilitates major changes in his biological body.

"We will now speak very precisely, but in the example with the ship travelling inside the Earth, a point where the necessity of having a very advanced technology will reach such a magnitude that the effect of the technology upon a person undergoing such travel completely transforms the way that he or she thinks."

"All right. But what actually happens when this personal evolution of each member of the crew takes place?" I asked.

My curiosity was legitimate , but I felt I already had the answer. By then, I figured that travelling to the center of the planet no longer had a quantitative aspect but rather a qualitative one; but I wanted to know how the material elements would combine with the subtle ones. How would the surrounding reality appear? What kind of perceptions would be generated?

Dr. Xien patiently explained the phenomena that would be taking place. The members of the crew are adapting to another energetic resonance frequency, and if this happens, they will then pass beyond this one. By that, I am referring to a plane or dimension vibrating with a superior frequency to the material plane. Their entrance to such a world does not happen because they crossed the lava deposit but because they have managed to break the condensation limits specific to the physical matter encountered up to that time, that is, the sediments, rocks, and lava. This way, they break through the vibrational frequency of that type of condensed energy that the matter we know represents. Pragmatically, they entered a new reality superior to material reality. They then enter into the etheric plane."

I was astonished and totally confused, but the conclusion was clear.

"It means that every time someone goes to the material center of the Earth, he will actually never get there because he will first reach the etheric plane, entering a realm superior to the material dimension."

"Yes, you understand. Advancing to the center of the planet in a material reference frame is conditioned by the necessity of personal evolution with regard to vibrational frequency because the intensity of the magnetic field grows very much. All along the way, the nearer and nearer a human being comes to the center of the earth, the individual mandatorily evolves. Otherwise, he just cannot go further on. He cannot break the restrictions corresponding to the vibrational frequency of the material plane from which the journey began.

THE INNER EARTH AND THE EVOLUTION OF CONSCIOUSNESS

After a short break, Dr. Xien looked me straight in the eyes, and in an even and detached voice said, "As opposed to the way scientists now conceive it, the universal laws of manifestation do not necessitate a literal geometric point of reference."

This was one of the strangest statements that I had ever heard, but I had already begun to guess the meaning of it. In order to clarify in my own mind as much as possible this new idea of the planet's internal structure, I decided to take advantage of the fact that Shin Li had left the room and ask a series of short questions. I did not want Shin Li to believe that I could not understand the explanations already given to me. So, I quickly addressed Dr. Xien.

"Maybe it was a bit too fast, shifting paradigms from materialism to the subtle planes. I think I pretty well feel the background of it, but I would like to clarify once again the precise position. Let's take it all over again. I want to know what happens if you go to the center of the Earth in a capsule without any advanced technology. For example, I am here on the physical plane of Earth and start a journey to the planet's nucleus with a machine that resists very high temperature. I plan to reach the exact center of the planet no matter what I find there. What happens on the way?"

"At a certain point, you would start losing your mind. You will no longer understand anything."

I opened my eyes wider due to the amazement of what he said.

"For what reason? Just because its environment and its frequency of vibration changes?"

"I told you before, and now I am repeating. You start here at the surface. The first part of the journey is going to be easy, crossing successive deposits of ground, rock, lava and other substances. In this instance, you are in the material level. There is heavy matter with a vibration similar to what your body has and your mind is thinking in terms of the laws of classical physics. Let's say that, after some kilometers, you would see the difference between solid and liquid matter and you want to go further on, but at one point you will stop because you will no longer be able to go if your vibrational consciousness level remains the same. You have reached the limits of the fundamental material world and what we know as day to day experience. You can perceive only so far. You can resist only so far. Beyond this zone or barrier of vibrational frequency, you will feel you cannot take it anymore, and if you insist, you will become unconscious. That reality you have reached no longer corresponds to your conscious vibrational level but has a higher one. You then no longer have the capacity to understand what is going on there. You cannot make connections. You would be like an Eskimo seeing a snake or seeing a tree growing on the moon. In both cases, your usual mental understanding is overwhelmed, confused and very probably shocked."

"Still, I don't feel like I would pass out because of this."

"These examples are meant just for you to have a comparable analogy to bridge your understanding. In reality, if you would travel in this particular condition, you couldn't take it after a certain moment, but this applies not only to you. The capsule itself and all the equipment in it will become stuck. Your capacity of seeing and understanding also becomes stuck. Everything is then blocked between the material reality from which you originated and this new reality that you have reached. There is a difference in vibrational frequency and your capsule's technology no longer resonates with this new frequency.

In order to further clarify this matter, I asked, "Is it an issue of personal adaptability and suitability or is it a state of consciousness?"

"One serves the other as much as the capsule's technology and your consciousness are at a certain vibrational level that is inferior to the frequency occurring by reason of getting closer to the center of the planet. At that point, you either have the real capacity of higher understanding and resonate to these high energy frequencies or you simply lose your consciousness because your mind cannot process the sensations and information it receives.

"In the end, the center is reached, but this represents another world entirely that has gradually manifested long before through the etheric plane as well as the more and more elevated subtle planes of existence. The vibrational frequency from the body to the mind has evolved. It is an automatic process, but still, it respects certain conditions. It is required that a person has a certain psychological or mental training and internal knowledge. Otherwise, the transformations are too strong to resist the accelerated evolution that occurs while going to the planet's interior."

"I got that, but I am interested in learning how such travel might appear to an external observer."

I watched Dr. Xien very keenly for several seconds. This idea had been pursuing me for a while, and I was very curious to find out the answer. I continued with my questions, offering an example of how this might play out in an actual situation.

"Let's say that there is a mission command center on the earth's surface with a crew monitoring what is going on in a capsule penetrating the Earth's center. This crew has no reason to be subjected to fainting as it has remained on the surface. What would they see in front of the monitors? At a certain point, they will no longer see anything on their screens."

Dr. Xien was silent for a moment, looking at the ground. He then continued with his uniform voice.

"I can see that you haven't fully understood. Have you already forgotten that the entirety of the technology in the capsule and all that is connected to it stops due to the incompatibility of the vibrational frequencies? Nothing is sent or received because the machines can no longer work together as you start to get closer to the center of the planet. The frequencies you meet there are much higher than those in which the actual technology was conceived. There are no longer coherent connections between the electronic components."

"If the frequency rises so much, then what happens with the solid matter inside the Earth?" I asked, continuing with my persistent questioning.

Dr. Xien smiled gently, just as he would always do every time he had the chance to appreciate a fine observation. I could somehow breathe more easily, telling myself that after having taken a cold shower, I was now taking a warm one and could get back to the discussion.

Even though what had been explained to me was not that difficult to understand, I was combating a lot of my own mental resistance concerning materialistic thinking and the deeply imbedded thought programming that surrounds the dense matter of the physical plane. Although most of what Dr. Xien presented was clear to me, I still wanted to have a more detailed understanding. At that time, however, I had no idea that what he was saying was such an important turning point in our discussion, and his ensuing explanations would amaze me. Up to now, I had reacted as if his information was akin to more of a mere novelty, as if the analysis offered was similar enough to the schematic of the material plane as we know it but in the context of also offering some possibilities. But now Dr. Xien wanted to go to a deeper level of explanations. From his first words, I recognized that I had to change my own mental register in order to carry on with the discussion.

"You go beyond the crust," he answered, "and after reaching the mantle or where it begins, we just approximate what is there as well as what is further towards the center."

"What kind of approximation?" I asked, interested.

Dr. Xien answered me, looking me in the eye.

"Mainly from that zone beyond where there is no more physical matter. From that level on, because the of the increasing frequency of vibration, you already are in the subtle planes. You enter the etheric plane, then the astral plane and then you get to the causal plane surrounding the center of the planet. It is a structure of manifestation that can be found in any celestial body but also in the human body. Inside yourself, everything is perfectly structured with a sequence of higher and higher vibrational frequencies, starting from the material body to the subtle causal body and eventually to the center of your being, the heart, and that is the essence. In her own way, the planet is also a being. It is the same type of matter and conscious organization, just that you are a human being and she is a planet. "This is the principle of correspondence which traditional spirituality talks about. As above, so below. With this principle, you can view everything as miraculous. What exists down here is like what it is up there. What is down or below refers to that which is small, the microcosm. What is above or up refers to that which is big such as a galaxy or the macrocosm.

"At any scale of manifestation, the structural principle is the same. If you understand this, you also understand what happens when someone travels to the Earth's center. After the material field of the planet, you get closer to and start getting into its subtle fields. I am referring to the etheric plane, astral plane and so on. But, you will only go as far as your own vibrational level of consciousness will be able to fulfill the resonant conditions. If there is something higher than your own individual conscious vibrational frequency, you cannot see it. You cannot understand it and go into it."

THE SINGULARITY IN THE CENTER OF THE PLANET

"Things are clearer now, but this being said, what is it that is right in the center of the planet?. I understand there is no solid matter nor any iron ball nor other material structures with the characteristics of friction. What is there? There must be something, isn't there? What is that source?"

Dr. Xien remained silent for a while, measuring his words. I felt that he was interested that I take in all the information correctly. If not, it could possibly cause certain concerns or delays in his plans. I could not help but notice this, but I was not concerned because I felt I could pretty well absorb all of the explantations he offered. In a certain way, I felt this was really about an important revelation; but still, I would not have expected it to be what he said it was.

"In the middle of the Earth, there is a black hole."

We were both silent again, longer now, but for different reasons. I was looking to organize my thinking and scientific ideas in order to correctly absorb these explanations so as not to sound ridiculous or appear vulnerable to mocking. On the other hand, Dr. Xien was relaxed and waiting, looking like he wanted me to take the time needed to digest the information and to prepare my questions. I decided not to hurry. That is why I asked for a certain tolerance regarding my recurring questions. Besides, I wanted some more time to adapt to this new level of discussion.

"I feel like we should take it as slowly and as precisely as possible. I want to clarify things in order to be sure that I have tied up all the loose ends before going further."

"Go ahead and ask me," said Dr. Xien.

I hurried up in order to avoid any surprises or changes in his direction. Digging deeper into the subject, I responded.

"I understand about the vibrational frequency rising, but exactly how does consciousness cross into the subtle etheric plane?"

Dr. Xien bent over the table and broke off a piece of paper. While drawing, he gave me explanations, keeping the same equal but almost hypnotic voice.

"Here comes another surprise. Scientists have already obtained information demonstrating that there is a huge ocean of water beyond the Earth's crust that separates the material consistency of the physical world from the subtle one, following from there to the center. They have, of course, asked themselves, 'Where does this huge amount of water come from?' and 'Was it from the impact of our planet with comets or asteroids from outer space?' I know this is the accepted theory even though there is nothing certain about it. To a small degree, the water of our planet has also come from comets hitting it; but in reality, the extant water — and this applies to the oceans on the surface just as much as the huge internal ocean — mostly comes from the black hole that exists in the center."

Perplexed, I just stood there.

"This is the cherry on top of the cake!" I finally said. "I don't know who will be able to swirl it."

"Those who feel that this is the truth and also those who have already

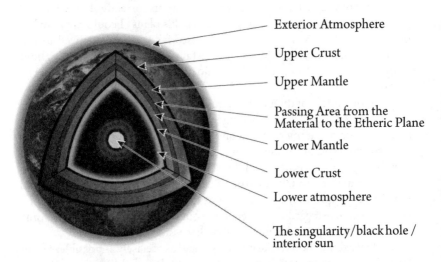

Exterior Atmosphere

Upper Crust

Upper Mantle

Passing Area from the Material to the Etheric Plane

Lower Mantle

Lower Crust

Lower atmosphere

The singularity/black hole / interior sun

THE INTERNAL STRUCTURE OF THE EARTH AS IT REALLY IS

experienced the planet's interior. Some of them have seen the central sun which is the black hole itself. Here is insipid intelligence where diplomas or academic honors mean nothing compared to real knowledge and direct experience. These things can be verified by those reaching a certain spiritual level of knowledge or even through very advanced technological means."

"Still," I replied, "the notion of a black hole in the center of the Earth is already very hard to accept, not to mention that the water in the in-between ocean comes from this black hole."

Dr. Xien continued, patiently explaining.

"Your indignation is due to not knowing, but listen carefully to me now and cast away the prejudices. These sorts of things overcome the actual materialism of science. They are esoteric. You cannot judge them through formulas nor other observations as scientists would like. Moreover, they are connected to other types of sciences that are discredited nowadays just as alchemy has been. While such do not talk of the huge ocean of water inside the Earth, there are clues given regarding radical humidity and how elements, metals and minerals are thereby formed. Almost all sources indicate the fact that, at the beginning, everything started from water, humidity. This is a great mystery with both metaphysical and scientific connotations. More and more, scientists are admitting that life actually began in the planet's oceans. Do you think, however, that anyone would be inclined to admit that we are expanding from a black hole; and more, that this makes water and water forms a very big ocean inside the planet?"

I quickly made a correlation.

"In the *Bible*, it is said that we were created out of clay, but after all, the clay is a mixture of water and earth. If we look from the perspective of primordial elements, this is exactly what you can find in the planet's interior; an ocean of water and the solid matter of the crust. The expression is obviously metaphorical, but I believe there is a core of real consistency."

"You would be surprised to find out how literal this expression is. It is not metaphorical at all. Water, created by the dynamic of black holes, does exist in cosmic space. Better said, the process to create water begins with a condensation of subtle water from the etheric plane through the dynamic rotation of a black hole. In the material plane, this condensation appears like an expulsion from the black hole's vortex and, right next to it, water is manifested in the shape of ice. So, water exists in cosmic space and in huge amounts. Even astrophysicists have noticed it, having a big surprise when they do. You cannot, however, expect for it be like 'potable water' because it has some special properties. It is, however, water. You will find the same process inside the Earth. The water is condensed beyond the dynamic of the black hole that emanates from the center of the planet. It's amazing. I know this is contrary to typical scientific notions and dogma; and while everything seems to be so phantasmagorical, it is obvious and simple enough if you make an effort to overcome the initial shock. Then, you should no longer be surprised over the prospect of a black hole residing in the center of the Earth. Any structure, no matter how big or small, is based upon the same fundamental principle. There is a black hole vortex in the center, and this is a principle of creation just as is the principle of absorption applies at the end of its existence. Any galaxy has at its center a black hole. Any atom has in its nucleus a tiny black hole that ensures its existence and manifestation of evolution. Don't guide yourself under the contemporary scientific paradigm. The way it sees the world is still at a relatively modest level which is focused on either the quantifiable universe or the microcosmic aspect because it is limited to a purely materialistic understanding of things."

"I think that man's general reaction to such aspects is to deny them by reason of his own prejudices, and there is then further resistance because of scientific dogmas," I said.

"Yes. This seems to be the reaction in most cases, but as I've already told you, this is not important to us. If a person doesn't make any effort to overcome themselves in order to intuitively understand these realities, how would you expect them to react positively? From what resources?"

"I don't know, but I still find the information confusing. Who would be willing to believe that, in the interstellar vacuum of space, there is water coming from the cosmic black holes? But first, how could a black hole produce water? As far as I know, a black hole only absorbs matter — it does not create it."

Dr. Xien stood up from his chair.

"You lose yourself in so-called scientific considerations. Until recently, it was considered that nothing could escape from the gravity of a black hole. Recently, a hypothesis was acknowledged that something could be released from a black hole. You have seen how many times science makes a determination. Then, after a while, everything is modified with an admission that they were wrong. It is irrelevant to bring up formulas, equations and scientific concepts as long as the general view of contemporary science is fundamentally flawed. Although we are in the 21st Century, there are still plenty of people still believing that elementary particles are colliding like material balls, and this is just a minor example. This, however, is not the time and place to speak about such things. I will later explain to you some of the very important elements in this field. You will first need to study other elements by yourself in conjunction with your own experiences with advanced technology."

I raised my eyebrows. I could not understand what he meant.

"When, where, how?" I asked.

"Be patient. You have already seen a lot of things, and you have already had a lot of special experiences, but still, you keep a dose of mental backstroke."

There was obviously a misunderstanding in our communication, but we no longer said a word. I was very interested to find out about the Earth's interior. I was imagining that it would be a relatively easy journey like the one to the occult room in Egypt, but as Cezar said, things were looking to be much more complicated.

WATER AND THE REAL WAY PLANETS ARE FORMED

I continued with the subject, accentuating the most sensitive point.

"No matter how tolerant I might be with regard to a scientific point of view, it is very hard for me to conceive that water exists in huge amounts in the cosmic vacuum and that, as you mentioned before, it springs from the black hole's dynamic."

"The process is not so complicated," said Dr. Xien. "The space-time reality is very distorted near a black hole which means that there is a passing to another dimension or manifestation corridor. Liquid water as you know it is just the material expression of a specific subtle energy which is indeed the subtle element named water. There are special energetic conditions surrounding a black hole where, under certain circumstances, the subtle water from the etheric plane is condensed into liquid water in the material plane. There already are clear observations regarding this."

"But how is this explanation connected to the water inside the planet?"

Dr. Xien made a gesture telling me to be patient.

"From the initial phases of what is to become a future planet, there is only the vortex of a black hole serving as a forming nucleus. The water is condensed and expelled into the cosmos in the shape of ice and it arrives mixed with other types of matter and cosmic dust. This belt of matter forms stars to gravitate towards the black hole; and by getting closer, it forms a sort of plug around the vortex. But some of these ice and matter objects escape and they start travelling through cosmic space. This is the case of comets for example. The rest of the matter and ice belt comes back to the vortex of the black hole and conglomerates in a crust from which the planet is forming. The crust somehow blocks the center of the black hole's activity just as a plug blocks the spiral flow of water in a kitchen sink. Or, if you wish, it is like when you build an arch and the last stone or keystone in the top of the arch holds all the rest in balance and keeps the entire structure from falling to the ground."

Amazed, I listened to this explanation but could not understand what to believe. Was I finding out about an actual process or was I smelling fantasy-like science fiction?

Sincerely, I shared my thoughts with Dr. Xien.

"Maybe even Galileo would have thought like you if someone had explained the theory of relativity to him at that time. Many times, science has assumed the supremacy of knowledge thus far obtained, and each time it has had to admit to the fact that new elements always appear revealing that there are evolutionary stages of development."

"But is that crust enough to ensure the conditions of life on a planet?" I asked, willing to go further to find out new information.

"Things do not happen as accidentally as scientists believe. The so-called spontaneity of creation is more like the fruit of necessity. Elements combine, starting from the destiny of that manifesting soul that the planet is to the distinctiveness of the cosmic region where it exists. In the meanwhile, an interior habitat is being formed following its evolution and having in its center the black hole. They all reach a balance because of the conscious activity of the central black hole: matter, water, lava and all the rest.

"Is this singularity also conscious?" I asked, astounded.

"Of course. It is an evolved spirit taking care of what it created, but we are not discussing this now."

"So, the central black hole regulates proportions. Does it also adjust the elements on the surface?" I continued, accentuating the most sensitive point.

"In time, the exterior of the planet is also created, and there is a habitat. The temperature can increase and create a favorable atmosphere to maintain material life, but this is not mandatory. It is always a balance of forces and influences between the exterior and the interior, marked by the specific destiny of that celestial body. That is why we meet an extraordinary variety of possibilities and manifestations. We are talking here of planets, natural satellites, asteroids, comets or other celestial bodies. In the case of the stars, the process is similar, but the central black hole is much bigger so the temperature and pressure conditions determine other manifestations of the elements from the subtle plane. In this case, the dominant subtle element of manifestation is fire, and this is why the stars light up and become the main support center sustaining the planetary system in the material plane.

"Stars have another mission compared with that of planets. Does the water not interfere in these cases? Only in the first phase of creation does there exist a transformation to the fire element when the star then lights up; but what I want to underline is the fact that in the case of our planet, almost all of the existing water comes from the central black hole inside the planet. Keep in mind that most of the water comes from the so-called interior of the planet. The interior planetary ocean, which has also been identified by scientists, contains water created in the way already described. Moreover, there are many other water sources at different depths and in different zones inside the Earth. Theses include lakes or even seas."

"What you have said is contrary to everything that is known about cosmic genesis; and also about everything that is known about the way in which a black hole works," I said with a certain concern.

"Don't worry about it. For now, just observe that your answers are from the modern sciences and that its thinking and conceiving of the surrounding environment and universe are still materialistic. It is really tiresome to see so much limitation and sometimes even stupidity in some people pretending to be intelligent for having reached certain academic levels. Science does not even understand the nature of a vacuum. It does not conclude what consciousness really is. How could it therefore understand the mystery of the nature of a black hole's action or behavior? When it comes to the universe or any other aspect of creation, it is as if you are talking to a three-year-old child about differential equations and quantum mechanics. No matter how you tell him about these things or even about a beauty contest, he will only show you what he knows and that's grabbing the shovel he uses to play with in the sand."

I definitely understood that the up-to-date notions of science cannot penetrate the meaning of such revelations.

"But still, how does water appear from black holes?" I asked. "I don't need to see equations but rather hear the natural explanations."

"I told you that it is a phenomena of conversion that can be understood as a condensation from the subtle plane to the physical material plane. The converter is the central black hole of the planet. The water is pushed out in different historical stages of the planet and in different amounts. At the beginning, it is pushed out as ice in the cosmos where it combines with cosmic dust and other material elements. After the crust is made around the central black hole, the water created in the black hole supplies the interior ocean. Then, through breaks in the crust, it supplies the oceans and seas on the surface."

A PARALLEL WITH MODERN SCIENCE

Obviously, Dr. Xien's observations have little to do with the accretion theory of astrophysics where planets are formed over a long period of time through the collision and gathering together of many boulders made out of rocks and ores. Still, there are also other theories besides the accretion theory which answer people's wishes to discover certain questions and realities from the surrounding universe. Unhappily, they look for answers according to the extant knowledge of a limited conceptual level. If something contrary to these ideas is said, the theory is considered to be either an impossibility or just nonsense. Just as Dr. Xien emphasizes in a following discussion, one of the main causes of such failed thinking is that they do not pay enough attention to the concept of a fifth element in the universe, something which they consider to be more of a philosophical theory with nuances of fantasy rather than something truly real. On the other hand, scientists do not consider anything else other than the phenomena taking place in the material plane of cosmic space, forgetting or not realizing at all that such does not represent anything else other than the ultimate manifestation of superior energies and influences. It is at this point that black holes come into the discussion in regards to what exactly they represent and what they really manifest. To a certain extent, calculations and equations can describe a material manifestation of the phenomena surrounding a black hole. For example, the crust and mantle of the Earth are formed through accretion because the accretion manifesting around the black hole in the center of the planet is, in a certain way, similar to an accretion disc surrounding a cosmic black hole sucking the plasmatic matter of a star, cosmic dust, particles, stones, or boulders of different sizes, as long as they remain at an appropriate distance.

The next information I then received from Dr. Xien was like a thunderbolt to the ideas I already had regarding these matters. It was a pretty fast meltdown of the prejudices I have had. Still, there was something missing for me. I tried to justify myself in a certain way. It is hard to overcome the materialistic ideology of today. I confess that it is also difficult for me to accept the idea of black holes emitting water in order to form stars and liquid planets, just as which happens with some protostars and protoplanets. And, even though I have had the opportunity to see extraordinary things and convince myself of many of the amazing aspects I have already stated, I still found it difficult. Even after having had the process patiently explained to me, it is still hard for me to understand how water could spring out of a black hole and stay at the base of a forming planet. It was as if I could not get rid of this question.

"It is not as difficult to understand as it seems to you," Dr. Xien answered with amiability. "You'll have a reference point if you consider that the composition of comets contains a lot of ice, meaning water. All astrophysicists have a certain origination point in mind for comets but always beginning from a certain stage and a certain area in the cosmos. But, for example, where did the comet take that ice from? Or how did the ice appear as subtle water in the cosmic vacuum? The accretion theory does not stand, and they know this very well because it does not explain the formation of the gaseous planets. You cannot say that telluric planets are formed in a different way than the gaseous ones, but if you consider what I have already explained about ice being pushed out in the initial phases of a protoplanet from the central black hole and what follows afterwards, you can then understand the origin of comets more easily."

"Then," I asked spontaneously, "what is missing from the actual science in order to understand these things? Is it only the fact that it does not apply to the theory of the elements?"

"That is just a particular case. Generally speaking, contemporary scientists have a materialistic set of antique or beat up principles and conceptions systemically opposed to a wide understanding of the universe. Only a few have begun to have a holographic vision of how creation functions. Most of them still do not have the power of understanding right now because scientists' minds are limited to a frame of reference of space-time events belonging to the material plane.

This was the first discussion I had with Dr. Xien about the interior of the Earth. I almost did not sleep at all the following night, analyzing again and again what I had just learned. I did not believe that the subject of the interior of our planet could be so complex, and I was starting to have a more consistent amazement of the condition of things, realizing how insignificant as beings we apparently are. In comparison to the big mysteries of the universe, we, at the same time, have access to these mysteries if we know how to develop our inner capacities and if we understand correctly the things.

I could not wait for the dawn of a new day to come so I could meet with Cezar and we could debate these new elements revealed by Dr. Xien. Moreover, we had already established our travel to the Bugeci complex to prepare for an expedition. Wanting to make the best use of the available time, I took advantage of the situation by continuing to talk about this subject.

HOW TO GET INSIDE THE INTERIOR OF THE EARTH

After planning some technical and executive details inside the base, I left with Cezar to Bugeci. We preferred to travel by car in order to have a free discussion. As Cezar loves to drive, he does so any time he has the opportunity.

With a lot of enthusiasm, I shared a synthesis of what I had learned from Dr. Xien and expressed my hope that my knowledge level would allow me to successfully realize these matters during our upcoming journey.

Cezar dismissed my possible doubts.

"Things are already set," he said. "The journey is all set up. I can even tell you that we are awaited, and for this first journey, there will be no problems."

I was silent for a few seconds before asking doubtfully, "What do you mean by 'this first journey?' Will there be more expeditions?"

Cezar approved, nodding his head.

"There are many access levels inside the Earth, and your accommodation is necessary. The internal structure of the planet is very complex, and if what you found out from Dr. Xien amazed you, prepare yourself for what is coming. The interior walls are diverse and surprising."

Filled with mystery and projected out of the daily reality of the regular man, I enjoyed the state or condition of anticipation. Even though it was pretty common to have such an expedition within Department Zero, there were still special moments like this one, of preparing for a new expedition where your inner sensations and perceptions would amplify.

I rapidly opened up a discussion with Cezar, intending to clarify an older question I had about getting into the empty interior of the Earth.

"I understood that not everyone can get inside of the planet, especially at greater depths, but what about the location used to get inside. Is it important? Has it got any specificity? For example, does the Second Tunnel respect any rule in this regard?"

While asking, I looked at a clearly focused Cezar who was emitting an enormous self-confidence and energy of honesty. In my opinion, he is one of the few human beings capable of understanding such complex situations at their true value, even if such complications and confluences are completely random and whether or not they are connected to the material world or the spiritual world. He answered me in the direct and simple way that I have known very well for almost twenty years.

"The easiest way to get inside of a celestial body is by following the lines of its magnetic field. It is the very same in the case of the Earth. If you follow the magnetic field lines on the upper side, you will gradually get through the subtle planes — the etheric, astral, mental and causal — to the center. If you want to go directly by chance, then you go through the crust; but then, at a certain moment, you stop because you no longer have the capacity of understanding what is happening there and you lose your consciousness. Everything stops. As Dr. Xien also told you, 'Machines, technology, and mental processes: you either have the real capacity of getting in and then going further — meaning your being is ready for that vibrational jump — or you stop there where you can even become crazy'. So, up there at the poles, it is easier to get inside."

Continuing to think about these matters, I then wanted to implement the same technique I used on Dr. Xien with Cezar.

"Let's say that someone could pass into the planet with no problems on this magnetic line. What would he see then? Landscapes changing?"

"The thickness of the crust and some parts of the mantle are materially crossed; but then, there is no more physical matter because you are entering the subtle dimensions — the subtle, astral and so on."

"But, scientists give a pretty clear structure of the planet. Are they so wrong in the theory they present?"

I was not attempting to cross-check Cezar by asking him pretty much the same things I had asked Dr. Xien, but I was eager to assimilate more of these matters by looking at it from many different points of view.

"It is just their approximation based upon extrapolation and direct obser-vations, but there are also other realities. You will be convinced by yourself," Cezar assured me.

I was excited in anticipation for these moments and wished to find out more about our imminent travel, so I asked him, "Does the passing to the subtle planes take place all of a sudden?"

Before he would give me an answer, Cezar took a short break. I was watching him trying to carefully choose his words in order to make me better understand.

"No, it is not done suddenly. If you adhere to a certain continuity in movement, physical matter starts to become somehow lighter, then a plasma-like condition manifests which is an even more rarefied condition. You then emerge totally into the subtle planes where matter is actually energy materializing on different vibrational frequencies conditionally based upon the dimension or plane of manifestation you have reached. You cannot, however, move further beyond the zone from which you are energetically prepared. The subtle field there acts in a sort of elastic way. If a rough energy comes to it, this rebounds elastically, meaning that it cannot get in there because it is not recognized by the vibrational frequency."

I remained quiet for a while, trying to assimilate this information.

"So, you cannot make use of force?"

"No, you will lose your consciousness if you do, or you are simply rejected. If someone were to have an adequate mechanism and start digging like crazy directly to the center of the Earth, at a certain point, the device would simply stop. It could not work because its vibrational frequency originated out of

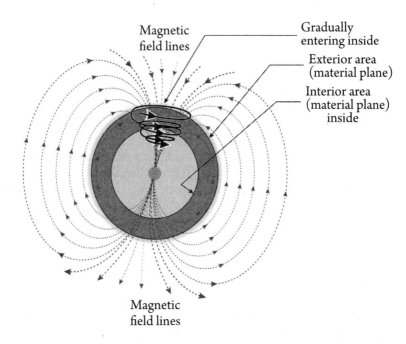

Magnetic field lines

Gradually entering inside

Exterior area (material plane)

Interior area (material plane) inside

Magnetic field lines

THE WAY OF ENTERING THE INNER EARTH
BY FOLLOWING ITS MAGNETIC LINES

the technology and constituent material and would no longer correspond to the internal layer that it has reached. You go as far as the frequency of your individual consciousness allows you to . This principle is valid as much for beings as for any objects made out of anthropomorphic matter ."

"I understand this, but still, I cannot imagine how such a device could be blocked from advancing."

Cezar thought for a little while; then offered me an expressive example.

"It is exactly like a space craft entering the atmosphere. If it comes in at too sharp an approach angle with a lot of energy, it will be consumed because of the intense friction. If the angle is too wide, then the gravity will reject it and the ship will bounce off the planet's atmosphere, but under a certain angle and direction, it can penetrate the atmosphere safely and reach the surface of the planet. This rule is primarily the same for entering the inside of the Earth where you can go through subtle dimensions, entering via the lines of the magnetic field, first on the etheric plane, then entering more and more subtle planes to the center. This, of course, depends upon the individual's level of consciousness being adapted to such a journey."

I interrupted Cezar, wanting a clarification.

"I know that man's subtle bodies cover the physical body, the last and most refined one being the causal body on the exterior, but from what I've discovered from Dr. Xien and yourself, it is not the same in the case of the planet."

"The human subtle bodies are presented as covering the physical body, and they extend more and more to the exterior, from the etheric to the causal body. Still, this extension is not only in one direction because the material body is also impregnated with the other subtle bodies inside. In the case of the Earth or another planet, things are just the same. Even if it is apparently reversed — in other words, that you start from the physical body and move to the center where the causal body resides — just the same, I can say that our planet also has an etheric body covering the physical body and that there is an astral body covering the etheric and so on. But, this is just a dimensional representation of the problem that the mind sets up in its need to understand the mechanism. The spiritual evolution of the human being, for example, is not designed to progress outward towards the exterior but rather in the direction of the interior of the being towards its spiritual core. From the perspective of the planet being an actual being, the fact that you can find the highest spiritual frequency in the spiritual center of the planet is perfectly justified. So, the problem is reversed but only in the mind's perspective which interprets it dimensionally, adding the ideas of inside and outside. That is why things seem to be opposed, but in reality, they are united."

I was now understanding the situation very well, and I thanked Cezar for his explanations.

CONCEPTUAL BARRIERS

For a while, we were quiet. Cezar was enjoying the driving and I was contemplating the notions I had learned during the last few hours. After several more minutes, we resumed our discussion on one of the sensitive points.

"I find it very interesting that this planetary forming process that Dr. Xien told me about doesn't have much to do with the current scientific conception of accretion theory."

Cezar nodded his head, approving.

"Interesting, isn't it? How far off the truth can they be with this, and how much can they struggle to restrict Mankind's consciousness by maintaining an antique and limited materialistic idea? In reality, all stars and planets either create themselves or are created starting with the black hole principle, but science understands phenomena only from the point of view by its obvious possibilities. Even their explanation of cosmic boulders colliding to form planets through accretion is obviously not enough. Still, it works out conceptually but only in the context of a very limited theoretical explanation. No matter how many errors, discrepancies or contradictory observations of this theory exist, they are stubborn in maintaining it, even if they figure out it could not work out."

"I wonder what makes them remain at this limited level of conceiving," I said, somewhat rhetorically.

I knew the answer, but still, I wanted to hear his opinion, too. I did not have to wait long.

"Hubris, arrogance and routine. The fact that some scientists obsessively beat up on thinking systems is absolutely materialistic. This stops them from having a wider vision of the universe. You can't keep forever asking for or relying upon proof through measurements as long as the measurement devices and technology are modest and relatively limited. In these cases, you only get what you wish for — I mean, at least as much as the devices can offer. This process requires noting down the specific frequencies of the phenomena you seek to observe. Only then can you become aware of the existence of such through measurement devices, but you also have to increase your personal vibration and frequency in order to make effective changes in the technology. In this regard, scientific scrutiny also requires a change in thinking and behavior; and only then will one be able to perceive this phenomena or superior reality. The main barrier to the scientific process is conceiving of the world with a completely materialistic view."

"Anyway, it seems to me that the idea of a small-sized black hole being a source of planetary formation is too much for them to accept."

"Astrophysicists also conceived an outline for such a model when they created a theory of stars forming from stellar dust clouds as a result of gradually rotating matter, but they tried to solve everything from a materialistic point of view and ended up going backwards. Actually, this fundamental vortex first appears like a singularity manifesting a field of rotating forces that become more and more intense until the first outlines of physical matter appear, namely stardust; and then, after a while, water also appears."

"It is very interesting and amazing how things actually happen in the cosmos; that is, how matter appears," I said, really fascinated with these mysteries.

"There are a few voices in science now who assume that the main elements of matter; namely electrons, protons and neutrons; are formed inside the intense magnetic areas near some very fast rotating black holes. Other scientists consider that these elements appear from nothingness and then melt back to nothingness. I am referring to the cosmic vacuum. Actually, this vacuum is real and it exists even if its energy appears to be magic. Any small vortex existing in the cosmos represents a small black hole, and the energy of the vacuum is condensed and manifests through it like a thing filled, a sort of liquid vacuum similar to a liquid surface always swirling."

"I somehow understand, but I doubt that modern scientists can even listen to such things. I also said as much to Dr. Xien."

"I studied the problem because it was of interest to me. To your surprise, scientists have already discovered this truth, but they don't understand what to do with it.* The fact that they are so stubborn in saying such things is not something natural in this universe. It's their problem and not ours. In the same way, they imagine that all events are a circumstance of 'coincidence,' a smaller or a bigger instance of chaos from which life just 'happens' to manifest, creating a star, planets or whatever."

I was amused because Cezar was using almost the same expressions as Dr. Xien, meaning that these teachings had deep roots inside of him, too.

"According to the conceptions of contemporary scientists, the only governing principles are the rules of the material universe as applied to a limited domain of reality. Variables always appear. There are always question marks. There are always unsolved mysteries, even if their laws say that a certain object, phenomena, or manifestation should not exist where it appears or in the shape it appears. You can't build a building by using only the chisel and hammer because you risk its breakdown. You have no connecting elements. You do not know the essence of the project. In such cases, scientists should study documents, engage in research and be open to other wider possibilities in order to realize a meaningful conceptual jump. Up to now, it has not hap-

---

* [From the Romanian editor] The author is probably referring to the Bose-Einstein capacitor which demonstrates a condition of matter different from the one's we know in nature where atoms begin to correlate and act in unison when the temperature is very close to absolute zero.

pened, but maybe there are chances that such will occur in the near future."

ACCESS TO THE INSIDE VIA THE POLES:
SUBTLETIES, LANDMARKS, CERTAINTIES

"I can't see how they could do this unless they can conceive of the existence of a subtle dimension of manifestation superior to the vibrational frequency of matter," I said. "They will have no access inside of the planet. They wouldn't know how to get inside."

"Indeed. People do not understand how the passing to the subtle dimension is done. They all imagine that the empty Earth should be like the inside of an empty coconut. Once again, this is due to the purely materialistic conceptions that they have about things. Look at those who have described getting to the inside of the world by boat. What do you think actually happened?"

"I know these sorts of stories too well and can also interpret them based

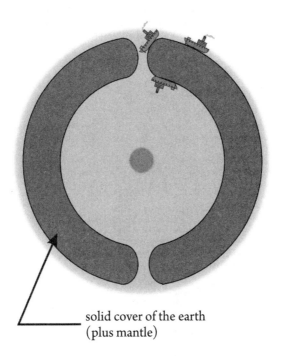

solid cover of the earth
(plus mantle)

**SCHEMATIC REPRESENTATION OF GETTING
INSIDE THE PLANET FROM THE NORTH POLE**

upon what we have just discussed," I said. "Floating near the Arctic center was an opportunity for them align with one of the magnetic and gravitational field lines leading inside."

"Exactly. At the poles, it is easier to get in if there is a shared resonance between the frequency of the etheric plane and the individual's frequency. It also depends upon the speed of the boat as it intersects with the magnetic and gravitational lines. If it fluctuates, you will miss entering the precise point where the magnetic lines of the poles are aligned with the gravitational field. The important thing is that the speed of the boat must be constant. You will not get inside at the equator because the magnetic field lines are perpendicular to the gravitational field and their influence does not produce this effect. Instead, biological diversity is encouraged at such a locale; but at the edge of the magnetic cone in the Arctic, right at the limit of the transition to the etheric plane towards the inside of the Earth, the magnetic field is strong and becomes aligned with the lines of the gravitational field. Their association and mutual influence is transmitted to the essence of the physical body which

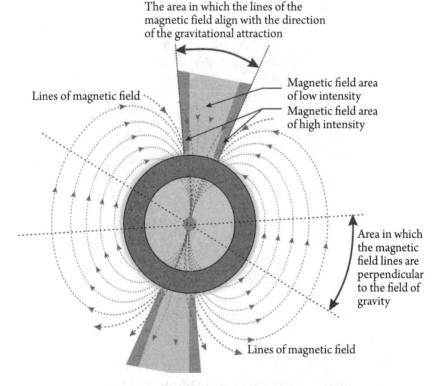

The area in which the lines of the magnetic field align with the direction of the gravitational attraction

Lines of magnetic field

Magnetic field area of low intensity

Magnetic field area of high intensity

Area in which the magnetic field lines are perpendicular to the field of gravity

Lines of magnetic field

"THE MAGNETIC CONE AND THE AREA OF ALIGNING THE GRAVITY TO THE MAGNETIC FIELD LINES"

is strongly energized. Then, as you enter the magnetic cone, the intensity of the field gets lower but the vibrational frequency of the body's atoms rises, allowing it to pass to the etheric plane along the magnetic field's lines."

"I got it. Let's say that I am at the edge of the magnetic cone and I respect the given conditions. Do I then enter inside the earth?"

"You have three possibilities. If your direction is not toward the pole, then you continue along on the ocean floating above the entry zone. In this case, you remain on the material plane. You don't understand what that area represents. You do not feel anything and you do not get inside the planet. If your direction is closer but not on the exact line going to the pole, you then enter a certain trance-like state in which you figure that something unusual has happened. You might even receive certain information, but that's about it. It is just an internal experience. Physically, you crossed the access area with your boat but without getting inside the Earth. But, if your direction is toward the pole, there are a lot of chances to enter the etheric plane, and through it, the inside of the Earth. But for this, you need your individual frequency to be equal or near to the crossing frequency. In other words, if your consciousness and level of understanding is compatible with crossing — I mean pure and high enough — you can align yourself with the magnetic and gravitational fields and move into the next plane which is the etheric plane. In this way, you access what is called the Inner Earth."

While Cezar explained all of this to me, I was preparing to mentally speak for myself with regard to such ideas. To make things clear, I drew a few sketches after coming back to the base. The illustration on the next page is the final version representing the three possibilities. But let us not forget that this is just a material drawing attempting to represent a subtle reality from one point of view. For example, the drawing suggests that when we get inside, we apparently turn around with the boat on the interior following the bending in the drawing. In reality, if someone were to have such an experience, they would feel neither bending nor such an upside down turnover. This is not because of the wide radius of curvature as some have tried to suggest but rather because, in reality, one has crossed through the entrance to the subtle etheric plane. Once there, one will not perceive the upside down turning but will just follow the magnetic and gravitational direction to the center to the Earth.

Water will also surround us. We will generally see the same sky, but before long, other elements will begin to appear, and we will know no reason for their presence in Arctic waters. Those who describe such experiences say they have entered inside the Earth, but they think this way because they continue believing that they are in the material plane. Actually, they have already entered another dimension, the etheric one corresponding to our planet in that area. Not knowing about such subtle reality, they try to associ-

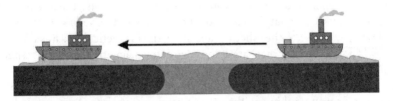

The ship goes above the entrance zone to the Inner Earth

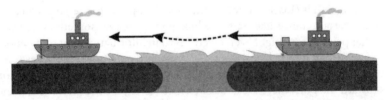

The ship goes partially through the entrance zone to the Inner Earth

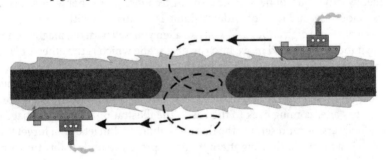

The ship gets inside the Earth on the magnetic field lines

THREE POTENTIAL OUTCOMES WHEN CROSSING THE POLAR ACCESS ZONE TO THE INNER EARTH

ate this with what they already know on the material plane, and this is why they are feeling that they, in a certain way, have arrived in the empty interior of the planet.

Cezar then explained something to me that might appear very strange and is also a primary factor causing people to misunderstand this phenomena. Shortly after reaching the etheric dimension of the Earth, if you look at the middle of the sky, you can see the central sun of the planet which is different than our sun in the sky in the material plane. In very rare cases, however, and for a short period of time under certain circumstances, you can see two suns. One is in the physical plane, the celestial body from cosmic space, and the other one is the sun from the etheric plane inside the planet. Soon, however, only the sun in the etheric plane remains because one is now travelling in a different realm, and this one has a less intense light and a smaller size.

"It is still not quite clear to me how the sun inside the Earth could represent the black hole at the center of the planet," I said. "I am just about certain that there be an error in the presentation. It is either a singularity, an absorbing black hole, or a sun."

I was apparently right. Inside, however, I was feeling that my thinking was somehow frail because of a "germ" of not-knowing.

"Neither Dr. Xien nor myself told you that there is a star in the middle of the planet," Cezar answered. "What is seen there, like a sun, is actually the illuminating expression of the central black hole in the etheric plane. Normally, you cannot see anything there because the vibrational frequency of the singularity is very high, overcoming the frequency of the physical spectrum."

"Why then is there a sun making light?" I asked, surprised.

"Actually, it is the radiation of light emitted by the black hole, and the light appears out of the matter absorption process. What you see exactly with this phenomena is a transmutation of bright etheric radiation because you are already in the etheric plane at that point. It is called the interior sun because we are used to naming something that generates light in the sky as a sun. The central black hole that is referred to as the interior sun has its own magnetic and gravitational field. It has an angular speed of its own and these elements determine the rate of absorption of matter which occurs gradually but it does indeed happen. The interior sunlight is a bit weaker than the sun you see in the sky in the physical plane. That is why the interior sun is also named the smoky sun."

I was quiet for a while, feeling almost dizzy from these explanations. I was looking to clarify this new precious knowledge out of the remains of either false or misunderstood information I had acquired up to that moment, courtesy of what contemporary science has provided and still does.

"Going from the physical plane to the etheric plane requires you to fulfill one more condition," Cezar told me. "If you are ready internally, and if there is a resonance between the vibrational frequency of your consciousness and the vibrational frequency of the etheric plane, there is a communal range of frequencies between those two planes which you will have to cross past without losing your consciousness. You must remain perfectly aware during that short passing. Getting into the etheric plane does not happen all of a sudden but is a rather smooth and gradual transition. It continues for a reasonable amount of time. The more ready the being is, the less uncomfortable is the passing. The transition can still be felt, however, especially when something strange happens. Things seem to remain the same in the beginning, but they start to change as new elements enter the picture and become flagrant such as vegetation in the Arctic, warm wind, warmer water, a new sun, and new animals as never seen before."

"And this is the world inside the Earth?" I asked out of curiosity.

"There are many such worlds inside our planet. It depends upon which you are referring to. There are civilizations, and I say that with a restricted sense of that word, which exist in huge cavities right inside of the terrestrial crust."

"The crust of the planet is physical; but a transition zone to the etheric plane already appears near the terrestrial mantle. This material portion of the planet is not too thick in section and appears to be like a honeycomb with many cavities of different sizes. Some of them are empty, others have living beings there, or there are cities with smaller or larger communities. There are also different types of beings. Other such bubbles inside the Earth are filled with lava or oil, and some of them also contain huge lakes within them. We can call them underground worlds if we choose, and there is a lot of diversity amongst them. Some of these communities that are closer to the surface are integrated into the material plane. Others situated deeper act as if they are already situated in the etheric plane or are interconnected to it."

ON WATERS, IN CAVES, OR THROUGH THE WOODS

"If this is the interior structure of the Earth's crust, then I believe that all of the beings living there do not just get in and out at the poles. They probably have other access points, just as we can enter through the Second Tunnel."

"Of course. Actually, these are three main ways to the center of the planet. The first is at the poles, and it is the easiest. We already described it. The second possibility is through some special places, usually caves or caverns inside the mountains, but such could also be on the surface of the ground, in the woods or even in the fields. Scientists call them space-time distortions or portals; and, in a way, this is exactly what they are. To be more specific, they primarily represent the intersection of energy vortexes in the material with those of the etheric plane. Sometimes, the energy vortexes of the astral plane are involved. There, where they intersect each other, a sort of energetic boundary is established on the physical surface of the Earth, a special zone. Some of these energetic boundaries continue to last longer than others with some lasting a shorter period. The strongest could last as long as hundreds or even thousands of years. Others might be a few minutes long."

"Is this the reason why ancient priests used to perform invoking rituals in the forest?"

"It is one of the reasons. This is why they say that there are forests where people are afraid to go. It is not because these forests have a problem but rather because a crossing to the etheric plane inside these forests either exists or once existed; and further, it contains a different reality. The vegetation or beings are different than those from the material plane; and most of the time, this frightens human beings. No longer in their accustomed space and time, people get confused. They do not understand what has happened to them, not realizing that they are actually in another plane of manifestation, one superior to the material plane. For example, some of these special forests could be relatively small-sized; and after getting inside, people could go on for days without getting to an end because they were already in another dimension, usually in the etheric plane where the forest located there had some different characteristics. But, the inverse could also happen. Everything depends upon the specifics of the cross-point."

After a short break, Cezar continued.

"If you get by or go in there, and if you are ready for such a thing, your crossing into the etheric plane is completed. You then get right inside the interior of the Earth; but for this to happen, I repeat, you must be ready. You must have the correct inner state to understand these aspects and in order to be in the right place at the right time. If necessary, all these elements arrange themselves, just as they should. For example, you walk through the forest and a path appears that is different from all the others. You follow it and reach a cliff where you see an ordinary entrance to a cave. That cave or entrance in the mountain did not exist until then. Following that entrance, you then go deeper and deeper; but as you go further into the cave, you get the feeling that its walls are getting narrower and narrower and that they are flowing like a river, flowing faster and faster, even if you go as usual."

"Are there many such special places?" I asked, fascinated by the discussion.

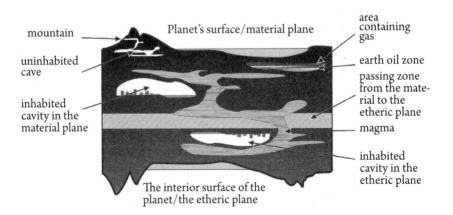

STRUCTURAL ELEMENTS IN THE CRUST AND MANTLE OF THE PLANET

69

"Their fluctuations are great, but some of them are well known, lasting for a long time and remaining very strong. Even if they have become well known to some people, however, the effect they create is first fear and even panic. The instinct of self-preservation then acts very powerfully in the man. The fear of the unknown, amplified by stories and other strange elements happening around one, creates a sometimes terrifying legend of such a place. The tendency of both the locals and the authorities is to block the access. The tension appearing at the shift of the vibrational frequency at these places generates a state of confusion, powerful emotions, mental chaos, and even more often, the strong feeling of fear."

I interrupted by asking something that seemed important to me.

"But, assuming you move through such an objective boundary, does the space-time proportion remain the same as in the material plane? I would say no."

"You are right. A relatively small distance crossed inside such an energetic boundary could means tens or even hundreds of kilometers in the material plane. Travel inside the Earth is usually fast if you have the right means or if you come to pass the right energetic portal."

After giving these explanations, Cezar told me about the third possibility of accessing the Inner Earth.

"This was used in antiquity, and it was part of their actual beliefs because it was natural to them. In this case, going inside of the Earth is done on water. For example, you are on a boat on an actual lake. Pretty soon, a strange fog appears, and once you are inside of it, you are in another place. This shows that you have already entered into the etheric plane, and most probably you are inside the planet."

"That could explain the specific situation with regard to the Bermuda Triangle," I said immediately.

"That is right. The only problem in such instances of planes going into the fog is that the machines on board no longer work because the resonant frequency changes. You have no idea where you are or where to go and even the engines tend to stop working, but as long as you are on a ship, you will simply float adrift through that fog until, at a certain moment, you get out of it. At that point, however, you are already inside the Earth on the etheric plane."

"These things seems to be sort of random to me. There is a large amount of unknown involved and even risk."

"Only apparently. Some of these zones are like energetic operating bases which are known very well by the inside inhabitants and that's why, in most of the cases, you are awaited and welcomed when emerging from the white fog. This happens not only on the waters but also in the distortion areas on land, inside mountain caves, or other such passings inside the Earth. You will convince yourself of it soon. A good example is that of King Arthur and his knights who knew how to go to the land or island of the wise men. That did not belong to the material plane but could be reached by crossing a fog on a lake. This was historically represented in an etching where their boat was depicted on a lake beneath the water and you can see a snake biting its tail, making a circle, or better said, an oval. This is the ouroboros snake from many energetic traditions, but its meaning is the same. It means the connection to the vacuum energy and crossing from the material plane to the superior plane of manifestation which is the etheric. It is done through such a void which is, in fact, a singularity."

I was amazed that people in that age had a special knowledge about planes and subtle dimensions and that they even knew how and where and were able to access them as they wished. Cezar then added some more specifics.

"Indeed. It shows some initiatic information that Arthur and the ones close to him had in those times. You know that, so far, his fortress Avalon has not been identified. That's why history and culture prefer to add Arthur, Merlin and their stronghold to the category of myth and legend. It is easier and more convenient, and their excuse is that no evidence was found; but the absence of such proofs — due to the fact that these citadels, cities or characters either did not exist or did not remain in the material plane but belonged to the etheric plane — can be found in many other cases. For example, there is the Incan city of El Dorado, the citadel of Troy and still many others that nothing is known of or where the information is contradictory."

The last twenty-four hours had been a very convincing and powerful ideological tour whereby my conception of the internal structure of the planet was totally reset in a certain measure. I felt ready to go for the first trip, but the departure was scheduled in a few days. Once we arrived at the location inside Bucegi, I asked Cezar for two hours rest and that is what I did. Then, full of unexpected resources and exaltation inside my soul, I returned to the magic atmosphere of the Projection Room.

CHAPTER TWO

THE GREAT CONTROVERSY:

SOLID OR EMPTY ON THE INSIDE?

After waking up, I verified and signed some official documents for a short while. The new executive and organizational structure in the secret base at Bucegi has now become an optimally functioning system. The tasks were therefore easy to assign as the command structure had been greatly simplified. Most of this was due to exceptional American technology that has been in use at the secret base. While some of these technological elements broach upon what is found in science fiction books, the reality is that we are now enjoying them. Everyone in the Department knows that this technology does not come from government projects but rather from some other quarter, but there is a tacit agreement between ourselves and the Pentagon's American officers not to exacerbate the sensitivity of this very delicate subject. Accordingly, I have an increased responsibility; and as there are certain aspects that have more to do with the American side, I will not mention the various technologies that have been specifically designed for this location.

UPDATE

The surveillance and security systems of the base are so sophisticated that the need for staff is greatly reduced. If one decides to go on a mountain hike and gets a chance to penetrate the area, they will not see the road leading to the location as it has been disguised in a very clever way. But, even if, in the event of some security breach, you were able to find and follow the short piece of road with its woodsy appearance, you will pass right on by the mountain without understanding that you have just missed what is perhaps the most important secret base on the planet now. To get to this security level, the thickness of the mountain was simply extended to a distance of almost thirty meters in order to fill in the entrance area; and on the left, the topography was turned into a curve of more than eighty meters that was then covered with soil and vegetation. These changes included a configuration of what seems to be a sharp cliff extending up to the mountains with firs atop it. I was there with Cezar when this change was actualized and was amazed to see how efficient this technology is. If they could manifest such things in such a simple and fast way, it means that, if they wish to, they would have no problem building bases on any suitable planet or satellite.

Neither conventional sources of energy nor materials are utilized for such construction. The entire operation was huge in size and would have been extremely difficult to put together with regular technological capabilities, but this state-of-the-art technology accomplished it in only two days. The first day was focused only on the setting, programming and layout by way of three mechanisms being successively utilized, none of which resembled anything from contemporary technology. The process was sort of like magic, the likes of which I have never seen. It overcomes the conceptual image that I had about both construction and matter. Two separate perspectives were taken into account with regard to this topographical change. The first concerned increased security for the entire base area. The second one was to create a new space inside for a command and control center. This space included energy resources and a functional redistribution of departments because the scientific analysis laboratory had been returned to the secret complex. Many years ago, it had been relocated to a specially arranged building in Bucharest, but it was observed that the procedures proved to be inferior without justifying any substantial improvement in the quality of the discoveries. It was General Obadea who brought up the idea of returning the laboratory to the secret complex, just the way it existed in its first years. His idea was brought to a happy conclusion by Cezar just more than a year after the General's death.

The research laboratory was returned to the three long rooms inside the hangar that had been dug into the mountain. These included resting spaces used for expedition preparations and a small dining hall that was created in the new space created by extending the mountain. These three rooms were transformed into larger spaces equipped with very sophisticated devices, and a big room was configured to house the original laboratory. The team of scientists was generically made up of three people who did not know what the secret location was really all about. They only received directions to study various artifacts and devices that were brought to the laboratory. The contracts that the researchers signed were six months long and included very severe conditions which were overseen by the American contingent. They were renewable only once for the same person.

The massive sliding doors at both the hangar's entrance and the tunnel in the mountain were also eliminated. In their place, a very advanced technology was used featuring energetic protection fields masked with holographic projection. A very interesting aspect of the security system is that these energetic fields are adapted to a resonant frequency specific for each of the individuals that have clearance to enter the Great Gallery and the Projection Room. Arriving at the secret location, those who have access inside wear a sort of bracelet like a flat watch which emits the frequency granting clearance. When in front of the energetic field at the entrance, it automatically allows access to that person. The technology is also a part of America's secret sect of high technology, allowing us to eliminate all other checking and protection barriers. For example, there were originally human guards provided for the entrances to the tunnel, the Great Gallery and the Projection Room, but they were all completely replaced by this amazing and very restricted technology. I am not, however, allowed to describe the devices that create the energetic field nor the unconventional sustaining source of energy. This radical simplification of security has accomplished more than just virtually complete protection. It also satisfied an older wish of both General Obadea and Cezar who were not agreeable to a big influx of people into the Projection Room. There was something very special about this secret architectural development inside the mountain. To a certain measure, in the earlier books I have written, I have tried to recreate the unforgettable impression that both entering or staying in this space gives you. It is radically different than the regular experiences one has in the outside world.

A sensitive person might say that "it leaves a feeling of nostalgia in your soul" while somebody else could describe it as "a mysterious hall to the unknown" and others could define everything as true magic. Personally, I think each of these descriptions contains a partial truth because, as I already mentioned, when you get into the Great Gallery and especially the Projection Room, it is like going into another world. The feeling is complex and amazing at the same time. You feel like you have been transported to a sacred place. Even the fact that there is no trace of dust or dirt inside the location is meaningful. But beyond all this, there is the uncontested sacred character. You feel somehow lighter and worry free, like you would not want to go back to the world of people. Dark thoughts disappear. Low down and petty or mean activities and plans also disappear. All you wish for is a continuous longing for good and harmony.

Getting back to the general structural elements of the location, one of the most sophisticated areas of the military complex in Bucegi is the control room that was built inside the artificial enlargement of the mountain. From this place, everything surrounding the location is monitored, including the access paths, the energetic functioning of such paths, and also all the energy that is emitted from this installation. It is hard to conceive that such technology could exist on Earth, but it is now a reality in our secret location. For example, it assures a psychological protection barrier, but the technology is radically different than what is known as HAARP which is, by contrast, more like a children's game as opposed to the subtle energetic protection that is provided for preventing others from getting too close to this zone. If a person does get too close, they begin to feel perplexed, misdirected and unsure; or a small light dizziness takes over the person, all of which is enough to make them draw back. The remarkable thing is that this technology acts in an intelligent way without human assistance either measuring or knowing if the intruders are heading to the secret complex. Only if this happens, and only from a certain distance, does the protective effect then appear, but this represents just one example of technology introduced there and one which is considered to be relatively simple. There are, however, others which are much more sophisticated and these have to do with defense, other types of entry or even military aggression into the zone. The entire location represents a completely self-contained and secure system.

Before entering the Projection Room, I had a meeting with Cezar and we ate together. There is no kitchen in the base. The meals are provided as that which an astronaut would have, placed into special packages. It was decided that relinquishing a series of facilities and functions that are otherwise common in a regular military base was absolutely necessary in order to minimize complications, especially with regard to maintaining minimum staff. The conditions at the base are so good and the technological facilities so vast that someone can live without problems in both physical and mental comfort.

THE PROJECTION ROOM, ANOTHER WORLD

After the meal, I entered the tunnel with Cezar through the energetic screen. Approaching it, the particular frequency emanating from the bracelet creates a slight luminosity of blue iridescence in a part of the energetic field that is rather pleasant, accompanied by a vague hum. One passes through the field individually. The only feeling accompanying this a very large sensation of tingling or numbness, but it only lasts for fractions of a second. Once inside the tunnel, the outside appears completely opaque. If you look behind, you see only a world of blue phosphorescent color.

The electric transport vehicles that I like so much were awaiting us, aligned on the right side of the tunnel. The light to the Great Gallery entrance, now less intense than the first years of the establishment, is discrete and pleasant. The red lights on the walls had been replaced by a nice LED system.

I slowly passed the short distance to the giant stone gate guarding the entrance to the Great Gallery. It was open, but the entrance was blocked by the energetic field that acts like a curtain undulating in slow motion but with a greenish semi-transparent color. This replaced the old and complicated laser system and, of course, the two military guards that had been part of the access protocol. At our coming, the energetic curtain acted just like when we entered the tunnel, becoming a bit effervescent and making that refreshing low hum. I went under the arch of the imposing stone gate and could not resist commenting, a bit amused, that not even now is the technology that we are using completely understood. I abandoned myself in the hypnotic magic of the path through the Great Gallery with those undulating "waters" of colors that relax the mind, body and soul until I arrived at the entrance splendidly framed by the bluish magnetic field guarding the access to the Projection Room. Just as excited as I had been each time I was there, I stepped into the immense underground space. Although I had been there many times in the previous three years, the feeling of the sacred never disappears. You do not get used to being there. You do not get either bored or tired. It is a real technological wonder and a spiritual marvel at the same time, something for which Humankind should probably pass through evolutionary stages in order to reach a proper understanding thereof. Cezar respected my immersion into this rarified environment and remained silent, walking slowly next to me. I was feeling myself emerge out of that silent tingling, from that light coming out of nowhere, and out of that energetic subtle field that invaded my being, my soul, and my heart. I had acquired the habit of, after getting inside the huge cavity under the mountain, not looking right ahead to the giant openings of the three tunnels within the Projection Room. I have also noticed that the consciousness goes on a sort of a strange hiatus with the senses, perceptions, and certain other capacities becoming slightly staggered from the regular and continuous way that they should be manifesting. Studies and observations showed us that this was common to almost everyone going inside the Projection Room; and that is why it was recommended that, at first, the gaze should be directed to the ground or to the side, laterally; but after the middle area of the hall near the podium with the cylinder is reached, the strange feeling or sensation of duality disappears. During two of the visits I have paid to this location, I was alone in the Projection Room. This was a privilege that only Cezar and I have enjoyed since General Obadea's death and after my investiture with the commission. It is, however, only by living through the direct experience of such an environment that you can be privy to the inner emotional state that overwhelms your entire being. As Cezar knew too well the extraordinary inner force that accumulates as a result of remaining in the Projection Room, he allowed my access; but still, he advised me to be watchful about my inner state of evolution. I stayed for many hours during each visit, experiencing very intense emotions and conditions that were also very profound. It was like a trance until exiting from the tunnel whereupon everything would fade away very quickly as I returned to the base with only an unclear memory remaining that resembled a night dream. I discussed this aspect with Cezar, and he told me that the difference between the individual frequency of my being and the specific frequency of the subtle space in the Projection Room is still pretty large, and it takes time for these factors to adjust; and further, that they do so by reason of exercise and repetition.

Even so, he considered me to be ready for the expedition to the Second Tunnel which actually is the central tunnel, the one leading inside the Earth. From inside the Projection Room, the openings of the tunnels appear to be immense, imposing and somehow hypnotic, the feeling being accentuated by the light green iridescence appearing at the tunnel openings which, in reality, comes from inside of them. From a certain distance inside the room, however, the tunnels cannot be seen. But, when you move around and see the openings under different angles, you notice that the luminosity is also different. It almost disappears completely sometimes, the opening then appearing to be dark. Other times, their light goes to turquoise.

I arrived at the consul and Cezar initiated the controls. In front of us appeared a holographic projection of the interior of the tunnel representing its first part, and only then could I see certain pictures. The first impression was that this, structurally speaking, was not any different from the First Tunnel leading to the occult chamber near the Great Pyramid in Egypt. Once inside, however, I observed major differences. The Second Tunnel or central one starts descending in a smooth decline a few meters after entering it. On the other hand, the space distortion device, similar to the "trumpet cone" at the entrance to the tunnel to Egypt, was not at the beginning section of the tunnel but rather a little further downward and was related to another specificity. Immediately after the distortion, the hologram showed the entrance to a space wider than the tunnel's diameter, a sort of cube with a length of about eight to nine meters. Observing that certain dates were constantly changing on the console, I guessed that there was an energetic dynamic element that was not represented.

There were diamond-shaped alcoves in which the quartz-colored crystals were similarly arranged on both sides of the access door, but we did not notice the grooves in the walls that exist in the First Tunnel, possibly serving as navigation markers. Also, the tunnel did not feature a sideways turn like the one to Egypt but went on in a particular direction after starting to descend into the interior.

My attention was captured by a sudden change of the hologram in front of the console where the image of a human being appeared in the interior of the tunnel. The creature had white skin and stood still, looking in our direction. As I estimated it, he was approximately 1.8 meters high and was wearing a long robe like a Franciscan monk. The garment was white-beige in color, featured a hood, and was long to the ground with a narrow center around the hips. The look of this figure was very intense as it rested still for a while at the beginning of our encounter. Then, he slowly lifted his right hand with the palm facing us from his chest as a gesture of alliance. Right after this, he made a gesture like a fan, and his image disappeared.

I remained staring at the empty image from the hologram. No question was needed because Cezar talked to me very naturally while closing the hologram and the controls on the console.

"His name is Dryn, but it is spoken like 'Drian,'" Cezar said. "He is one of the wise men we are headed to. We have met many times before and have

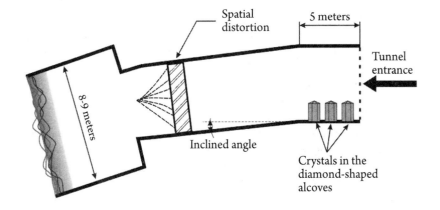

Spatial distortion · **5 meters** · **Tunnel entrance** · **8-9 meters** · **Inclined angle** · **Crystals in the diamond-shaped alcoves**

THE TUNNEL STRUCTURE INSIDE THE EARTH

collaborated. The travel we will make now has already been programmed. He only confirmed that they are awaiting us."

Cezar then took a big briefcase that he had brought with him and placed it on the ground inside the tunnel, leaving it there. As we walked to the exit, I was silent. I knew that it was not necessary to insistently question with regard to certain matters. If it was really necessary, Cezar would have explained to me what I needed to know. Some of the information in the Department was restricted to me because I did not yet have the security clearance to know it.

MYSTERIOUS MEETINGS

Based upon what Cezar has shared with me about his travels over the last few years, I have learned that the connections, relationships and alliances to those existing inside of our planet are complex; and maintaining them is a very difficult task because of the high level secrets involved and the fact that the governments of the great powers are especially interested to know them. The biggest problem in this regard is generated by the interest of some occult groups and organizations who exercise very strong control and even have an agenda of conquest. There are also issues involving national security, the concerns of which are much more profound.

As the years have gone by, the situation is even more complex than we originally thought. Although not asking for more than what was needed, I was still informed about the discussions on this subject between Cezar and General Obadea while the latter was still alive. I also knew about the strictly secret meetings of the Romanian-American selective group that had only a few members. These meetings took place especially after Cezar's return from his expeditions inside the Earth, two of them after returning with his crew from the tunnel to Tibet. Although I was in charge of the logistical organizing of these meetings, I did not participate in them nor am I allowed to offer any details regarding the place, the numbers of persons or the participants involved.

I can say, however, that these meetings had a different rhythm and criteria than those we are accustomed to at this diplomatic level. Sometimes, things just cannot be solved through common methods because they belong to a different level of knowledge. This was the main reason why these meetings were not recorded and why no stenography was allowed, except for the last one of them where an agreement at the highest level was secured. The technique used to make it secure was amazing because, obviously, a lot of other countries want details about what happens here. At two of these meetings, Cezar came accompanied by a man who was not wearing a suit or a military uniform, and he seemed to move and talk differently than the other members. Initially, I was surprised because the person was not included in the very strict diagram or grading structure of the meeting and Cezar had not announced anything to me. Inside the secret services, you quickly understand when you are not supposed to ask uncomfortable questions. I was, however, very interested to observe this person because I noticed his special way of being. I did not get a chance to understand this first man very well because I was in a neighboring room as he passed through the corridor with Cezar. I could follow him for only a few seconds as he walked with a unique footstep that was somehow imperial, imposing, towering and thoughtful. But I was luckier with the second character because I was right near the heliport taking care of security.

As Cezar and the mysterious character descended from the helicopter, they were welcomed by General Obadea. Before entering the building, the General and Cezar stopped for a few seconds to discuss an issue, and from what I figured, it involved a certain choice. During that short time, the stranger remained at a certain distance from the two. Keeping his hands and arms at his back and his head slightly tilted in a forward direction, I was looking from the back and admiring his elevated and confident attitude, seemingly very detached of this world's uncertainties. To my big surprise, he turned to me at this moment, looking exactly at me with a kind but bland manner and exhibiting an imperceptible smile on his face. The man then turned his back; and immediately afterwards, all three continued their way to the building. I then wondered how fast my heart was beating without understanding too well why.

A MORE PROFOUND UNDERSTANDING

Returning to Alpha Base, we were welcomed by Dr. Xien who went with Cezar into one of the offices. I then noticed that the Doctor was holding something in his hand which seemed to be a map, but I couldn't figure out what it represented. On the following day, when Cezar went to Bucharest for certain official meetings, I found this the right time to clarify some aspects about the interior of the planet. The expedition was about to take place in two days, so I had enough time to settle down and take my last opportunity to secure what knowledge I could about the internal structure of the Earth. Taking advantage of the beautiful weather in the evening, I accosted Dr. Xien while he was in a more private area of the base, appearing motionless while looking at the distant setting sun.

"I have been imagining a certain situation by which the Earth could be viewed in a way that the factors we talked about a few days ago do not apply."

Unperturbed, Dr. Xien made a gesture to continue our discussion.

"Let's say that we are in outer space, about 2,000 kilometers in altitude; and hypothetically, the planet is cut in half by a laser beam. It is an action in the material plane. My question to you is, 'What could be seen from outer space if the Earth could be sliced into two pieces like an apple?'"

This idea had come to me on my way back to the Base, but I was not ready to start a discussion then, willing to think about it by myself first, in a very special way. Passing from the physical plane to the subtle plane of manifestation, how could such a thing be seen? How should we understand this transition area? After arriving at the base, I spent most of the night contemplating this problem from different perspectives, but I was not convinced that I had found the right answer. The following day, I decided that I would open the discussion and ask for an explanation. Finding out that Cezar had gone to the capital, I went to Dr. Xien to hear what he had to say. After all, it was even better this way, considering the fact that the entire discussion about the interior of the Earth had started with him.

Dr. Xien answered, looking at the red disc that was the sun.

"First, you need to understand that, theoretically speaking, you cannot carve the Earth into two pieces with a laser because the laser cannot cut into a black hole. The singularity that is in the middle of the Earth represents the real source of its forming. If the laser beam were to enter inside of the black hole, its photons would not come out. So, the action of cutting would be compromised from the start."

I was silent for a moment, impressed by this very simple point of logic that I had not thought of. Instead, I was concerned about how the successive planes of manifestation would be affected as the laser might approach the center of the planet. That is exactly why I insisted on addressing this matter.

"We could assume that scientists do not know and do not think that, in the center of the planet, is a black hole. Theoretically, they would start cutting into the Earth, being curious to see what is inside of it. Anyway, the transition from the material plane to the subtle planes is done long before reaching the nucleus of the planet."

"What would they see from outer space then?"

Dr. Xien discretely smiled. He then offered me a description very similar to the one Cezar gave me a few hours earlier.

"You have presented yourself with a challenging theoretical exercise, but this is a good thing. It helps you understand what you will soon be living by yourself in a real way.

"If such a cross section of the planet could be rendered, at first the physical matter of the crust would be seen. Afterwards, the structure of the crust begins to look like swiss cheese with empty spaces of different sizes inside. In some of the cavities, water that was generated from the initial dynamic of the central black hole could be found. In other cavities, you would find lava, gas pockets or even different types of rocks and metals. Others would be inhabited by different types of beings; but I think that this no longer represents a surprise for you. Inside our planet, you can find a pretty diverse and rich life."

Indeed, the idea of life inside the Earth was not new to me, and I was accepting it without any problem, but it still was not clear to me the way in which it exists, the zones in which it manifests as well as other aspects related to the kind of beings and their nature. The rather sparse information I have received in conversations up to this point has offered only a general context of the issue and one that is often evasive.

Having the opportunity to clarify many details, I could now do different correlations through the good will of both Dr. Xien and Cezar. I understood too well that an ideological and proper theoretical education would help me very much to correctly assimilate the sensations and real experiences that were awaiting me on our upcoming expedition.

Dr. Xien continued to speak, thoughtfully, and looking far away.

"If you go deeper, you will see that these empty Swiss cheese holes become larger as you get closer to the transition points to the subtle plane. In this crust zone, at a small distance from the surface, the central black hole's influence is not felt enough, and the matter is therefore heavy, hard, and physically pure, but as you get closer to the lava bed in the interior, the physical matter becomes more rare and the sizes of the interior caverns become a lot bigger."

"I understand, but when does this influence of the central black hole become noticeable? At what depth from the surface can we talk about the transition to the etheric plane?"

"You can't talk about a line of separation but rather more about an area. The influence of the singularity inside the Earth becomes clearly perceptible at about 1,800-2,000 kilometers deep, when the transition to the etheric plane begins. Up to that point, as you get closer to this area, you notice certain transitions to the subtle plane; and at that level of the terrestrial mantle, it could be said that an effective entering to the etheric plane occurs. From there on, if we talk from a strictly material plane point of view, you no longer see anything."

"Still, I need to perceive something," I said, expressing my curiosity.

"It does not make sense to say that, if you head to the center of the planet, as I assume scientists imagine, that you would continue digging through solid matter until reaching it. This is not just a huge conceptual mistake but also a point of considerable stupidity. It is like saying that you can get closer to the fire by using ice and that it continues to remain ice. You can't. It automatically becomes water and then vapor or steam. It is just the same when travelling to the center of the Earth. As you move inward, there are transformations to higher states of vibrational frequency that are imperceptible to ordinary instrumentation or perception."

"Then how do I see this transformation?"

"Assuming that you could see something, everything you see related to the material plane is an immense blank, a sort of vacuum in which, at the very most, you see or sense how light is absorbed by the central black sun. It could be said that you are then at the event horizon. You see some lights that, acting like a whirlwind, head to the center, which is the effect of matter being attracted to the center of the black hole."

I was well aware that what I was discussing with Dr. Xien was at the limit of what could be considered crazy by scientists, and not just by them. I was, however, attracted to the subject, seeking to better understand the subtleties involved. I continued, coming back again and again to my initial thoughts about the hypothetical cross-section of the planet.

"But, if we keep in mind the model with the cross-section of the planet and are looking at it from outer space, how would this reality appear to us, theoretically speaking?"

"First, you would see the section through the solid crust. Then, you would see the interior cavities or 'swiss cheese' getting bigger and bigger, and at a certain moment, you will reach the area where the liquid lava bed resides in the mantle. Still, its thickness is not so great. The existence of this lava bed, by the way, shows not just the lava transformation from solid to liquid within this aggregation of matter, but it is also indicative of moving into another plane. Then, from a certain moment onward, you will no longer see anything other than an empty space and the way in which the mantle is absorbed by the black hole in the center of the planet. This absorption will look like wires of light, and at the limit, you can see a bed of rocks, but these are really the peaks of the interior mountains situated within the lower part of the mantle."

The problem of the central black hole's influence was an aspect that confused me right from the start. After Dr. Xien told me about the real internal structure of the Earth, I began to realize that this information encapsulates

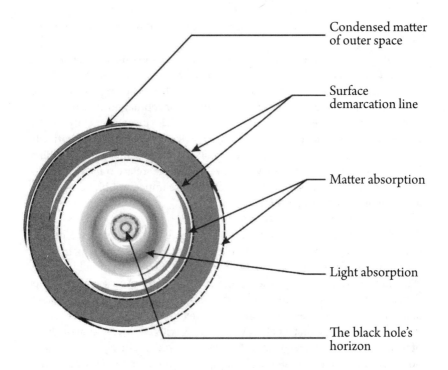

Condensed matter
of outer space

Surface
demarcation line

Matter absorption

Light absorption

The black hole's
horizon

***DIFFERENT DEGREES OF ABSORPTION IN THE SUBTLE REALMS BY
REASON OF THE SINGULARITY IN THE CENTER OF THE EARTH AND
THE CONSEQUENT DISTRIBUTION OF MATTER IN THE INTERIOR
AND EXTERIOR OF THE PLANET***

the actual mental block to correctly understand the reality of this structure. The concepts and prejudices we have on the effects of black holes make them appear to be utterly devastating when related to our planet. For example, most of us would imagine that, if a black hole really did indeed exist in the center of the Earth, we would all be crushed very fast.

In reality, as Dr. Xien explained to me, the absorption of matter in the center of the black hole occurs slowly because all the processes are correlated. It would make no sense that what the planet gives birth to by virtue of its energetic central vortex and singularity would then turn around and destroy it brutally as if to evoke the "wrath of God." Astrophysicists think that a black hole is produced through the implosion of a colossal aggregation of matter; but what they seem not to understand is the fact the black hole itself, when it manifests in the material plane, is what starts to absorb gases and cosmic dust from the exterior world in order to start the process contributing to the forming of a planet or star. Everything that manifests in the material plane:

the sky, the planet, any other celestial body, or even an atom or elementary particle, is born because of an energetic vortex that appears in the material plane that we associate as a black hole."

With precise movements, Dr. Xien drew a simple sketch of the planet's cross-section; then continued with his explanations.

"The role of the central black hole is to serve as a converter of matter. By absorbing matter at a certain speed, and through its rotational and gravitational features, it also gets to create matter. This phenomena is not known to astrophysicists even though they have taken the first steps in their observations regarding the emission of waves and chains of particles from black holes.* It is through these special characteristics of the central singularity that a certain size, weight, and balance of our planet is maintained. If things were not this way, you would expect the size of our planet to exemplify what amounts to billions of years of accumulation of matter and cosmic dust. It is not enough to say that it has constantly eroded, having therefore remained about the same size."

Once more, I was amazed by the ignorance of this elementary observation of which I had not even thought about up to that point. Generally speaking, science always finds excuses that leave you more or less mixed up with regard to anything that has no credible explanation from the perspective of classical laws and principles. It does not want to analyze the ideas that are outside the bounds of what they consider to be "normal" thinking.

After several minutes of contemplating the drawing, I asked, "If we were looking from outer space, what precisely would we see in the center section of the planet?"

"A black vacuum, but some could still see a weak sparkling light, like a mysterious point of glitter, but this could happen only if they were to get closer to the center. You don't see the glitter from far away."

"Why is it that only certain people could see such a thing?"

"Because of their very strong indoctrination into the conception of materialism. For many of them, everything represents matter and with this comes a heavy nature. Even if they were to figure out that matter is actually energy, they still treat the phenomena and situations as if they could only belong to their material world. The break between scientific conception that is limited only to the material plane and spirituality is dramatic, and it stops any meaningful progress with regard to deeply understanding the universe."

I figured that the answer coming next was important because Dr. Xien turned around and looked at me in the eyes.

"Because when you overcome the material plane to the subtle plane in order to see what happens beyond, you would inevitably have to adjust your individual vibrational frequency or you don't see anything. If you observe

---

* [From the Romanian editor] The is the so-called Beckenstein-Hawking radiation.

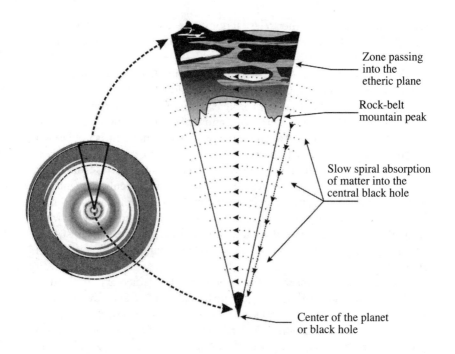

Zone passing into the etheric plane

Rock-belt mountain peak

Slow spiral absorption of matter into the central black hole

Center of the planet or black hole

CROSS SECTION OF THE EMPTY INTERIOR OF THE EARTH —
THE ORDER OF THE PLANES OF MANIFESTATION AND THE WAY IN
WHICH MATTER IS ABSORBED BY THE CENTRAL BLACK HOLE

a phenomena related to a particular space and the time, you must correlate yourself with the relativity of this phenomena. This means that the structure of the time and space changes. Then, the vibrational frequency changes. Let's say that you align to the new vibrational frequency. Then, you start to resonate with it. All of a sudden, you observe that there is no more dark, but actually another kind of reality on another frequency."

I remained quiet for a while, thinking about what Dr. Xien had said.

HOW WE CONSIDER AND MEASURE SPACE

What I had found out about the interior of the Earth was extraordinary, but I could not totally ignore what science presents as the internal structure of our planet.

"Scientists do not even think that there could be something inside the Earth other than physical matter, let alone that in its center would be a black hole!" I cried out. "Even if though they have no direct access to observing the phenomena there, they still rely on pretty precise measurements of seismic waves. How could we ignore such a thing or how could we say that they are not correct?"

Dr. Xien gently smiled at my honest query and responded.

"I see that you maintain the doubts you had two days ago, but all you have to do is to give up dogmatic thinking. We don't deny the results the scientists obtain, but there is a very important difference with regard to the nuances of how to interpret them. What they have discovered as clues to some sort of material reality that is inside the Earth could also result from another reality which is not material but rather purely energetic, just as is the black hole from the center of the planet as well as the intense field that it generates. The researchers start from the premise that they have to measure something, but in order to do so, they must be able relate to that something. It is not possible to start an experiment without knowing what you want to measure or to find out. For this, they need a mathematical space within which they do all these approximations, measurements, formulas, and laws, etc. So, right from the start, science designates a mathematical space specific for what it wants to find out.

"They cannot be blamed for this," I said. "After all, that space is abstract. It is a space that we all use in order to account for the way in which we understand the world around us and its dynamic movement."

"It is truth, but still, it is a space designated by the limitations of knowledge of this particular moment. In the exact moment in which you want to measure a certain phenomena, the abstract space that you measure is then created. It is as if I were to tell you that you only exist because I am talking to you right now. In other words, by the very fact that I talk to you means that you exist."

"That is inconclusive. Could you say we do not exist if we shut up?"

"Who indeed does exist and related to what? Perception is relative, but it represents an experience. Intent activates the reality that you want to find out about; so, when scientists look to find out what is inside of the Earth, they already have made up their minds that there can be nothing other than that which is solid or, in any case, something that is made up of physical matter. With total conviction, they project this set of fixed ideas into the abstract space specific to this reality. They cannot perceive, however, that this mathematical abstract space was created exactly because they wanted to measure something. The idea that such a mathematical configuration was precisely created by them in order to justify their own concepts and principles seems crazy to them. The prospect that this might be a possibility does not even enter into their minds."

"I understand. This is what people call one hand washing the other but without realizing it. Still, why is it so hard for them to modify their ideas?" I asked, surprised.

Speaking with an attitude of detachment, Dr. Xien clearly pointed out the underlying factors to the situation.

"I know that scientists generally either despise or disregard spirituality and metaphysics; or, at the most, find it ironic because, in their world view, such cannot be measured. But, if they were to study even the most basic notions of spirituality with an open mind, they would see that all of these things are not only possible but are actually true. Unfortunately, they not only will not do it, but they even fight fiercely in order to prove that spirituality is false, that it is a dreamy game, or an invention of those who are unrealistic."

I heartily approved of Dr. Xien's assessment, knowing well myself of many such examples. He firmly continued.

"The evolution of the human being, and that includes the scientific paradigm, cannot take place without spirituality being involved. The concepts of materialistic science are much too limited and primitive. In such instances, it is as if you would want to measure the diameter of the sun using a yard stick. You can't. You are materially and technologically limited. Using such primitive means, it is possible that some might dig their feet in and stomp on a chair in protest. This is the case with today's science with its set of ideas, conceptions and materialistic prejudices. No matter hard and often they would hit their head on the upper jamb of a door without being able to explain a lot of things, they will remain stubborn and continue to hit their head rather than to give up their limited concepts that maintain the status quo."

In perfect agreement with what Dr. Xien had said, I was thinking that, to contemporary physicists, there does not seem to be any difference between how they would measure the circumference of the Sun, such as with a tailor's measuring tape, and the space between two orbiting particles within an atom. The way they understand the reality surrounding them makes them think that space, such as is found on the surface of a planet or in the atmosphere, is identical to the quantum space within an atom or inside its nucleus. For them, the only difference would be that the latter is "smaller." According to their mentality, the metric of the two spaces is the same, the only difference being the delicacy of measurement. Dr. Xien explained to me that this is a major conceptual error based upon the fact that all of the laws, constants and principles issued by physical science are based only upon approximations giving the apparency that phenomena occurs or behaves in a certain way a certain percentage of the time.

"Okay, but what about the rest of the percentages? What explanation do scientists have for that?" I asked, thinking that this was a point of view that could not be ignored.

"They have no explanation, simply saying that they will analyze those percentages at some point in the future when science has progressed to the point where they will see where they fit in. They do not even think of dismissing their materialistic thinking. You cannot pretend to solve everything through materialistic explanations when you are surrounded by an ocean of different energy frequencies and vibrations. Those percentages that cannot be explained by science are actually an essential point of reference."

I then thought then that the situation with these percentages might be like comparing them to a twig making the great chariot of materialistic science shake and eventually overturn. A good example is that all but 3% of human DNA is considered to be "junk" because no one understands its purpose as an essential macromolecule of life. This "junk," however, actually contains fundamental information about the human being. Similarly, we can think of Einstein's formula predicting that, near the speed of light, mass tends to grow infinitely. Although mass increases as one approaches the speed of light, it is not particularly significant until the very last few "percentage points" whereupon it grows suddenly, tending to infinity. Therefore, the essence of phenomena in general is contained in the small or remaining percentage phenomena that is ordinarily not recorded. Is this not really the true mystery of Einstein's formula as opposed to the typical percentage of phenomena in which physical "reality" is not compromised?

Dr. Xien continued, extending this line of logic to the elements about the Earth's core.

"You can also apply this point of view to the black hole in the center of the Earth. To a considerable extent, you can approach a black hole without the surrounding reality changing too much from what you are normally accustomed to. Eventually, strange phenomena will appear, but to get to that point, you have to first be prepared to understand such. This, however, does not apply to contemporary scientists. When they want to see and measure something about which they have already made a preconceived opinion, they will achieve results in line with what is expected. This exactly as it goes with quantum physics experiments: you observe what you want to see or what you suppose you should see."

CURRENT SCIENCE — WHAT AND HOW IT "SEES"

I now understood the situation quite well, but I still could not understand why science does not persistently and boldly pursue the avenues of investigation that it does not master. Dr. Xien explained to me that this is the result of two converging tendencies.

"The first is ideological indoctrination. Some scientists are not necessarily predisposed nor willing to break conceptual barriers in order to penetrate an unknown field. Rather, they prefer to stick to what is already accepted, to occupy themselves with what is already known, and to analyze what they already understand. Oriented to make so-called practical inventions for the purpose of mass consumption, they thereby justify their role in society. They dislike the unknown, the challenge, and the mystery, save only to the extent that they want such explained to them through concepts they already know. There is a kind of scientific aggrandizement with everyone beating their own drums, excited about what is inside their own garden and the parameters of that knowledge. This attitude, however, leads only to stagnation and eclipsing a deeper understanding. It's like spinning around your own tail. Spontaneity disappears, and the sparkles of genius are stifled."

"Yes. I somehow know this problem, and I wonder if researchers still exist who have the courage and energy to have their voices heard so as to make a big impact in the scientific world," I said with a bit of bitterness.

"The chances are slim. Very few scientists allow themselves to bring novelty into their thinking. Generally, this only happens when they are old, either when they are considered to be credible or when they do not care what society says. Until then, they are obliged to align themselves with the classical and palpable requirements so as not to disturb the very foundation of the status quo of materialistic science. This is the second tendency of contemporary science and it refers to an unspoken habit of contemporary science and society: you are not allowed to either think, study, analyze, nor present what is not within the materialist framework of thought. To this end, all kinds of means are used ranging from ignoring, marginalization, irony in the scientific environment, blackmail and even harsher methods. Real scientific advancement is blocked right at the start, not because of a lack of genius or illuminated minds who are capable of understanding such but rather because they are not allowed to progress in such a direction."

Continuing, Dr. Xien offered me an excellent example using the case of imaginary numbers in mathematics. For scholars, these numbers belong to the abstract domain and are used only for mathematical computations. In the vast majority of cases, contemporary science works only with real numbers that offer possible solutions in various equations.

Dr. Xien then pointed out something rather remarkable.

"Any phenomenon appearing in the physical plane is somehow 'parallel' to all of the other phenomena in that such are not completely self-referential. On the other hand, all phenomena in the physical plane 'are placed' there and develop accordingly on that plane of existence. They are just effects. The fundamental misconception of scientists is that they believe that cause and effect lie in the same plane; that is, the physical plane. In other words, if there is an effect on the physical plane, scientists say that the cause of it is in this plane. This vision is a profoundly wrong vision."

"Indeed. They seem to mix the cause and the effect in the same soup," I said, amazed that such obvious aspects had never occurred to me.

"Yes, but that soup is not edible. In order to have access to the causes of the phenomena, you have to rise vertically. You must access a plane that is superior to the material plane. Only by looking from above can you understand what coordinates a certain effect that happens below. What we perceive in the physical world is actually a step-by-step condensation of causes emerging from subtle superior planes until these materialize in the form of phenomena which we call effects. This is the right vision."

"Do you mean that they do not recognize the existence of other planes of existence besides the physical plane with its three spatial dimensions?"

"Yes, they admit that there are spaces with many more dimensions, but they only consider it from a mathematical point of view and with an attitude that these spaces are not real. For contemporary science, real means only the physical space and time in which we live in and that people are aware of. Scientists do admit there are other planes parallel to the physical plane, but in their conception, they are nothing more than variations of our physical space and time. To them, a parallel plane has the same space-time structure or 'fabric' as our plane. Time flows the same way and space is measured the same; therefore, it is not a plane above our plane, but it simply another physical plane parallel to ours. In this way, science does not take into account the frequency of vibration which is, in fact, the main element in the structure of Creation.

Recalling some of the notions I had read in esoteric texts that I thought were related to what Dr. Xien was telling me, I interrupted him.

"Maybe that explains the exact meaning of certain ambiguous expressions in various writings, all of which obscure, hide or deflect the reality of the situation. They talk about the lower realm, the middle realm and the higher realm. In my opinion, this is a deflected or compromised representation of the planes of manifestation, each with their own specific vibrational frequency."

Dr. Xien nodded his head.

"Right. These are different planes of manifestation, each with their own different frequency of vibration. The lower realm does not mean that it is

Linear space-time events lying in the material plane

THE WRONG VISION OF CONTEMPORARY SCIENCE: THE CAUSE AND ITS EFFECT ARE IN THE SAME PLANE, THE PHYSICAL PLANE.

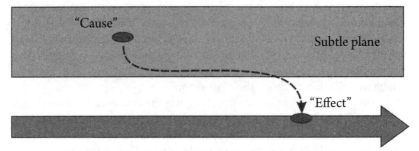

Linear space-time events lying in the material plane

THE RIGHT VISION: THE CAUSE ORIGINATES FROM A PLANE SUPERIOR TO THE PHYSICAL PLANE.

further south but refers to the telluric realms, that is, to the physical plane. The middle realm is the etheric plane, and the upper realm refers to the higher etheric plane as it passes over to the astral plane. Elves, for example, correspond to this realm."

We stopped talking and headed toward a building at the base. Outside, it had already turned dark, and air was pretty cold. Feeling my thoughts, which were gravitating around scientists, their measurements and their hypothesis concerning the internal structure of our planet having a solid core of iron and nickel, Dr. Xien spoke to me with great patience.

"You are still thinking about the scientific theory concerning the interior of the planet, but do not forget that what they say is nothing but an approximation of what might be in the center of the planet and its surrounding layers. From the point of view of physics, chemistry and geology, these approximations are valid, but in reality, what they imagine does not exist. Our planet is not a dense mass of physical matter."

I replied to Dr. Xien, saying what I had said to him many times before.

"Scientists have built their theory of the inner structure of the Earth based upon the seismic waves that they measure. After all, they can say that they have what amounts to almost sure evidence in their hands."

Dr. Xien did not let go and refreshed my memory.

"They can say this, however, the evidence they invoke is just an apparency. I have already explained to you that what scientists measure as response waves can either be the result of the reflection of another reality or a known material one. Besides, if we think intelligently, seismic waves are the only means scientists have to make assumptions about what's inside the planet. This is far too little to make claims that you have categorical answers."

I then thought what a crazy thing it would be for a team of scientists to travel through the tunnel to the center of the Earth. At the very least, the fabric of their modern scientific thinking would then be overthrown in an implacable and definitive manner. The shock would be huge, and the results unpredictable. Unfortunately, Mankind is neither yet ideologically nor spiritually prepared to understand and correctly assimilate the subtle realities of our planet. Its exclusively materialistic vision on the planet's interior is not only primitive, it is also meaningless; although, to a certain extent, it seems perfectly justified by the measurements and results that the researchers obtain by analyzing seismic waves. On the other hand, the idea of the Earth being empty on the inside must not be treated simplistically either. From the explanations has Dr. Xien given me, the idea that the interior of the Earth contains a huge hollow cavity surrounded by a crust of a relatively small thickness of about 1500-1800 kilometers is indeed unrealistic. In such a case, the shell of the planet would be too fragile, and the phenomena would not correspond to the reality we know.

From this point of view, the scientists' observations are correct because, once the seismic waves that are transmitted only through physical matter would overcome the crust of the Earth, they could not propagate further inside; but the measurements show with clarity that the seismic waves still propagate and they are perceived on the opposite side of the planet from the place in which the earthquake started. Actually, it can be said that seismic waves propagate to almost any area of the planet and that has convinced scientists to incorrectly believe that the Earth is indeed solid inside. They

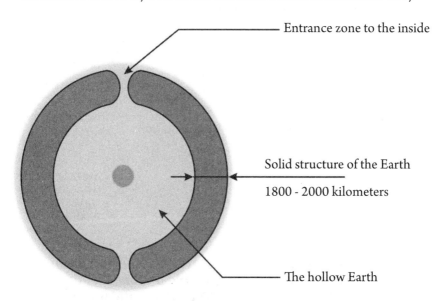

Entrance zone to the inside

Solid structure of the Earth

1800 - 2000 kilometers

The hollow Earth

THE HOLLOW EARTH — AN INCORRECT VISION

see our planet like a billiard ball, rigid inside and filled with solid matter, especially stratified rocks.

At this point, some observations can be made revealing that things are not as clear as science wants to assure us.

CAVENDISH EXPERIMENT

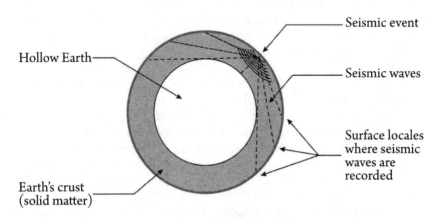

Hollow Earth

Seismic event

Seismic waves

Surface locales where seismic waves are recorded

Earth's crust (solid matter)

THE ABOVE EXAMPLE DEMONSTRATES THE (INCORRECT)
THEORY THAT SEISMIC WAVES CANNOT PROPAGATE
THROUGH THE HOLLOW INTERIOR OF THE PLANET

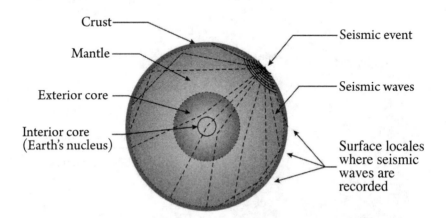

Crust

Mantle

Exterior core

Interior core
(Earth's nucleus)

Seismic event

Seismic waves

Surface locales where seismic waves are recorded

SCIENCE VIEWS THE EARTH AS A FULL, SOLID AND RIGID
SPHERE IN THE INTERIOR, A CONCEPT BASED UPON
THE SURFACE MEASUREMENTS OF SEISMIC WAVES
THAT ARE REFLECTED INSIDE THE PLANET

We can start with the assertion by scientists that as one descends towards the center of the Earth, the pressure increases immensely and to the point where matter itself becomes more and more dense. While the logic is apparently reasonable, the reality of the situation contradicts it. It is interesting to observe how scientists come to these conclusions and what they are based on.

Sometimes it takes only one experiment or theory to instill rigid dogmas into scientific thinking, especially when it is of materialistic origin. In the case of the scientific theory of the inner structure of the Earth, it is based entirely on a single experiment from two-hundred years ago as well as the three-hundred year old theory of gravity of Isaac Newton.

Wanting to measure the density of our planet, English physicist Henry Cavendish designed an experiment that resulted in establishing a certain average value for the density of the Earth.* Having the density, it was then possible to calculate the mass of the planet. Cavendish conducted the experiment in 1799; and since then, it has remained the only method science has at its disposal for calculating the Earth's mass. Moreover, there is no other way to verify the results obtained in that laboratory experiment.

The problem with Cavendish's experiment is that he relies on a whole series of assumptions. First, it is obvious that the two lead balls involved in the experiment are electrically neutral. On the other hand, it is equally obvious that planets carry intense electrical and magnetic activity, both in the atmosphere and within them, even if scientists consider them to be electrically neutral. If this is the case, then how can we talk about the similarities between the two lead balls in Cavendish's experiment and our own planet? Even if we were to consider only this single aspect, which refers to complete difference in electricity between the lead balls and the electricity for Earth, the results of the experiment would not make any sense.

For example, Earth displays giant electric currents within it that have intensities that can even reach up to one billion amps. By comparison, the lead balls in Cavendish's experiment show no electricity. In this case, what kind of "similarity" can there be? This reductionist view of science offers us only a rough approximation. Accordingly, they consider the Earth to be electrically neutral; and such a view gives credibility to Cavendish's experiment because a certain "electrical similarity" or relationship could then be considered to exist between the lead balls and the planet itself. As long as the Earth is continuously passing through giant electric currents, as has

---

* The Cavendish experiment used a torsion balance to measure the weak gravitational force between lead balls and was the first laboratory experiment to measure the force of gravity between masses and to produce definitive values for the gravitational constant and the mass density of the Earth. A torsion balance consists of a bar suspended at its middle by a thin wire or fiber. Twisting the wire requires a torque that is a function of the wire width and material.

been demonstrated by various measurements, this proposition is, at the very least, inadequate. Therefore, if it can be demonstrated that the intense electricity affects the force of gravity, Cavendish's experiment becomes irrelevant and its results are invalid. This view has been strongly supported by certain scholars who really wanted to demonstrate this through laborious observations and experiments.

A first observation in this respect can be made in nature. It is known, for example, that static electricity has a gigantic force compared to that of gravity and that it is capable of influencing the latter. But, in order not to complicate things, scientists believe that the planets are electrically neutral and that static electricity is not in question. In other words, they consider the force of gravity rather than that of electromagnetic force. It is well known, however, that electromagnetic force is trillion times the force of gravity within an atomic nucleus; nevertheless, scholars prefer to ignore this aspect at the macrocosmic level. Instead, they rely only on assumptions that are meant to support the results of Cavendish's experiment.

On the other hand, we cannot ignore the influence of the magnetic field of the Earth on the force of gravity. High intensity electric currents are a measurable reality within our planet, and that is why magnetism and electricity influence gravity in a certain way. It is virtually impossible for these fundamental forces of Nature to be independent because everything in the Universe is correlated and acts harmoniously.

Such "news," however, is not to the liking of scientists because, if it is recognized that the planet's own electromagnetism influences gravity, the consequence is that the Earth does indeed weigh far less or much more than that which was estimated by the Cavendish experiment, and the findings of such will have to be declared invalid. Since there is no other way to measure the density of Earth and its mass, science would be embarrassed. With all of the current scientific progress and advanced technology we have at our disposal, scientists would no longer be able to tell us how much our planet weighs or what its average density is.

THE PROBLEM WITH GRAVITY

Although this fundamental force of nature is especially courted by scholars, too little is known about it at present. For example, the real nature of this force is neither fully elucidated nor is the way in which it works. Only the effects it produces are known. Ever since Newton formulated the famous Law of Gravity, science has not taken significant steps in developing this theory. For example, the source of this force is not known nor can its behavior be described in the quantum realm. Additionally, neither the magnitude nor its speed of manifestation are deeply understood.

One of the delicate points in these studies is connected to what is known as the "gravitational constant" which defines the magnitude of the force of gravity. This results from a formula, but all such formulas have severe limitations because they support approximations and adjusted figures, such as is the case in rounding numbers. Falling into slave-thinking by rigidly adhering to formulas is a big mistake that scientists routinely make. In and of themselves, formulas are not meant to serve as an argument to be invoked in a scientific discussion, especially when the field or scope at hand is much more complex than what particular scientists might be able "bear" from their traditional conceptual point of view. Scientists who are really well trained and who have developed a certain inner sense come to know when and where to grasp the limits of applicability of a formula. They also know where to insist with calculations using various equations and formulas. It is, however, very difficult to change old opinions deeply rooted in people's minds and replace them with new ideas, and this is all the more true with scientific dogmas.

There are, therefore, many variables that can affect gravity. How can any-one claim, through an automatic and stupid application of Newton's formula of gravitational attraction, that gravity acts within the Earth just as at does at its surface? What good scientific sense is it that two lead balls that are a few centimeters in diameter, as in Cavendish's experiment, are similar to our planet which is over 12,500 kilometers in diameter? In this case, there are so many variables, forces and effects that are not taken into account that you have to wonder what the experiment is actually measuring. For example, how is it possible to consider gravity at 3,500 kilometers deep inside the Earth as being identical with that which exists at 1-2 centimeters deep as in Cavendish's lead balls? And, as a rhetorical question, how can this simple and unique experiment ascertain the theory of Earth being solid and rigid in the interior?!

Curiously, either for lack of inspiration or for fear of ridicule, such questions have not been asked by too many scientists. Some avant-garde researchers, however, such as Jan Lamprecht and others, have shown a lot of courage and determination and have succeeded in shattering such scientific "automatisms" that give science a great disservice.

It can be argued that when the experiment was conceived, it was natural to make certain assumptions in advance and to consider certain approxima-tions, but the fundamental mistake of scientists is that they do not just stop at these assumptions but then consider them to be strict laws.

In reality, the reasoning upon which they base their "vast knowledge" of the inner structure of the Earth is extremely fragile. Apparently, the calcula-tions, methods, diagrams and measurements are numerous and complex. Additionally, the technology and methods of measurement used might seem superior and defining; but in reality, they say nothing real, only offering some clues which are then interpreted in the wrong way. For example, who can possibly know that g (the symbol for "gravitational constant") is indeed a constant in both Paris and 4,000 kilometers deep? There are already experiments proving that g is not constant, the best known of these having been carried out in the deep mines of South Africa, at the bottom of the oceans or at the base of the ice caps. All showed an increase in the value of the "constant" of the gravitational attraction of g. There is therefore no obvious reason to speak of a "constant." Even more interesting is the fact that different values of g appeared at much lower depths. What about other factors of influence that are not known in detail?

Accordingly, there has been what amounts to a "unanimous consensus" that g is a constant anywhere on the planet and also within it. If scientists were to recognize the fact that a planet's electromagnetism influences gravity, as Einstein was fully convinced, it would overwhelm all of the calculations and the carefully constructed theories up to now. That is why contemporary scholars deny the possibility that electromagnetism will influence gravity despite experiments conducted some fifty years ago by the Austrian physicist Erwin Saxl. These produced very strange results involving electrically charged pendulums. Although the results are controversial, these experiments were comprehensively designed and repeated, being conducted over a seven-year period. Besides this, clear variations and deviant behavior of pendulums have been observed during solar eclipses, a time when massive electrical charges are occurring on a planetary level. While all of these results and measurements are clearly a fact of life, they are not taken into account because scientists to not want to break out of their dogma.

PLANETARY HEAT — WHERE DOES IT COME FROM?

Volcanic eruptions throw melted magma which obviously comes from the deep. It has an average temperature of 1000-1100° Celsius depending upon its type and composition. This information, however, presents a formidable question. Where is the very high heat that can melt the silicates that make up most of the volcanic magma inside the Earth?

The existence of layers of molten magma does not prevent the movement of seismic waves, rather only a certain category of them. This has led scientists to conclude that the Earth's crust is mostly solid in nature; and more to the point, it is rare to find instances where seismic waves do not penetrate the magma.

Accordingly, another question was asked. What is the origin of the heat that melts the silicates and rocks inside of the planet, thus transforming it into magma? There are two scientific theories for it, and as both have elements to support them, they could be true. The idea that magma would come from the center of the planet, however, cannot be true because, as scientists have pointed out, it would lose heat over the enormous distance that it would have to travel and would solidify long before it reached the surface. It is therefore obvious that the lava that is expelled out by volcanoes comes from deposits within the Earth's crust which is only a few tens of kilometers thick or, at most, from the top layers of the mantle.

On the other hand, our planet's age is estimated at about 4.54 billion years, but even after this enormous period of time, it seems that the Earth has a sufficiently strong source of heat powerful enough to melt matter and produce fused or melted magma. The planet obviously generates heat from within; and, moreover, its temperature proves to be relatively constant. This shows us that our planet is not just a hot sphere of melted matter which gradually cools and solidifies over time such as might be imagined or mistakenly believed by many people. As current measurements and observations prove, reality is proving to be quite different.

In fact, the source of the Earth's internal heat remains a mystery to modern science, and all the more due to the fact that it can only be researched or measured indirectly. Science currently admits that it cannot penetrate the inner depths of the Earth beyond some 18-20 kilometers deep because, due to increasing pressure and temperature, the rocks melt and the cavities in the solid bark would fill up so that a drill would hit a semi-solid mass of molten material and melt it, too. In practical terms and according to scientific theory, it is impossible to drill deeply towards the interior of the Earth because, beyond a certain depth, the drill could not remain in the hole it bores because this would be filled with magma that comes from a certain depth. So far, the observations and conclusions of scientists are correct, but they do not explain, as did Dr. Xien, what else is going. Furthermore, the scientific theory is valid only for a rather narrow branch of the crust. It is not a generality that can be applied to the whole planet. This is actually a great problem for scientists as they extrapolate upon the Newtonian theory of gravity and apply it to the rest of the planet's interior, claiming that the pressure and temperature increase coincident with linear depth and that, according to Cavendish's experiment, which sets a certain average value for Earth's density, there is matter within which possesses a much higher density than the rocks at or near the surface.

For example, many scientists imagine that the Earth is full of volcanic magma starting from a certain depth. They think this way because they have noticed that when you descend into a mine or dig downward, the temperature rises constantly. This led them to extrapolate that this would apply at depths of hundreds or even thousands of kilometers inside the Earth, thinking that everything would be the same and that a gradual increase in temperature would continue all the way to the core of the planet. It was also assumed, historically, that the Atlantic Ocean continued to the end of the world. And the ancient Greeks also assumed that the warm weather in the Sahara desert would continue to warm up as it progressed southward to what we know today as the Antarctic.

The big problem with today's scientists is that they assume they have a logical and rational basis upon which they base such extrapolations. First, even the deepest mine does not reach much more than eight to ten kilometers inside the Earth, and this is almost nothing in comparison to the Earth's radius of 6,300+ kilometers. It is far too small of a sample with which to consider this shorter depth as an appropriate starting point for doing extrapolations. Just because it has been observed that the Earth's temperature increases at the rate of about 1° Celsius per 100 meters, this does not mean that this rule applies at any greater depth inside it. Even though no one can verify it, no one seems to doubt the proposition that the temperature increases as we move deeper towards the center of the Earth.

Let us entertain a simple exercise of logic. As I have said, the volcanic magma originates from the crust of the Earth which is about forty kilometers thick. As lava has an average temperature of 1,100° Celsius when it is expelled by volcanoes, it invites us to ask a question. If the crust has this temperature, then what temperature should be inside of the planet at depths of 2,000 kilometers or more (keeping in mind that modern science is using the principle of extrapolation in this case)? Obviously, all of these values and theorizing on this phenomena are assumptions that are based upon Newton's theory of gravity.

DRILLING COMPLICATIONS

Several decades ago, some countries invested funds to drill into the Earth in order to verify the scientific theory of our planet's internal structure. Drilling into the crust, however, has revealed a notable difference between actual experience and the assumptions of scientists.

As I said above, the universally accepted theory has been that the temperature inside of the Earth increases by one degree Celsius for every hundred meters. Drills conducted by Russians, however, showed that beyond three kilometers, the temperature increases 2.5° Celsius for every one hundred meters, two and a half times faster. At a depth of ten kilometers, the temperature was already 180° Celsius and not 100° as would have been expected so as to be in line with modern theory. This proves to be almost twice as great as what scientific theory implied. Considering such facts, what value can be placed on such a theory?!

Despite the above experiments, nobody has done anything to inform the public about such information nor has the subject been debated or explained in any way. Instead, the same degree of misinformation and scientific ignorance has been maintained.

The Germans have also drilled into the crust of the Earth and with remarkable results. At a depth of four kilometers, they discovered that the temperature already measured 100° C, but at a lesser depth, for example 3.5 kilometers, the temperature was yet higher, having a value of 118° C. During this drilling in Germany, it was found that the temperature rises rapidly from the depth of 500 meters; and after that, it decreases. Such results appear to be unbelievable, at least in relation to what science had predicted. Not only do these findings fail to converge with scientific theory, they prove to be opposed to it.

The density of matter has also proven to be inconsistent with scientists' predictions. They assumed that the density of rocks should increase as the pressure increases, but the Russians have discovered that up to five kilometers deep, the density of the rocks was constantly increasing. After that, it decreases, probably due to their higher porosity. Neither of these outcomes, however, have been able to break the stubbornness and rigidity associated with certain concepts of scientists. In principle, they do not want to give up on the basic ideas upon which their theory is based; and instead, they firmly hold that both the temperature and density of rocks increase as one penetrates deeper towards the center of the Earth. Even though these are just simple assumptions, they are universally accepted as undisputed truths. And this is besides the fact that no scientist has verified whether such a theory is true. Additionally, even simple verification with superficial drilling tests have totally invalidated this scientific model.

Therefore, nothing in the theory that science has assumed, as it seeks to understand what is within our planet, is valid nor is it based upon observation. As has been noted, inconsistencies with this scientific theory occurred even in the first ten kilometers of drilling. Accordingly, what should we say for what might occur in the next 5,000 kilometers? How is it possible that such a scientific farce is maintained in such an aberrant and disrespectful manner and by omissions or false hypotheses used in order to manipulate all those who show a certain intelligence and good intention to learn the truth?

SEISMIC WAVES

The situation is almost hilarious, and Jan Lamprecht synthesizes it very well. We have just one single experiment, 200 years old, upon which science relies upon in order to support the current theory that the Earth is solid and rigid inside. This experiment of Cavendish is itself a direct product of Newton's gravity theory which also has its limits.

The only methodology that is somewhat acceptable, whereby certain assumptions can be made about the interior of our planet, is the "seismological method" whereby seismic waves are analyzed and measured as they propagate and spread both at the surface of the Earth and within it. No one actually knows how and where these waves travel. All that can be done in this regard is for seismic stations on the surface to measure their intensity or strength and the direction of their propagation. The results can then be correlated and analyzed by computer and, in turn, be subject to complex mathematical models in order to help scientists understand how the Earth is structured inwardly.

Current seismology is based only upon Cavendish's experiment and a set of assumptions. The behavior of seismic waves is also interpreted mathematically. Therefore, absolutely everything in the current scientific theory about conditions inside the Earth can only be described as mere interpretation and assumption. Under these conditions, if Newton's theory of gravity is not observed to be applicable within the Earth as it is on its surface, then we can assume that when it comes to the internal structure of our planet, the entire edifice of modern science is fundamentally wrong.

Moreover, mathematics and seismology, however laborious their methods of computing and interpretation are, cannot by themselves explain what lies within our planet. There is a limitation in this regard because it would lack common sense to provide such a complex theory about the interior of the planet that are simply the result of extrapolations that are based only upon blind suppositions.

In turn, these hypotheses were issued by scholars; otherwise, they could not have begun to develop theories and studies of the internal structure of the planet. All are but assumptions of what they thought might be there, nothing else. In the spirit of materialistic theory, this is how they thought it should be and then considered these assumptions to be true.

For example, Newton's theory of gravity gave Cavendish's "experiment" a so-called "mass" of the Earth with an average density of 5.5 grams per cubic centimeter. The only place where scientists can actually measure the density of the Earth is at its surface, and here it has the value of 2.7 grams per cubic centimeter which is half the value given by Cavendish. In order to "balance" this average, scientists have deduced that the density in the Earth's depth has to progressively increase from 2.7 grams per cubic centimeter to a certain value so that, in the end, the Earth's average density will correspond to the value found by Cavendish two-hundred years ago. By making the necessary calculations, scientists have concluded that the average density in the middle of the planet should be 8-10 grams per cubic centimeter; and, accordingly, have provided a whole theory that the inner structure of the planet contains concentric "layers" with different densities. Starting from these models, which they assume to be real, scientists have begun to interpret seismic waves. If, during their research, their model proves to be wrong, they then change its characteristics to fit what they measure, but all of their models, conceptually speaking, are the same.

When a strong earthquake occurs, the seismic waves propagate everywhere, both on the surface and inside the planet, but this propagation is not uniform. By analyzing its characteristics, scientists strive to understand what is inside the planet, and for this they appeal to other scientific notions such as the speed of seismic waves as they move through various layers of rock. In other words, they measure the time it takes for a seismic wave to travel a certain distance. It has been observed, however, that the waves suffer sudden variations in velocity at certain depths. The conclusion of scientists is that seismic waves cross layers of different density. This could be a decent explanation, but it turns out that these changes do not happen exactly in the same places, thus demonstrating that the Inner Earth has a different "relief." If the "relief" inside the planet is different, this means that there is enough empty space within to allow for changes, thus implying that the density, compactness, rigidity and solidity of the planet's internal structure do not respect the modern scientific theory.

All of the results scientists obtain are based upon two assumptions which no one knows the truth about. First, scientists deduce the speed of seismic waves moving inside of our planet based upon their own model and in accordance with Newtonian gravity as mentioned above; but no one has the means to verify that these waves even reach those depths and propagate inward with those speeds. On the other hand, no one can be sure that the changes in wave velocity are due to the change in density of matter inside the Earth. How do we really know how deep these seismic waves actually go and what is the density of matter in that location? For example, no one knows where the seismic waves travel inside the planet or what they are actually going through. The only aspect that can be measured involves the effects of these waves which, again, are perceived at the Earth's surface by seismographs and seismic stations.

Naturally, we expect these waves to be refracted, and there is even an entire theory showing precisely how this happens when density increases as materials are impregnated with seismic waves. But here, we could ask again: how do we actually know, like science assumes, that the density rises as the depth becomes greater? As even the superficial drillings that have been done up to this point demonstrate that what they have found does not conform to the theories given, how could they then rely on something that proves not to be real?

Scientists have assumed that changes in seismic wave behavior are due to the structure or "relief" within the Earth, and they view this in the context of physical nature in accordance with Newton's theory of gravity. So, it is no surprise that science bases its entire conception of the internal structure of the planet on this classical theory. In reality, however, nobody has tested anything in this regard, and there is no chance of something happening in this direction, at least with the technological means currently at our disposal.

The deep drilling conducted by the Russians that I have already referred to was a shocking blow to contemporary science. They have shown very clearly, based on the data obtained from penetrating the Earth's crust on Kola Island, that the density of rocks did not, as was expected from the scientific theory, increase in proportion with depth; nor did the speed of the seismic waves increase. Moreover, and once again contrary to the predicted theory, there were no changes in the physical properties of the rock layers that were drilled.

Such data and conclusions are the kind of information that is immediately suppressed and unpublished in the broader environment, or simply ignored. Not only is it embarrassing to modern science, it also raises serious credibility issues in scientific theories and in many other areas, especially in the quantum and nuclear fields. The data from the Russian drilling has clearly shown that the traditional idea that geophysical measurements carried out on the surface should correspond with the natural materials in the terrestrial crust materials is, in fact, completely false and must be changed. Even so, contemporary science continues to work with this idea, paying no attention to these results. People are still taught these theories in schools and universities but without any of the details; and instead, by presenting just the model which the researchers consider to be viable.

For example, the science of geology presents the theory that continental plates are characterized by a great discontinuity in the velocity of seismic wave movement at a depth of five kilometers which is attributed to a change of rock layer from granite to basalt. The drilling on the island of Kola showed that such a discontinuity does indeed exist but at a much greater depth (between 8.5 and 9.5 kilometers).

The Russians, moreover, have detected other discontinuities of this type, in addition to the aforesaid erroneous depth postulated by science. The final death blow to their theory, however, comes from the fact that the basalt layer that had been predicted at a depth of five kilometers did not even appear at a depth of 9.5 kilometers; and further yet, it did not even appear at a depth of twelve kilometers, the deepest drilling depth to which they had drilled. While there is indeed a zone of discontinuity that exists between tectonic plates, it turned out that, after the drill passed beyond this area, the nature of the rocks did not change as the researchers had expected.

This example shows how far and how fast scientists can be deceived when a theory is not supported by practical evidence. If such a mismatch between scientific theory and experimental evidence occurred at a depth of ten to twelve kilometers, how can we believe what science tells us is happening or what exists in the center of the planet at a depth of 6,300 kilometers?

Results that invalidate this pet scientific theory were also obtained by the Germans who also dug to a great depth. Guided by this theory, which states that there should be a delineation of the rocks at a depth of 3 kilometers, this was not yet identified at a depth of 3.5 kilometers. The problem is that, whenever scientists fail to discover the internal structure that they predicted, they say that "perhaps this will be found at a greater depth." But if so, then why did they not achieve their expected results that was based upon their measurements and analysis of the duration of seismic wavelength propagation? If they really were so precise, there should have been no problems, and any errors would have been detected immediately.

OTHER ISSUES THAT DO NOT "FIT"

Another example of theoretical disparity concerns the pressure inside of the Earth which they say is so great that it would practically close or seal any hole made by a drilling hole as well as any naturally existing exit, fracture or porosity. In fact, nothing of this kind was discovered as result of deep drilling; and moreover, geologists were disturbed by the fact that, when such drilling was done, they encountered the totally unexpected: fluids in circulation such as highly mineralized water and also gas. The hubris of Western scholars, however, has not been diminished by these obvious results. They then blamed the Russians for using an inferior drilling technique, but the same result was also obtained by the Germans who discovered hot fluids in open fractures at 3,400 kilometers deep, a depth at which scientists did not even dream of finding such.

The subject of the Earth's core is also controversial, having been described in various ways: in the form of an ovoid, a sphere or even as a hexagon. If the measurements of the seismic waves are as accurate as is stated, then how does one explain such "scientific" babble?

On the other hand, the issue of "topographical relief" existing inside the planet began to surface when it was discovered that rocks actually have a "flexibility" factor of five percent when they are traversed by seismic waves, even at very deep depths. While the science of seismic tomography provides the possibility of viewing the structure of the Earth's mantle in a three-dimensional format, it is not yet clear what these images represent. Are they showing that there is a "relief" landscape in the mantle or the pressure changes in those areas? Some scientists are even talking about continental-sized objects in the center of the Earth or about mountains and valleys at various depths of the upper mantle or lower crust. Thus, we can now say that the first doubts about the true reality within our planet are beginning to arise within the minds of some researchers who are, in turn, asking serious questions. As there is no actual evidence that the pressure inside the planet has the enormous value that science expects, these doubts are all the more justified.

There are other serious questions that have not been answered so far by science. Amongst them is the problem of the planet "shaking" as it rotates around its own axis, as if something of a liquid nature within it would cause these slight variations in movement over the years. Although scientists have searched for all sorts of explanations for these small perturbations in the axis rotation, they did not bother to think that the Earth might be "empty" inside, and further; that the immense mass of water inside or "inner ocean" could lead to this slight alteration of movement.

One of the greatest mysteries that science struggles with, which invalidates the scientific theory of the solid and rigid structure of the Earth on the inside, concerns the observation of deep sea earthquakes. Normally, ordinary earthquakes occur up to a depth of 100-150 kilometers, beyond which, according to scientific theory, the pressure and temperature would be so high that the tension between the rock layers would cause the tectonic plates to slip over one another rather than fracture. Science tells us that rocks at these depths somehow become elastic or ductile in a certain sense; mainly, that they "soften" and that their sudden and catastrophic fracture is no longer possible. That is why theory teaches that, because there is no tension, earthquakes should no longer exist beyond the depth of 150 kilometers.

Over twenty percent of earthquakes, however, are deep-sea earthquakes. Earthquakes with the intensity of 8.2 on the Richter scale have been recorded, for example, at a depth of 650 kilometers. Another strange fact is that these deep-sea earthquakes have similar properties to shallow ones, including the fact that they have fracture characteristics. These measurements virtually abolish the scientific theories of laboratories which state that such a reality cannot exist at those depths due to the very high pressures and temperatures there. Nevertheless, such earthquakes are still perfectly possible and do indeed happen; and it is science itself that makes this all known as if they, in this way, seem to be nailing their own sole. Deep sea earthquakes show exactly the opposite of scientific prediction: namely, that the pressure inside the planet at those depths is not nearly as great as it is believed and the temperature is also quite low.

Scientists believe that if seismic waves can reach any point on the planet, it then means that the Earth is completely rigid and solid inside. For example, they say that if it contained a lot of lava, large seismic waves could not move and would not be able to reach different points on the globe. They therefore conclude that, for the most part, the Earth must be solid in the interior so that such seismic waves are crossing solid matter and reaching various points in the world, all according to the measurements made.

A computer model, however, simulating an Earth with an empty interior with a diameter of about 1,200 kilometers, revealed a different story. In such a case, the simulations showed that the seismic waves would also spread across the entire surface of the planet, giving the impression that the Earth would be solid inside. In this model, the density does not rise constantly toward

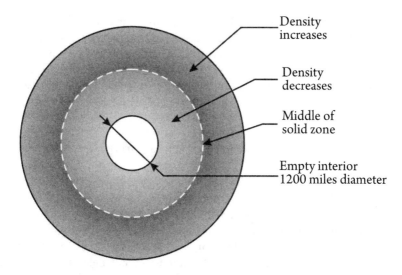

Density increases

Density decreases

Middle of solid zone

Empty interior 1200 miles diameter

A HYPOTHETICAL, BUT MORE VIABLE, PHYSICAL MODEL OF THE EMPTY INNER EARTH

the center of the planet, as scientists think, but it increases toward the outer core and then drops as it approaches the inner core of the planet. This model would also explain the very large deviations of waves that show their reflection and strong refraction from the core of the planet.

The whole idea of the structure of the Earth being based upon an "outer core" and "inner core" is, in fact, only an invention of scholars relying on certain assumptions. They have measured different types of seismic waves and have seen that the primary waves, which propagate only through solid matter, do not pass into certain areas while the secondary waves, which can propagate through a liquid medium, do pass. From here, they deduced that it must be a molten environment and thus invented the theory of an "outer core" as molten metal that surrounds an inner core that is solid. The model of the Earth with a solid inside, however, features the inconsistency of the seismic waves reducing their velocity in the inner core while, on the contrary, this should increase due to it being solid matter. Scientists have determined this mysterious slowdown to be an effect of change in the elasticity of the core, a factor contributing to the change in speed. The empty Inner Earth model, however, solves all these mismatches and predicts results that are in agreement with various types of measurements that have been carried out and without the need for the theory of an outer core and an inner core.

All of these problems arise because scientists are stubborn about accepting or finding a model of the Earth's internal structure that fits in with the enormous mass of the planet that was indicated from Cavendish's unfortunate experiment. In this case, they have to find a way of explaining how a lot of matter is condensed in a given volume so as to verify the value of Earth's mass that was provided by the experiment. Their only possibility in this regard is to find evidence that matter is changing its density within the planet and that it grows enormously towards its center. In this way, they could also explain incomprehensible changes in the speed of seismic waves at certain depths within the planet.

THE SITUATION TODAY

Some scientists realize that the reality within the planet is different from what current theory supports, but if they were to dare to present another viewpoint, they would be ostracized by the reaction of the scientific community. In this way, it seems that one hand is washing the other and, under the tangle of terrible manipulation and a very oppressive control of progress and scientific ideas, Mankind is actually held under an embargo on the knowledge of reality and scientific ideas. Dr. Xien has repeatedly specified to me that the "evidence" and measurements regarding the internal structure of the planet only seem to portray a certain reality, the one that scientists want to impose, but the truth is completely different. It has already been demonstrated that the planet, which is believed to be a compact full-faced planet, might be hollow at its center by reason of the existing data and measurements that have been recorded. Therefore, it is only a matter of interpretation by contemporary scientists who prefer the solid Earth model, even if it exhibits innumerable inconsistencies and even if it is proven by experimental evidence to be false.

An eventual recognition of the model with an empty interior of the planet would automatically attract many awkward questions to which science is still far from providing competent answers. What follow are just a few examples: How did that "void" form inside? What's there? What is the heat and energy source of the planet? What makes up her magnetic field? What are the environmental conditions in that "empty" environment?

Avoiding such challenges, scientists do not even want to recognize their own conceptual boundaries. Nor do they not want to abandon the obsolete and horizonless paradigm of materialism, a mind-set they seek to maintain desperately in any explanation or scientific hypothesis they express, both on the inner reality of the planet as well as the outer reality. In fact, this "curse" of a dusty vision has even extended into the quantum domain where phenomena is not understood in terms of the essence of its subtle energy but rather tends to be interpreted in the spirit of purely materialistic ideas and principles.

When I replied to Dr. Xien that we ourselves cannot provide concrete evidence of how things happen inside the Earth, he had a lot to say.

"This is true. You cannot show what is unseen, but there are still many people who have gone through these experiences in one form or another, more or less consciously. They usually sense these experiences when they either become conscious while dreaming or consciously recognize the etheric or astral plane at the time they are led to the inside of the planet. Sharing many delicate common points of agreement, these experiences cannot be explained by reason of access to the collective subconscious because these elements do not belong to daily activity. Many of these people, however, either do not realize where they have arrived nor do they understand the subtle mechanism that is involved here. Upon returning, their memories are usually blurred or, if they are clear, they are not fully understood. Many of the distinctive elements I have explained to you such as visions, perceptions, or situations related to the interior of the Earth are the same as some people already experience. They do not, however, know what it all means.

"So, why do such people not tell others what they have lived?" I asked Dr. Xien.

"For fear of appearing to look ridiculous. The lack of a certain initiatory knowledge or understanding the conscious power of entering makes them unable to correlate all of the aspects of their experience, and they therefore prefer to remain silent and conceal what they know."

Desiring to clarify this issue, I asked Dr. Xien a question.

"Does the one who travels this way know where he is and understand that he has entered inside the Earth?"

"They often do not realize this. It depends upon the nature of what is experienced and the level of consciousness of that person. That is why a traveler to these realms is accompanied by one or more guides, i.e. other beings of the interior or in the celestial worlds whose mission is to lead and sometimes inform that being about what is happening, but this is not always enough for her to understand or remember. Often, at some time after the experience, everything tends to be concentrated in the category of interesting dreams; but, in reality, the being has lived a real experience from which he can learn a lot. Instead, when access is direct, starting from the physical plane through a portal or internal passage as is the case in Bucegi, the situation is highly advantageous because then you "translate" the whole structure of the being, including the physical body. This is important, provided the continuity of consciousness remains."

I realized that, in the end, everything seems to be a matter of inner preparation for the being, an aspect that involves our level of consciousness. Our access to the spirituality within the Earth depends upon the stage we have reached. This led me to the following rhetorical observation.

"I suspect that not any such conscious experience means going inside the Earth."

"Not at all. Such trips are dedicated, have a precise purpose, and the people involved have certain affinities or tendencies towards those regions within the Earth, whether they realize it or not. Everything has a meaning and nothing occurs by chance. Such experiences do not happen anytime or to anyone, but even so, I assure you that there are many souls who have experienced such experiences and not just once. But, you cannot discuss this with scientists because it is a non-existent domain for them.

"But, is there anyone who has penetrated the planet directly from the physical plane? I am not referring here to our tunnel."

Dr. Xien had an almost imperceptible smile. His answer was very close to Cezar's comment.

"There are but very few cases. Such entrances to the interior of the Earth, starting from the physical plane, are well guarded and blocked from outside access. Actually, they are more like 'buffer zones' between the physical plane and the etheric plane that lead to the interior of the planet. You have to be there at the right time and under the right circumstances to be given access; for example, when entering caves and usually in mountainous regions. If it is on a wide and open surface, such as on water or in the air, then most of those who experience such do not understand what is going on. Their astonishment becomes very great, and it is not clear what phenomenon has happened. Most return to the surface world, but some remain there in one of the worlds within the Earth."

"Are they the ones who choose to do that?" I asked out of curiosity.

"No, it is a matter of destiny, but in certain cases, there is the possibility of choice."

"And, if you pass through such a gate, coming from the surface of the planet, you consciously come into subtle planes and arrive inside it," I said.

"Just as I have described to you, but only if you have the level of consciousness for that, and only if you can understand what is happening then."

I was to soon convince myself of it. I left Dr. Xien and retired to my room to rest. The last two days had been challenging both mentally and physically, so I wanted to be in shape for the expedition that was about to happen. Falling asleep immediately, I slipped into a wonderful dream, but I know for sure that I had not yet gotten inside the Earth.

CHAPTER THREE

TOMASSIS, THE ANCIENT ROOT

I spent the rest of that night meditating on the real structure of the interior of our planet as had been explained to me by Dr. Xien and Cezar. Practically speaking, this includes almost no points of convergence with the theories of modern science. With great power, the dogmatism and the stubbornness of scientists oppose a broader and more effective vision that would propel Mankind to a higher level of knowledge and achievement. Perhaps the balance will soon incline to the brighter side of life with the ignorance and narrow judgment being cast away.

THE SURPRISE OF THE SECOND TUNNEL

Cezar arrived the next day around noon, and we both worked on organizing the expedition, leaving behind the necessary instructions and orders for those at the base. He told me that, in principle, we would only be away for a few hours. Upon hearing this, I was amazed and even a little disappointed because I thought we would not be travelling too far inside the planet.

"You will see that this journey is different from the previous one you took through the tunnel to Egypt. It is done differently, and in the first phase, we will only go through the secondary branch of the tunnel.

Busy with certain orders he had to give, Cezar did not give me any further details at that point. I had no idea how we were to travel or what he had meant by "secondary branch." My expectation, however, was short because we were already in the Projection Hall by 9:00 A.M. the next day. This time, we arrived at the secret location in Bucegi by helicopter. I had slept well; but for no apparent reason, when I got to the front of the console, I was suddenly imbued with a deep emotion that melted me. I believed it to be the influence of a subconscious and egotistical defense reaction which was manifesting itself vigorously as a result of the actualization of the information I had previously received about the true internal structure of our planet. It was obvious that this expedition, even short-lived, in some way implied an alteration of ordinary consciousness, and it is very likely that my own subconscious was reacting in this way so as to defend my ego-centric conceptions and prejudices that had been fostered and fixed by living in modern society; and further, it was trying to stop me.

UPDATE

Managing as best as I could, I became aware of the orders that Cezar began to set on the console. The graphic responses on the glossy screen were different in shape and color, and I did not recognize any of them. After several seconds in front of the console, a holographic projection of the Second Tunnel appeared, its trajectory shown only up to a certain point.

Unlike the other holograms that I was already familiar with that depicted the entrance to the tunnel, this one presented the structure for a longer distance. The first major difference from the tunnel to Egypt was that the space distortion appeared at a certain distance after the twelve crystals, not before them. As I have said, the tunnel descended on a relatively smooth slope, and after a distance I approximated to be a few dozen meters, a cone or funnel was followed by a large cubic space larger than the diameter of the tunnel, inside of which we saw a strange phenomenon: the image appeared as if one reality was offset by the other, and the common area vibrated slightly. Then there was a bifurcation which was undoubtedly the "bifurcation" that Cezar had referred to: a branch of the tunnel with a small angle of inclination downwards as well as a second branch continuing in the initial direction of the tunnel. Here, at a short distance from the bifurcation, the hologram had a new distortion. It was vertical, but its surface was slightly undulating and was dark blue with purple tones. I suspected that the purpose of the distortion was to facilitate an earlier attempt to penetrate the subtle etheric plane, a sort of "shortcut" to the center of the Earth.

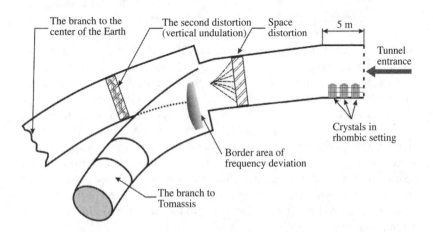

**STRUCTURAL DEPICTION OF THE SECOND TUNNEL
WITH THE BIG CUBE AND THE BIFURCATION**

Indicating to me that we would enter the branch with the slight angle, Cezar spoke.

"It's important to first get used to this kind of world and with the frequencies inside the planet," he explained. "These are inhabited worlds and each one has its peculiarities."

He told me that we would be going to an area inside the Earth, a living city called Tomassis. Such trips are based on well established protocols as visits involve different levels and domains: information, political, administrative, commercial, and military. I was the beginning of only my second expedition through the tunnels inside the secret location in Bucegi, but Cezar had already done thirty-four. Having personally documented the general reports in the Department's archive, I knew that he had explored practically all of the possibilities offered by the three tunnels in the Projection Room. Most of his trips to the Inner Earth were either with Romanian-American mixed teams or, especially after 2010, by himself. In his new position at the level of the Department and due to the information we had access to in the last few years, I know some elements about the nature and implications of Cezar's twenty-seven singular missions within our planet. I do not allow myself to reveal them, however, nor to present any sensitive details in this direction. I can give descriptions up to a certain point, in the name of informing people correctly and presenting some of the secret elements, but these disclosures should not point to delicate strategic information or to details that might disrupt ongoing plans.

After several discussions we had over time, Cezar and I set a series of parameters in order to balance the information I am presenting. Even though the books I am writing do not necessarily represent what the Secret Service wants, there is a limitation of disclosure which allows for a tacit approval by the latter. The reader may have noticed a certain lack of detail of sensitive points, but I have tried to supplement this with several drawings to make it easier to understand the elements presented. There are, however, limitations that cannot and must not be crossed at the current juncture of our world.

While much of the information is a state secret, it does fall into the category of general knowledge, at least at the conceptual level. While it cannot be used in a literal sense, it can contribute to a change in the mentality of the population towards its higher evolution. For example, even nowadays, many of the American and Romanian military officials and other senior officials of secret government agencies involved in these projects do not correctly understand the true nature of the planet's interior nor the subtle phenomena that is going on there. Lacking solid esoteric knowledge and having a habit of treating such elements as either potential physical threats or as issues to be dealt with by control and domination, they are prevented from believing or having a deep understanding of what actually happens when they interact with the reality within the Earth.

I have noticed that there is still much opacity and doubt with regard to correctly perceiving information from the ultra secret reports that reach decision makers. On the one hand, this is due to a lack of conceptual training of military leaders and heads of agencies or departments. On the other hand, it has to do with their habit of trusting and relying too much on the advanced technologies they have at their disposal as well as the modes of action that are specific to the physical plane.

The technology and huge funds that are allocated represent neither a guarantee for a good understanding of the situation nor for correct decisions being made with regard to certain negotiations with those inside the Earth. This requires many explanations, meetings, discussions and clarifications; but as life in the military and intelligence agencies is by itself very agitated and concrete, it does not easily allow for the assimilation of sensitive information on the surrounding reality. Generally speaking, military chiefs and Earth leaders are tributaries of mental habits and the education system in which they live; so, it is difficult for them to conceive that there might be another reality than the physical one that they are accustomed to and in which they act.

There is also the matter of interference from the state. It is very difficult to combine the reality of subtle higher dimensions and worlds with physically concrete desires and ideas and tendencies that are characterized by a low vibrational frequency which includes conquering new territories, controlling the population, discretionary use of energy resources, and political and military influences. Due to this incompatibility, the Earth's leaders do not understand almost anything about the phenomena that occurs when the Inner Earth is penetrated, and that's why they do not have access there. In other words, they do not seem to understand that oil cannot be mixed with water.

The very special protocol that exists between Romania and America regarding the secret location in the Bucegi Mountains, as well as the discoveries that have been made during the expeditions through the three tunnels, has solved some of these aspects and has also created some extraordinary opportunities. Suspicion and occult interests from state-run chains, however, which have their own understanding of the situation, still represent a strong barrier to openness and direct action. When it comes to such a level of collaboration between civilizations, problems can only be solved if there is a qualitative leap in the consciousness. The old way of thinking and acting, with divisions of territories and geo-strategic influences among the world's leading leaders, is not only awkward in such a case but also completely ineffective.

Cezar and Colonel Obadea had long grasped these aspects, and this is precisely why they sought to alter the bellicose vision of decision-making emanating in both Romania and the United States. The unexpected death of the General has made it difficult, but Cezar did not give up. Gradually, through sustained efforts, he managed to maintain a certain balance of conception and intent with the higher decision-making bodies, especially the military ones. There is an almost primal fear from the military when their technologies are either greatly out-dated or when they cannot understand a certain reality of things. The fact that they cannot know or have access to something creates the false impression that something is threatening and should therefore be treated with hostility. It's like an instinctive security need that, in fact, reflects the hidden desire to conquer and have power.

There is a huge difference between this kind of world vision and the reality that exists in the worlds inside the planet. To some extent, I was aware of the complex ties, especially at the diplomatic level, which Cezar has in this respect, as well as the discrete but extremely effective help that Dr. Xien has offered at key times. I had long guessed that this mysterious character from the Orient, whom I had known as Repa Sundhi, has missions that are far more complex than they seem at first glance. The powers and ramifications of the links between the exterior and the interior of the planet are extraordinary; and even if such circumstances seem unreasonable and strange in the context of today's world, such beings do indeed exist and manifest their presence and influence at critically key times in order to sustain the good.

After the General's death, there were some opinions in the secret services that sought to induce the idea that Dr. Xien's intentions were not sincere. When that occasion arose, I was very surprised to learn that Dr. Xien's deeper identity was also independently known and even documented to a certain extent. Up to that point, I was convinced that the only ones who knew that Dr. Xien was actually Repa Sundhi were those in Department Zero. Moreover, Elinor's existence was known of, and even though I did not have access to the entire file, which is from another section of the Secret Services, I saw some references about his presence in Switzerland. I do not want to go into details, which are quite complicated, but the information about his presence in Switzerland was conjectural and inaccurate. He is indeed in Europe but not in that country.

From a certain level up, the game of information within the Secret Service becomes very delicate. It is sometimes like a kind of barter between the parties and can even be constructive with mutual benefits. This balance is usually maintained until military interests arise, at which point the weight of arguments tend to bend in one direction. The nuances and psychology of the game increase at high levels of diplomacy; and when discussions are held with representatives of other worlds, emotions also play an important role.

In recent years, there have been several distinct phases of these conversations. Although progress has been difficult, there is a positive trend at work. From what I have learned from Cezar, the present phase requires a process of "educating" human beings who are in leadership roles with decision-making power, but this is done only in accordance with their own will and power of understanding. In such cases, it is most appropriate to utilize patience and perseverance.

Taking advantage of a relative "lull" from these encounters and very complex discussions, Cezar decided to grant me a higher level of access; and so I came to know very important elements about the planet's interior. Now, I was with him right before my first trip to such a world. To be honest, I thought that everything would be more "spectacular" or "grander," but the circumstances now seemed so natural that I was slightly disheartened. Cezar behaved very naturally, seeking to make me calm and able to reasonably approach the events at hand. As I would later learn, emotional behavior is very important in such expeditions and meetings. It is one thing to go to a safe place in which there are only objects, as in the case of the First Tunnel, but it is another situation entirely to go to a place where complex energy interactions and relationships are involved. Because the energy frequencies of the physical plane are merging with the frequencies of the subtle etheric plane towards the interior of the Earth, the energy balance of the being is very important, and it requires a stability of emotions. This is why Cezar had chosen a short period of time for our journey inside the Earth, probably so as not to overpower my subconscious and to avoid reactions or other undesirable emotional manifestations of being.

We were both on the threshold of the Second Tunnel which enveloped us with its diffused green light. Cezar took the leather diplomatic bag, the contents of which I did not know, and looked inquiringly at me. Breathing deeply and shaking my head, I told him that I was ready.

As I headed for one of the special vehicles that were parked there, Cezar said to me, "We do not need them for this trip. The road is shorter than you think."

He was amused by my astonishment, for it is true that I did not expect to walk to the middle of the planet.

"On this branch of the tunnel, things are simpler. We do not have much to go after the first distortion."

Walking into the tunnel somewhat hesitantly, I suddenly noticed an almost completely soundproofed ambience. My ears seemed to be covered with earphones, and I could hear my heartbeat. We both walked silently and swiftly past the gorgeously colored crystals that shined mysteriously in discrete light. As I was walking, I perceived a doorway effect; and while it was not disturbing, it made me feel somewhat insecure. Looking down, I saw that the material covering the ground was solid, smooth and almost glossy.

The sound insulation began to disappear immediately after we passed the crystalline area. The tunnel descended smoothly in front of us, but after about forty meters, what we saw seemed to make no sense. The tunnel seemed to be "offset" or "doubled" upon itself, but the area was unclear as if it were blurred. Intrigued, I hurried a little ahead of Cezar to get to that area faster. I stopped about a meter away from the passageway, staring at a reality that I could not interpret. It was like looking at a neon tube with indigo light. I could not see the contours clearly, but I found that this was valid only for the vertical surface, like a screen that delimited the area. Looking "beyond" that surface, I saw a cube-shaped space larger than the tunnel itself, a sort of antechamber at the bifurcation beyond the cube. I approximated the depth of the cube as being almost ten meters. What surprised me was the fact that, beyond the "double," the outlines were clear again.

"All you have to do is go ahead," Cezar said with a smile. "This area is an example of how technology replaces reality and quickens it."

I realized that the transition area somehow made it possible to "alter" the physical plane as a passage to the etheric plane and admit that I was shivering a bit before going through the "double," but I noticed only a slight dizziness when I passed through it . Beyond the transition zone, the soil was also solid and yet different. I suppose I could say it was more refined. It is hard to explain, but the impression was that matter had a less dense consistency.

"Those who built it had access to a very advanced technology, but they also had a profound knowledge of the universe," Cezar explained. "The Projection Hall and tunnels are some sort of legacy that they left behind by establishing fixed access points. They created several spatial distortions that increase vibrational frequency in order to facilitate travelling through the tunnels. The first distortion is general and exists in all three tunnels, raising the vibrational frequency of the body to prepare it for the underground journey. The one you just passed through brought your being closer to the etheric plan and made a kind of 'jump' between dimensions."

"A jump?" I answered, intrigued. "What kind of jump?"

"Take the keys out of your pocket and throw them back through the 'double' area," Cezar told me.

I threw the keys back into the tunnel, but I was amazed to find that they disappeared as soon as they passed the surface of the screen.

"You'll find them in the tunnel when we get back, but you cannot see them from here. It seems to be just a relative continuity, but it is actually quite a jump in space."

I began to understand why we did not necessarily need electric vehicles to move through this tunnel, but as I looked towards the mysterious space distortion on my right side, I could see that this was blocked by a discontinuity of an indigo-violet color which seemed to be crossed at certain points by short fast moving waves.

"That's where we'll be on our next trip," said Cezar. "It is more special and leads right to the center; but first, you have to prepare yourself through this branch."

We both entered the slowly descending left corridor. The tunnel seemed to be getting darker and narrower; but after about twenty meters, I saw bright yellow reflections on its walls. As the yellow color got stronger, the light in the tunnel became more intense, even to the point where it was shining right in front of us. I stopped again, hesitantly. Cezar urged me forward, telling me that we had reached the "first station."

"We only just left on the expedition," I replied. "Too short a road!"

"So it seems if you are thinking about the laws of physics you are familiar with. The reality is that we made a 'jump' and now we'll be making a second one. It is important to remember that things and phenomena in the etheric plane no longer have the same characteristics as they do in the physical plane.

"So Dr. Xien was right!" I exclaimed, forgetting the slight hesitation I had just had in front of the bright light. "Inside the planet we can even get into subtle planes!"

In what was a surprisingly rare moment, Cezar had a short laugh.

"Did you even doubt it?" he asked. "The truth in this case is that our passage into the etheric plane was not due to advancing through the thickness of the mantle and crust of the planet, but it rather has a more practical purpose in order to make the movement very efficient. This branch of the tunnel and the sequence of distortions have been precisely designed and planned. Originally, when it was made, it was not known exactly what it was that was beyond, but you can now convince yourself of what is there right now.

Saying this, he put his arm around my shoulder and we passed through the blinding intense light at the entrance, into a gateway that has no exit at the surface.

DRYN

The crossing was smooth, like a kind of slow-motion, and the light did not blind me. When I stepped out to the other side, I felt a return to something familiar. We were in a large room, like a hemisphere resembling a tall but well chiseled cave. I approximated the length of the room to be about 30-35 meters. Looking back, I could no longer see the intense light but only the oval outline of a slightly bright surface with metallic reflections.

When I returned to the room, I saw two men of medium height moving forward toward us. Their skin was light olive, and they had black hair. One of them raised a hand with his palm facing forward, making a sign for us to remain in our place. He seemed to be listening carefully to someone via a small rectangular device that was attached to his right temple, and I suspected that various transmissions and commands were being made through it. The man seemed to have received a certain order with something being explained to him. He gave a brief reply before both of them stopped before us, making a sign to wait.

Comfortably waiting, Cezar and I remained there for about a half minute. I took advantage of this opportunity to examine the area better. It looked like a natural cave that had been artificially widened. The rocky walls of the mountain were sanded and polished to some extent, but traces of the modification were still visible; the rocks being neither glossy nor perfectly smooth. We seemed to be in a passageway that also served as a storage hangar. In the back, I saw several crates and boxes of great size, one above the other. There were also parcels and other objects, but I could not tell what they were nor did I notice any vehicles.

The place was austere, even having a Spartan look. As a matter of fact, the impression that it was a military area was reinforced by the uniforms of the two men. Additionally, I noticed three other people who were wearing the same type of uniform and moving around the room, performing different actions. The slight military style was particularly noticeable in their boots which featured double straps around the ankle area. Their clothes appeared to be made of a lightweight beige-colored material with dark brown stripes, without being complicated like military uniforms in our world. The two men in front of us wore black belts and in the chest area, they wore tunics with several pockets.

I did not notice any weapons neither in the room nor amongst the equipment that was there. I asked Cezar if this was the usual procedure for this facility, but even before he answered, I noticed another character approaching from a large group of crates stacked one above the other. Taller than the two soldiers before us, he wore a garment similar to a gray-white coat with a belt at the waist. From his dignified bearing and the specificity of his clothes, I tended to think he was a monk, perhaps a spiritual mentor of the place, or a distinguished member in the spiritual hierarchy of that community. Looking at him, I recognized him as the one who had appeared for a few seconds a few days ago as a holographic image in the Projection Hall. I already knew from Cezar that his name was Dryn.

I noticed that his robe had a hood, but it was not on his head. His hair was whitish blond and was longer than the other two men who were in front of us. He seemed to be a man of up to about fifty years old and had black eyes with white skin, but it was not a pale white but rather vivid and even shiny. As he approached, I felt a sudden empathy for his gentleness and his wisdom. I was not surprised by the nature of these qualities but rather by the clear and direct way in which I was perceiving them, much easier than would have been the case in the surface world. As Dryn came before us, he gave a slight bow to Cezar as a welcoming gesture but then turned and spoke to me, as if responding to my inner inquiries.

"All your sensations and capabilities are somewhat amplified here. The vibrational frequency of the matter here is slightly higher than the frequency of the physical matter at the surface. It is still physical matter, but more refined, getting very close to the frequency of the plane that you call etheric. Functions are easier to carry out due to the lower density.

I was watching and hearing him speak a language I did not know it even though it seemed to me to be somewhat familiar as some of his words were close to ancient Greek and Latin. What amazed me the most was the fact that I perfectly understood what he was telling me even though I did not know that language. Somehow, the man gave me the meaning of his words telepathically, but for my convenience and to preserve the appearances and nature of that reality, he was still using the spoken language even though I realized that he could just as well have used telepathic transmission.

Reflexively, I was thinking that he did not introduce himself, but he promptly responded.

"You already know my name. You have found that out."

He had a very direct way of being, and I could sense in him the presence of an extraordinary force of will which, although not dominating, still produced a gentle unrelenting firmness. Making a gesture with his hand, Dryn pointed to the left towards a sort of platform on the wall of the room where I saw a construction that looked like glass.

THE DIMENSIONAL ELEVATOR

As we headed to the platform, I was experiencing a certain degree of mental confusion with regard to how I was able to understand the meaning of the spoken language I had been listening to even though I did not know that language. I was preparing to ask for some clarification, but Dryn was showing me that he had not exhausted all of his surprises because I then heard him speak in Romanian without almost any accent.

"Okay. In this case, we will communicate directly in your language. We know it; and, in a certain way, it represents us."

I was just about to answer him as we arrived at and ascended upon the platform at the end of the ramp. My attention was attracted to a kind of cabin with transparent walls, apparently embedded in the rock. It looked like a fairly large elevator and had a rounded entrance, like a semicircle. When we came to the door, it glided and Cezar and I entered that space, followed by Dryn and the two soldiers. The cabin was quite wide, measuring about 2.5 meters wide and two meters deep, and I immediately realized it was not made of glass but of another perfectly transparent and durable material.

The door was closed automatically even though I had not noticed any control panels, buttons, nor any other device that might activate it. The elevator then began to descend in the first few seconds at a relatively slow speed; but then the speed increased until I could no longer distinguish the details of the areas I was passing through. All I saw was a very fast roll of layers of different colors. The only noise I was feeling was a slight buzz, or rather a murmur, apparently created by the very high speed of travel. I did not, however, feel the strong acceleration as would be expected at that speed.

Several questions spontaneously appeared in my mind. First, what kind of "lift" was this which seemed to be break through and into the planet? Is there a deep shaft inside the Earth through which this elevator runs? How deep is it and how was this accomplished? What was the technology that made the lift move at such a very high speed without friction becoming critical? What was the source of energy that propelled it? What kind of "grip" or attachment did the elevator have on the corridor through which it was moving?

While these questions appeared in my mind, I was looking with great interest through the transparent walls of the cabin. I saw beds of rocks moving by at a very rapid sequence, and we passed by lava streams twice, feeling a slight increase in temperature but in a pleasant way. Sure, passing through lava without touching the walls of the lift was another issue that I wanted to decipher in later discussions, but I really enjoyed the impact of the radiation that the lava was emitting, perhaps because of the intense orange color which had gained a special glow as I passed through it at such a high speed. The heat that the lava beds emanated was different from that of radiators, a stove or the usual fire. I do not know why, but the two phases in which we crossed through layers of lava impressed me deeply, even if each such crossings did not last more than a few seconds. Our elevator trip took only about half a minute. As soon as I had barely begun to dazzle myself, I felt the deceleration but only for a very short distance and without unpleasant effects. During the last portion, I think no more than a meter and a half, the lift was moving at the same slower speed that we experience in the elevators in our world, just before they stop.

The door then slid to the left, and we went out of the cabin. For a moment, I thought my heart was going to stop with amazement and delight. We were on a mountain plateau, about halfway up that mountain, and a wide valley opened before us with a city that was stretching out to the shore of a calm sea in the distance. I was engrossed in deep emotion, not just for the sight we were seeing but especially over the fact that we knew it was inside our planet.

THE CAVITY AND ITS PECULIARITIES

As much as I wanted to associate what I was seeing and feeling with nature as it appears on the Earth's surface, there were still a whole series of elements that appeared strange. Moreover, I had the unmistakable feeling that things in general were different, including the vibrational nature of this environment. On the surface, what I was viewing was ordinary; and yet it all seemed wrapped-up in something peculiar. I also had the impression that I was seeing a highly evolved and clean ecosystem.

When we stepped out of the elevator, we were on a platform that was an extension of the rock wall, and what we saw was a human designed landscape but without artificial materials. For example, the soil was a mixture of sand and fine pebbles, and the rocky sides of the entrance to the elevator were slightly arched. The rocks had not been polished, but they seemed to be carefully carved. In the valley that opened up before us, I saw an inhabited city which spread to the left and to the right. Looking up, I saw a cloudy but bright sky of luminous lightning with a quiet reddish yellow color. The light was not bright nor did it have great intensity.

In the distance, close to the horizon and especially to the side, I could see how the sky seemed to bend in a way that is confusing and hard to describe. I could not distinguish clearly where the sea ended and where that strange atmosphere began. The entire landscape somehow creates the feeling that it "closes" somewhere in the distance. For example, I saw the rocks making a curved line as they tended to close into the horizon. I already had the impression that this was not too big of a cavity inside our planet, and I was beginning to wonder, with some disappointment, if this was the hollow interior in its center which has been the source of so many legends.

I saw Dryn turning to me, and for the first time, I noticed a fine smile on his noble face. As before, although those observations and conclusions were only in my mind, he still answered me loudly.

"No, this is not the empty interior in the center of the planet. You will probably end up there later on, and it will be special trip. What you see here is a big empty space inside of the solid bed of the planet. You call this layer inside the Earth the mantle, but your science does not understand either its structure or its functioning. As you can see, life has no problem developing here. You are not yet in a higher plane, and this is not a subtle plane of manifestation. You are still in a physical world, but it is more elevated than what is on the surface, and its vibrational frequency is very close to that of the plane you call etheric.

"Are there other cavities of this kind inside the mantle?" I dared to ask.

"Of course, and some of them are even bigger than this one. Many of them are inhabited and have their peculiarities. After you get used to the specifics here, you will then find out more.

Staring silently, Cezar did not interfere, and the two soldiers stood by, waiting respectfully. From the way Dryn had addressed me, I understood that my presence there had been discussed beforehand, and I realized that Cezar had called for that meeting so that I could gradually learn the mysteries

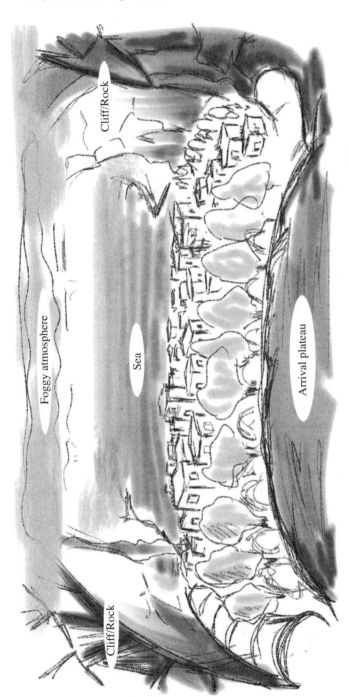

GENERAL VIEW OF THE CITY OF TOMASSIS INSIDE THE EARTH

of the planet's interior; and in this process, Dryn assumed the role of a guide. Cezar probably had a plan for the future, but he did not reveal it to me.

From my point of view, just as in the other amazing experiences I have had in Department Zero, I could not be anything other than deeply grateful for the extraordinary chance I was being offered. I do not exaggerate when I say that, to a certain extent, I was experiencing the impression of a "dream" that was as real as possible; and the truth is, in that case, the sensation was particularly amplified by the nature of the experience and the elements involved. I am referring in particular to the repeated crossings from one plane to another and to crossing spatial distortions that are likely to influence the ordinary perception of consciousness as well as its degree of vibration. In the absence of adequate training or familiarity with the respecting frequencies, passing through such spatial distortions can lead to a kind of "sweet dizziness" and even a slight euphoria during the first phases. Thoughts tend not to follow the usual course, and logical connections are sometimes strange. This condition, however, only lasts until the individual system manages to "reset" itself so as to accommodate the new demands it has been subjected to. One learns quite quickly, and if the level of consciousness is sufficiently evolved, the return to normal is fairly rapid and easy.

So, I took advantage of the short respite that Dryn had offered me to accommodate the new reality. Having many questions that were facing me, I decided to sort and organize them because I felt intuitively that I did not have much time to spare. Such expeditions are not like a holiday stay or a relaxing weekend in the mountains.

I realized there were two elements that intrigued me in particular: the "sky" above and the vegetation on the ground. For example, I did not see any sun, but the atmosphere was made up of a relatively thick blanket of "bright clouds". The light seemed to be uniform and did not come from "something" in the sky but was evenly distributed in the compact mass of clouds, giving them a slightly orange tone that was not shiny. It was more like a radiant diffusion of light as opposed to an emanation from a dedicated and powerful source of light.

Actually, after a closer look, I realized that the term "clouds" was somewhat improper. What I saw in the sky was more like a continuous fog such as a mass of fog at a certain height that was diffused and uniformly lighted. Still, that compact mass of fog was not static but was visibly animated by certain atmospheric currents, and I could even see formations that were moving to its outer side with a weak reflection. The impression was that there was a mist of clouds; and in the background, there were "clouds" moving under the influence of high currents just as there are clouds on different layers and at different heights in our atmosphere.

One of the first things that attracted my attention was that the general light inside of the cavity was of low intensity, making me think that we were there on the threshold of either the evening or early morning. I associate that quality of brightness with the light that our sun emits about an hour after it rises on a cloudy day, thus signifying a relatively low intensity of light.

The second element that struck me was the vegetation. In the areas of the mountain to our left and right, it was missing. There were only cliffs and rocks without biological elements. The atmosphere was relatively moist, but I also noticed the presence of some winds, more like a light breeze. I estimated that the temperature in that space corresponded to a subtropical region, even if the flora and fauna were different from what you might find on the surface. Somehow, the ecosystem of that inner cavity ensures an optimal fit under the given conditions.

The vegetation began in the valley below and continued up to the city but also extended inside of it. I immediately noticed that the color of the plants was green but a brownish green. Combined with shadowy light, the colors seemed dull and without brilliance, but this does not mean that the plants or atmosphere were not lively. Vital energy emanated from every pore of that cavity, and I felt it as a clean, pure and profound energy. The colors, however, were not as vivid as in our world, and I did not see a great deal of nuances in that respect. Even the seawater had a dark color. It was not blue but a dark blue-green, and in some distant areas, towards the horizon, it was gray.

The vegetation was neither lush nor tall. Rather, I could say that it was dwarfish, like a juniper. The tallest trees were like shrubs. I noticed that the plants developed more horizontally, having large and broad fleshy leaves with strong fibers, something like the aloe leaf. Perhaps that particularity

THE TYPE OF PLANTS PREDOMINANT IN TOMASSIS

was due to the need to absorb as much light as possible in order to achieve photosynthesis, the leaves therefore requiring a larger surface.

Those plants, shrubs, flowers, and the entire ecosystem there produced a sense of solidity, a sort of "power of life" that was, in its essence, simple force but with purity. As the minutes passed, I felt more and more clearly the infusion of a beneficial energy into my whole being such as I had never before felt on the surface of the Earth. This phenomenon probably contributed greatly to the balancing of my psycho-mental and energetic structure because I felt very confident with a great lust for life but, at the same time, internalized and focused. Even if I perceived the feeling of inner euphoria, which was probably due to the abundance of vital energy in that environment, I noticed that I naturally controlled my state and felt a conscious internal distribution of this great energy. The good mood that had appeared in my being was nevertheless effectively retained and channeled, and all of my faculties benefited from it. I was not sure if this process was controlled and directed by Dryn, but I tended to think it was a peculiarity of the place, something inherent in that space within the Earth.

One of the unusual features I had noticed was the lack of animals, but I did see some middle-sized birds flying at low altitudes. I cannot say for sure whether or not there is a rich fauna in that place, but I still tend to think it was sparse. The specificity of the vegetation and life of those people seems to have prevented the proliferation of animal species, at least in this particular cavity of the inner planet.

Feeling already in full form and being eager to find the answers to my questions, I wanted to find the source of the light in that place that I had not yet identified. That was one of the elements that struck me from the beginning: the uniformity of light across the sky at a low altitude. According to my estimations, the mist that formed was at the height of typical storm clouds, not more than two or three hundred meters.

"There is not a sun in the sky to give off light, such as you have on the surface," Dryn explained. "Here, the light comes from the strong radiation of the massive lava layer that is above our cavity. Temperature and light radiation is transmitted through the rocks, and the balance is ensured by the natural intelligence of the living energy and forces that do not belong to the physical plane. Because light does not come from an isolated source, it diffuses uniformly into the mass of clouds. There is a special process of interaction between the powerful lava radiation passing through successive layers of rock and the particles in the atmosphere here that ionize and create this twilight-like luminosity.

I smiled to myself, noting the style of Dryn's explanations: clear, concise, direct and very precise. His mental abilities must have been truly remarkable. Still, I did not want to persist with such thoughts, knowing too well that it was not a problem for him to perceive them whether or not they were spoken. I was preparing to ask the next question when I noticed something very interesting.

IN FLIGHT OVER THE CITY

In front of us, four objects floated through the air which I would compare to small platforms. They first attracted my attention through their color and the fact that they seemed to be the only objects in the environment that shined to a certain extent. I do not know who had summoned them and did not know how they were guided, but they were emerging from the town and headed for us. I guess it was a common protocol for people arriving from the special elevator and who were supposed to get to the city. What I saw, however, was a giant leap in relation to the technology of the surface world as these inhabitants seemed to have mastered the secrets of anti-gravity very well and also had devices that functioned with this technology.

I was able to better see these flying objects when they came right before us and stopped, standing at a height only a few inches above the ground. They looked very much like the antigravity platform that I had seen in the Occult Chamber when we made our journey through the tunnel to Egypt. Rather small, they were oval in shape and about one and a half meters long at the large diameter of the ellipse while the smaller diameter measured about one meter. I did not noticed any other moving parts or attachments other than the oval disk plate from which they were made.

There were, however, differences from the platform I had seen in the occult chamber in Bucegi. The most obvious of these was in respect to the construction material which, in this case, was very special. It seemed to be a metal, but it gave the impression of being transparent. I noticed that this sensation was due more to the interesting color which was a combination of golden and silver yellow, but the golden yellow also had a reddish tint. The specificity of that material and its color created a strange visual sensation as if the sight could penetrate superficially into the first layer of metal which, in reality, was not happening. It was more of an optical illusion caused by the characteristics of that material.

Climbing the platform beside me, Dryn climbed behind me onto the same platform. Cezar and the two soldiers each mounted on a separate platform. Dryn probably wanted to make sure there were no problems with me on my first flying experience with such an anti-gravity device. I confess that I had a slight grip on my heart during the first few moments when I climbed upon that platform, but I immediately noticed that it was very stable; and moreover, it provided enough space for me to feel that I was in relative safety. I thought that, at worst, I could sit on the surface to keep my balance or feel safe, but it turned out that I did not have to resort to that.

Immediately after we all got onto those anti-gravity transport platforms, they moved silently and perfectly through the air, flying at a speed that I approximated to be about 30-40 kilometers per hour. Once you experience that feeling of free flight, you cannot forget it. It was a feeling of freedom and openness, of ease and even happiness. I then wished to travel on that platform over the entire city, but I immediately felt the answer from Dryn — this time telepathically — informing me that I could not do this.

We flew to the city a few dozen feet above the ground and traveled for less than ten minutes. I did not feel any sense of loss of balance nor dizziness, and the air flow did not bother me at that speed at all. Perhaps we were helped in this way by Dryn's presence, and perhaps the material from which the anti-gravity platform was made had some special properties of a psycho-mental nature. It is certain that my whole being was filled with great joy and positive emotion, amplifying my affection and willingness to share it with others.

I watched the approaching town from a high altitude, and I noticed its streets, a big market place, people, and normal activity to which I could relate. It was not a metropolis, nor even a bigger city, and the tallest buildings had no more than two floors. Their shapes were different, but I noticed that squares prevailed. The dominating color was white or white mixed with beige or gray. Blue, with varying nuances, was also used for some buildings. Generally speaking, there were no loud or shining colors. There was a certain similarity to some of the constructions found on some Greek islands. That is, white houses in simple straight lines, generally parallelepipedic. I felt, however, from the way they were arranged, their mood and their shapes, the general atmosphere that this community was generating was a kind of precious information wave conveying stability and balance with great trust and a calm thanksgiving.

BRIEF HISTORY

While I was feeling and taking in the "pulse" of the city in this way, a thought entered my head which I had not considered before. Contemplating what was before me, I wondered precisely what that community represented and how those people came to live at this place inside the planet. My mind had already begun to create some images of lines of people advancing through hidden colors in the Earth's crust, wielding lit torches like during an exodus or when conducting a desperate search. My thoughts were then interrupted by Dryn's response.

"It would have been too difficult to do that. You cannot travel through the bark of the Earth like an endless subway tunnel. We've benefited from some shortcuts, just like you have in your travels. We have been here for thousands of years, and we have a very old and rich history. Everything is documented. Your historians and scientists would be very surprised if they were to see the documents in our archives."

"But why precisely those living in Romania?" I asked, a little surprised.

Until that moment, I had in mind the general idea that this city was somewhere inside the planet, in a random area of it, associating the displacement with the expedition we had made through the First Tunnel to Egypt.

"Where do you think that this city that you are now seeing is located in relation to the surface of the planet?" asked Dryn.

"I do not know," I said hesitantly. "Probably near the equator."

I had no basis for my assumption, but that was the idea I had as soon as I stepped out of the elevator.

"No, but you are actually pretty close to home if we are talking about a few hundred miles of depth beneath the surface. This cavity is under the territory of your country. More precisely, it corresponds approximately to the place where the ancient Tomis was located."

This was a new surprise, a wonderful one. Quickly, I made a possible correlation with the name of the settlement that Cezar had mentioned.

"Is Tomassis related to the old settlement on the surface?"

Dryn nodded.

"Yes, although it is located inside the Earth, it corresponds somewhat vertically with the old city on the surface. The cavity, however, has been populated since ancient times, well before Tomis even existed. We are the direct and pure descendants of the ancient Dacians. In a way, you can say that we are your ancestors. The people you see here in town descend in a direct line from the Dacians of 2500-3500 years ago.

For a few seconds, I looked at the fog and clouds above me thinking that, just a few hundred kilometers over our heads, we could find the theater or square of the city of Constanța* as it is today. The historical disparity was enormous, and as I understood it, the roots of that settlement inside the Earth go even deeper, linking back to time immemorial.

"The secret of penetrating this place was known by certain monks who were initiated during the wars between the Romans and the Dacians.** Prior to them, this inner cavity was visited only by the great sacred priests of old times who were serving in an area near Tomis. There are still ruins of an extremely old fortress from those times.*** The beings who lived here then were very small and came from the so-called First World which followed a great

---

* The current city of Constanța developed itself on the place of the ancient port of Tomis on the Black sea. It was a settlement of Dacians contemporary to the Roman Empire.

** These wars took place between 101-102 and 105-106 A.D.

*** The author is probably referring to the city of Histria, a former colony on the mouth of the Danube River. The word *Hister* means "Danube" in Latin, and the etymology of the word *history* is, ironically, intrinsically related to the place name of this ancient city.

cataclysm from the surface of the planet.* But even before them, this space was inhabited by other beings that did not come from the surface world and were highly evolved. Up to that point, the atmospheric conditions in this cavity were different from the ones now and were not favorable to human beings; but at that time, there were some transformations in this area of the planet's interior that led to some changes in the composition of the atmosphere, the characteristics of which could no longer ensure the livelihood of those special beings. They left this area at one point; and in fact, the planet itself. This new ecosystem rapidly formed, and it become accessible to surface beings. As I told you, a so-called 'colonization' of the area began gradually, but the number of people having access has always been small."

"I now see a whole civilization here," I said, curious to find out how this had been accomplished.

"With the loss of the war and the entry of the Romans into Dacia, we had to do this. There are other cities under the territory of Romania which were populated in the same way. Even though access to such locales was very secret and esoteric, the priests decided under special conditions that some Dacians would have access to this place and continue their lives, cherishing the same values as before. They considered that they were too important and valuable to be forgotten. Over time, the number of inhabitants has increased."

"What population is there now?"

"About two hundred thousand inhabitants. Genetically speaking, there is no difference between the Dacians of two thousand years ago and the people you see now on the streets. It was an act of retreat and preservation, and with it, many gates of communication with the exterior world were closed. Evolution, however, has followed its own course in all its aspects."

PEOPLE, ACTIVITIES AND OTHER
DISTINCTIVE FEATURES OF TOMASSIS

I wanted to ask about the technological level, but I noticed that the platform was beginning to descend to the ground, heading for the seashore. As we descended, I could see the structure of the city much more clearly, and it was very similar to what we see nowadays: streets, intersections, and people with various chores bustling about with focus as opposed to irritation. I think that the population could well apply the famous Latin motto: *festina lente* (which translates as "make haste slowly"). I did not, however, notice any vehicles, at least from the aerial vantage point I had. All of the men and women were walking on foot.

It seemed to be an unusual society from our modern point of view. For example, I saw nothing industrial, no factory, no smoke-free chimney, nor

---

* This possibly refers to the final drowning of Atlantis that specialists date to around 11,500 B.C.

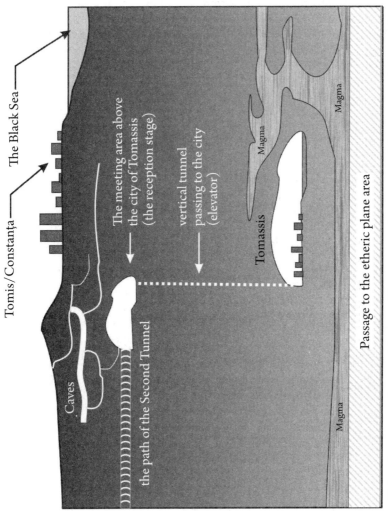

The Black Sea

Tomis/Constanța

The meeting area above the city of Tomassis (the reception stage)

vertical tunnel passing to the city (elevator)

Tomassis

Magma

Magma

Magma

Caves

the path of the Second Tunnel

Passage to the etheric plane area

Related correspondences of the city of Tomassis to other structural elements inside the Earth

any workshop. They probably had areas devoted to study and technological research with manufacturing and production being done elsewhere; or perhaps they have simply reached a higher level of civilization which no longer involves the cumbersome and complex mechanical devices that we use, and all of it without conventional fuels. Their antigravity platforms are an excellent example.

Generally speaking, the impression that the city left on me was that I was in Ancient Greece. I mainly saw buildings and constructions with a style very similar to what I knew from illustrations, books and articles, but everything was integrated with very modern systems and devices. This somewhat paradoxical state applies to both the perspective of the city itself as well as the behavior of people. For example, while the streets were not wide nor paved with asphalt, they were all made of cobblestone. It is true that their stones were perfect, but it was stone pavement without asphalt or other synthetic material. There were no "concrete and glass" buildings, no glittering contours, no skyscrapers, no complex highway intersections or clover leafs. Everything was steady and intelligent with inherent simplicity and a certain kind of elegance, somehow blending into the ancient style.

As we passed by the last of the building and headed to the seashore from the right, our platform approached very close to the ground and stopped. Neither upon our arrival nor at landing did I have any idea who had facilitated our transport or how it all worked, and I did not ask. I figured that it was probably a predetermined program and that the platforms followed a kind of schedule revolving around arrival and departure points, but I found it hard to believe that, with such advanced technology, the inhabitants of that place would have been constrained by fixed points of travel.

I stepped onto the sand of that beach. It was fine, clean, and yellow. The waves were not high, and later, I learned that there are never storms, whirlwinds or other destructive manifestations such as we are accustomed to on the surface of the planet. The sea water is always calm, just as I saw it. Near me, on the beach, there were a few small rocks with vegetation growing amongst them.

From the city, we noticed a group of three people, a man and two women, who seemed to know about our presence there. Observing their behavior and attitude, I could see them walking in a very relaxed matter with a balanced mood. I could also see the technological devices they wore. Each of the three people had a small triangular shape at their right temple which was attached to the skull in some manner. I saw no other elements that might support it. The man had a greenish shirt opened at the top and a little over his chest. It was not closed with buttons, but had a sort of vertical band that seemed to stick, like Velcro. On the lapel of that shirt, I also noticed a small device that had two bright lines, one blue and one green, flashing with different lengths. The man wore trousers of the same color as the shirt, but a darker shade, and he had brown shoes that resembled moccasins. Everything created the impression of perfection. I did not see anything that was disharmonious.

Based upon certain technological aspects that I have mentioned, it was logical for me to assume that their clothing was futuristic in style, similar to a "fashion of the future." Still, their clothes showed a simple and conventional design but one that paid careful attention to detail. If I were to make a concise description of what I saw in Tomassis and its inhabitants, I would say that it was the image of something that looks old but that is made with new things. All of these aspects created a slight sense of anachronism, but it was not disturbing.

The clothing of the three had good taste and also involved a knowledge of proportions, even an elegance of detail. The women were wearing a sort of traditional blouse for women which we call an *ie* (pronounced ēēya) in Romanian, and they had long black hair. I noticed that one of them had two beautifully braided ties that were decorated with two fine chainlets, one of gold and the other one of a red material.

The three approached us, bowing their heads slightly, and Dryn began talking to them in the unknown language that I had also heard him speak when I met him in the passage. This time, however, I no longer understood the meaning of the words, but I noticed that they often ended in *es* or *isos*, resembling what we know to be ancient Greek.

Meanwhile, Cezar told me that he would have to discuss some aspects of collaboration with Dryn and other representatives, and that meant he would have to go to another place in town. He told me not to worry and said that he would come back shortly. He considered the meeting to be important because it concerned opening up some possibilities for technological collaboration. From what I learned later, Dryn, serving as a high representative of the To-massis civilization, was offering documentation of anti-gravity technology. It seems that the issue at hand was not necessarily of a conceptual nature but was mainly related to the material or alloy that had to be used.

Turning to Cezar, Dryn made a gesture of invitation with his hand and climbed onto one of the platforms which then ascended into the city. Behind them, the man and one of the females, the one with the beautiful hair adorned with those precious metal chainlets, climbed onto the second platform. Their platform closely followed in the same direction of flight to another area of the city which I figured to be the central era.

"THE 30-YEAR-OLD WOMAN"

I was alone, somewhat out of my element, with the second woman in the group. The two soldiers stood at a distance from us, on the edge of the water, speaking slowly between them. Not knowing what I should do then, I looked inquiringly at that woman who did not seem to be more than thirty years old. The brunette, with big eyes and delicate features, had a very slim and even athletic body from which I deduced that her function was to serve in a protective manner like a security guard. The light blouse she wore had no sleeves, and on the upper side of the right arm, she had a spiral-shaped bracelet made of a reddish-colored material. Her black eyebrows were well contoured and when seen up close gave her a very determined air with a specific dynamism. The hair, tight on her temples and head, was trapped in back in a long queue. In her ears, there was a pair of long, elegant and very refined earrings; and upon the right temple, I noticed that the same device with the triangular shape was attached, just like the two men.

I was expecting her to somehow come forward, but she did not do that. Instead, she spoke to me in Romanian with the same strange accent that I had also noticed with Dryn.

"We can take a short walk until they come back."

I accepted and we started to walk slowly along the beach, somewhat parallel to the shore of the water. I was a little overwhelmed by the situation, not knowing how to proceed or what to say, but the girl was very natural and began to explain to me that some of them travel to the surface at different intervals with different missions. As the conversation unfolded, I realized she was not a telepath like Dryn, and then I became more relaxed. Asking her if she had ever been to the surface of the Earth, she answered that she was well acquainted with the regions of our country and with those in other countries.

"Last time I was in northern Scotland for three years. There is a well-established mission cycle, and my turn comes once every ten to fifteen years. I'm just getting ready for a new departure."

Something did not fit. I told her I recognized her as being young, but I could not understand how she could have missions to foreign countries during her adolescence.

"Our energy capacity is different, and our lives are longer," she answered. "You estimate my age to be thirty, but I am actually fifty-four."

I was deeply amazed but did not show much surprise as I myself was perceiving an infusion of special energy that made me feel deeply revitalized and full of good cheer. I changed the subject because I assumed that she did not want to give me more information about what they were doing at the Earth's surface during those missions.

TRADITIONS, ORGANIZATION OF SOCIETY, AND EVOLUTION

"I have not seen children in the city until now but just in the distance, on the shore," I said, curious to know details. "Is there a place for them?"

"The conditions here are limited to only a certain number of inhabitants so that life is balanced. We pay attention to this, but the great majority of children in our ranks were born on the surface. They are brought to our city when they are three years old. Those born here are more special."

I raised my eyebrows, frankly wondering what the reason was. The woman explained it to me with a warm and calm air.

"At birth, the child must benefit from astral influences. It is very important to achieve an energetic contact between his or her structure and the energetic influences that come from the stars. This is like a kind of a necessary footprint for its existence and everything that follows is under the sign of that influence. Your science still does not understand these aspects, but those born here have gone beyond the necessity of astrological influence because of their spiritual transformation. Such a being is Dryn."

"Okay, so how do you know who's supposed to be born on the surface and who's born here?" I asked.

The girl smiled and explained that this was determined by the wise people of that community, and this surprised me. I had the impression that I was viewing a documentary film about archaic societies, and my mind was beginning to look distrustful of what I was finding out. The woman probably felt my distrust and responded accordingly.

"In all of our history, for thousands of years, there was not even one case where the wise men were not right. Everything has come true just as they said; but you, on the surface, tend to regard almost everything as a product of technology and matter. That's why you often fail, and your conception of the universe does not allow you to understand any of its mysteries."

Having no choice but to accept her statement, I hoped for an accelerated evolution that could be helped by proper communication between Mankind and their society. I quickly realized, however, that things are very complicated in this regard, so I abandoned this topic, a subject for which I did not have any accreditation anyway.

Taking advantage of the opportunity I was offered, I asked a question.

"Have you actually progressed all alone in a closed system over the last 2000 years?"

"It's not a closed system," replied the woman. "There are connections both on the surface and within the Earth. We are not the only ones here. But we also have the advantage of special materials that cannot be found on the surface or extracted from your mines. It is a special knowledge that has long been transmitted."

"Dryn told me you are descendants of the Dacians."

She nodded with a noble and determined gesture.

"We are their direct descendants, but on an evolved spiral. Everything is like a mirror image. Just like our city, you have the surface city of Tomis on your sea, and we have Tomassis down here on our sea. The spirit of our ancestors and the Empire has been preserved."

I was not sure what empire she was referring to, but I suspected it was the Thracian one in Burebista's time, not the Roman one because, if it were otherwise, what she said would not make sense. But, to be sure, I asked her.

"It is the ancient Empire, and we have everything documented: tablets, metal plates and other objects from that time and even previous time periods.

We also have evidence of what followed. Everything is documented and archived and includes an entire history of thousands of years. We have continued the existence of the people, but only in this place, within the planet. Our organizational structure is the same as in the old days.

"What organizational structure do you mean?"

"Chain of command. The way in which decisions are made. We have a hierarchy, but the concept is that of our ancestors. It has no failures."

I could not contradict her since I had proof right before my eyes: a big city inside the planet which was perfectly functional, technologically advanced, and in which peace and tranquility reign, emitting reason and wisdom. Its inhabitants were beautiful, calm, relaxed, and intelligent. It was impossible not to compare what I saw with the sad reality of today, with the so-called ideologically "advanced" society in which we live with the stupid "democracy" of the existing political system, so complicated, useless and creating endless conflicts and problems. If such a political and governance system, with the hundreds of laws encompassing it, is truly valuable and effective, then how do you explain the continuous floundering of today's society with all sorts of problems and short-circuits in the decision-making chain which abounds all over the world? And if you see something that is obviously lame, would not it be normal to want to modify it? Unfortunately, the chain of inter-state dependencies and obligations, especially of an economic and financial nature, is so tough and manipulative that it becomes very difficult to make such a major change, even when it appears to be perfectly rational and make common sense.

The woman explained to me that their leadership system is based on "the principle of wisdom": the one who is the wisest leads the city. Asking about the way in which people determine the wisest, she told me that, generally speaking, they are chosen from the so-called "group of wise men" who are usually the elderly. It is that "old man's advisory group," well known from ancient times in our tradition but also in others, and they seem to have strictly maintained this tradition with remarkable results. She then explained to me that subordinate to the Wise Man there are what can best be described as ministers in our organization system. Each of them has a region, but it does not mean a space region but rather a field of activity: one for construction, one for science, another for research, and so on. The system is designed and applied so that each of these administrators take on their subordinate people in accordance with what they need to do.

"Of course, we also have a defense system that is very effective," she said. "There is a Special Guard and an Analysis Group. Those in the Guard are fighters who are well trained and have a very advanced technology available to them. Those in the Analysis Group are comparable to the analysts in your world. They monitor surface communication systems, access ways, and a blockade that we set up a long time ago in the event of possible intrusions or attack plans from your leaders. Fortunately, very few people know or believe in our existence here, and that is mainly due to the major disability your world has in terms of science. Your scientists do not understand reality as they should."

"Yes, too much hubris and arrogance," I said softly, mostly to myself, actually repeating the words of Dr. Xien.

After that, I wanted to make the bitter pill a bit sweeter.

"We still have a pretty advanced technology."

"The basis of our technology is completely different from yours," said the woman. "Its conception is parallel to what you know, at least up to now. First, you probably need to figure out where you block yourself or get stuck and then to look further. We are ready to help you and to respond to your appeals, but this has to be done with great care because, in the way you view existence, something very dangerous has slipped in over the past few hundreds of years."

I implicitly deduced that this had everything to do with the diplomatic contacts initiated by Cezar and General Obadea with the civilization of Tomassis, and I thought there was a high probability that the meeting Cezar was attending now represented a stage in these discussions and negotiations. I did not, however, have any further information at that time, and I understand that such things are very sensitive and cannot be discussed under any circumstances. The woman remained silent for a moment and lightly touched the device at the temple with her hand. Looking behind, I noticed one of the platforms approaching us, and behind it, on another platform, came the two soldiers. They stopped for a few moments in front of the woman who spoke to them in their pleasant tongue, after which they bowed respectfully and moved on. I understood then that the woman had a certain hierarchical rank and that she was even the superior of the two. She turned to me and spoke.

"We are not the only ones to have built this sort of living arrangement for ourselves. There are many more urban settlements beneath your country at different depths. When the 'exodus' occurred, many of us withdrew from virtually all of the regions of the surface territory, and we came to such secret places inside the planet."

"I am certain that almost no one on the surface knows about your existence. You have no connection with them."

"Before the wars, a connection between the inside and the outside existed. The cavities and the access ways to them were known by many people. There was another level of thought and action. After the arrival of the Romans, we were forced to withdraw and close these access ways. We blocked the entrances to the cities inside the Earth, but we also deposited here a lot of

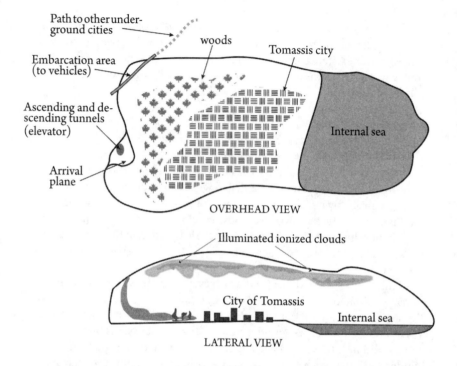

UPPER AND LATERAL VIEWS OF TOMASSIS, MAIN ELEMENTS

evidence, writings and documents that are not known, especially since that time after the conquest. Only a small proportion of what you know as the history of that time is true, but the greatest part of it is unknown. You just simply do not know how things really happened. When the time comes, all the evidence we hold will be made known."

We were both flying on the platform to the city; and more precisely, to the edge of the city where I noticed an area like a train station with several tunnels entering the mountain. Near two of them, I noticed some lift vehicles. There were no rails or other guidance devices.

We slowly descended to the ground which this time was well polished stone. The two soldiers were waiting for us at one of the vehicles. I looked inquiringly at my companion, and she invited me to enter that vehicle. I understood that we were going to travel; and impatiently, I rushed to the spot.

CHAPTER FOUR

APELLOS, THE CRYSTAL CITY

Approaching the vehicle, I could see that the design was very modern and unlike the generally simple and old-fashioned style that generally characterized the community. This was a real technological jewel. At first glance, it resembled the famous Shinkansen Japanese trains, but its capsular shape and more complex construction differed from them.

The woman explained to me that this was a sort of commuter or shuttle vehicle that links the cities inside the Earth, each of them corresponding to the approximate territory of our country. She did not, however, tell me whether it also was used for other settlements inside the planet that were situated at greater distances or depths than the place in which we were then. Logically, if such cities are spread out in a particular region, they should also exist in other areas of the planet.

AN ADVANCED TECHNOLOGY

The departure station was very much like the one in which we had arrived by the elevator. It had the shape of a semicircle, spreading out like a fan, being guarded by the vertical wall of the mountain. The capsule was floating at about ten to fifteen centimeters above the ground due to an anti-gravity effect.

The vehicle attracted my interest in a most special way and that is exactly why I have carefully analyzed it. Over all, it resembled an ellipse, but it had certain specific lines at the ends. I estimated its length to be about seven to eight meters and its height to be about three meters. It was compact, massive, perfectly polished, and it even asserted a certain dynamism because of its aerodynamic shape. While it was built out of a white material, it featured a white-cream color in some areas.

From the start, my attention was caught by the peculiar construction involved in building that vehicle. The external shell was covered by identical "packages" of joint-like scales in a way resembling the tiles on the roof of a house. I figured that this had to do with the specific technology related to its energetic source. Initially, I thought that the technology involved in building this shuttle was like the Maglev magnetic system that has been used by the Japanese, but I was wrong. The woman told me, however, that it is another type of technology based upon different physics. Your science still has not understood it, she told me. It is a force that distorts space and time.

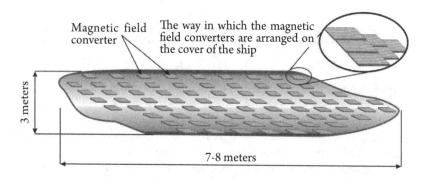

Magnetic field converter

The way in which the magnetic field converters are arranged on the cover of the ship

3 meters

7-8 meters

VEHICLE USED BY THE INHABITANTS OF TOMASSIS TO DRIVE INSIDE THE EARTH

Looking to understand what she meant, I was observing the special plates on the outer shell of the ship. They were compact and perfectly smooth. Rectangular in shape, the plates were adapted to the curvature of the cover upon which they were placed. The thickness of each of them was no more than two centimeters. The shuttle had no windows, skylights, nor other openings. It was like a sort of compact spindle that had been spread out, appearing to be made out of a single piece. The vehicle was positioned perpendicular to the mountain off of a massive dark opening that I initially identified to be a tunnel opening. Coming closer, however, I recognized that the surface of the mountain was polished in a circular pattern within which was a reddish-brown circle of about five meters in diameter that was much darker than the surrounding rocks. Actually, there was no tunnel dug into the mountain nor was their any unevenness or access path. Instead, the circle delineating the "tunnel opening" had several identical devices placed symmetrically on its circumference. I suspected that these were in a certain resonance with the plates or scales on the cover of the shuttle.

As it was not clear to me how such a vehicle would operate and to where it might travel to inside the solid interior of the Earth, I asked my companion.

"Obviously, the problem of digging mud-like tunnels through the mantle and the crust was not considered. Here is where the conceptual and technological jump that I told you about comes into play. We utilize the gravitational field; and precisely, its interaction with an electric field, just like the interaction between an electrically charged body and a magnetic field. In such an interaction, certain vortexes of electric and magnetic fields are generated. We have applied this principle, but in this case we are using gravitational fields. We realized that when an object crosses a gravitational field, a certain magnetic field is generated.

At this point, the chasm of my ignorance appeared to becoming deeper and deeper. Bewildered, I asked her a question.

"What do you mean? That — just like that — a magnetic field results from this interaction?"

"Not automatically, but through a conversion that is facilitated by these pieces," she said as she pointed to the scales on the exterior of the shuttle. "Just as you convert a magnetic field into an electric field, we also figured out how to convert a gravitational field into a magnetic field. There is a lot more to it than the simple electromagnetic induction your culture is familiar with because it this technology which allows us to bend space and time."

While the woman was speaking, I walked slowly by that capsule-like vehicle, carefully looking specifically at the unique characteristics of its construction. It was mostly like an elongated spindle or spike, a compact unit without any opening, perfectly sealed. When I arrived in front of it, the frontal part resembled a fighter plane's nose cone but with more rounded lines. I went around the vehicle, going parallel to its body, observing the exceptional finishing of the exterior wall. The "scales" were perfectly joined and arranged, one on the top of the other, covering the entire surface of the shuttle's body, but I could not figure out precisely how they were converting the gravitational energy into magnetic energy. I wanted to ask my guide about it, but the thought struck my mind that my interest could be regarded with suspicion and wrongly interpreted. Such apprehension, however, was unnecessary because the woman, obviously perceiving my anxiety, smiled and started to explain things to me in a very relaxed way.

"I can explain the principle to you, even if your science hardly accepts the possibility that such interactions can involve gravity. Before it starts, the shuttle generates a fluctuating magnetic field around itself which is augmented by high frequency ultrasonic waves which enable it to "enter" the solid environment of the Earth's crust."

"What sort of fluctuating field is that?" I asked immediately, very attentive to the explanations she was providing.

"It is a complex field formed by the combination of two magnetic fields: a rotational vorticity field and one other featuring a special characteristic which presents itself like a monopole because, at the exterior of the ship, it is always 'north,' and in the interior, it is always 'south.' This combination of fields, which is facilitated in a certain proportion and at a certain intensity, creates a kind of "space-time cell" that delineates the shuttle."

I suspected, to a certain extent, what the effect was and I told her.

"Does the vibrational frequency change in such a way that the capsule is able to cross through matter without interacting with it?"

"Yes, this is the phenomena. First, a local space-time distortion is facilitated by raising the vibrational frequency."

"Is this initialization a facility of the device? What creates the two types of magnetic fields? Is it the small plates on the surface of the shuttle?"

"No, not them. The walls of the shuttle are thick and they have three distinct areas. The inner one is the resistance structure. The middle area is very thick and includes magnetic field generators that initiate the distortion, but you cannot see them here because they are integrated into the construction of the wall. The outer area contains the plates on the shuttle's body which actualizes the conversion of the gravitational field into a magnetic field while traveling."

Based upon her description and out of the images that I later saw in certain holographic projections, a vertical cross-section from the body of the shuttle generally includes the features illustrated below.

I was curious to find out what was going on during the trip.

"After creating the distortion, the shuttle starts and then charges itself by moving and crossing the lines of the gravitational field," the woman explained.

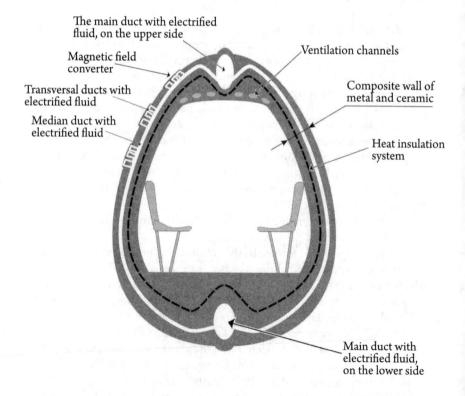

The main duct with electrified fluid, on the upper side

Magnetic field converter

Ventilation channels

Transversal ducts with electrified fluid

Composite wall of metal and ceramic

Median duct with electrified fluid

Heat insulation system

Main duct with electrified fluid, on the lower side

VERTICAL CROSS SECTION THROUGH THE SHUTTLE BODY

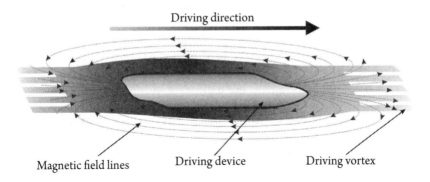

Driving direction

Magnetic field lines   Driving device   Driving vortex

THE PRINCIPLE BEHIND THE SHUTTLE'S DRIVE

"The small plates in the outer area then convert the gravitational field into a magnetic field."

"And what does that do?"

"It is used to maintain the process of generating the space-time bubble in which the shuttle resides in while it is in motion. The energy requirement to facilitate this phenomenon is very high. Only an initialization of the process can be done within its own means. Then, the energy requirement is met from the conversion of gravity into a magnetic field. The constant movement of the shuttle creates a kind of virtual tunnel or a kind of medium through which it advances at a high speed. Accordingly, the links between underground cities are easy to facilitate whenever they required."

Then, with a certain sense of surprise, I began to wonder how she knew all of these scientific details. Even though they concerned just the basic principles, she demonstrated a certain knowledge about the construction and conception of the shuttle. You could not offer such explanations without somehow being involved in the field. Relying upon the familiarity we had already established in our discussion, I dared to ask her about this.

"I coordinate research in the security and defense area," she said in a natural tone.

"But this seems to me to be a civilian transport vehicle," I commented, not understanding too well about the connection with defense.

"It can be used for other purposes," she said. "It is basically a transporter. We often use such shuttles to transport goods. Only a small part of their internal space is dedicated to travelers."

After saying that, the woman gently lifted her left hand on the body of the shuttle, approximately at chest level, and the wall glided to the left, leaving an opening to enter the vehicle.

IN THE PASSENGER COMPARTMENT

If you were looking at the capsule from the outside, it was virtually impossible to realize that there was actually a door that allowed entry. It did not overlap the wall but penetrated inside of it, after first withdrawing a few inches deep. There was almost no sound involved, just a pleasant wisp. The shuttle's interior was fully illuminated. I did not notice a special source for the light which was uniform and came from everywhere. The first thing I noticed was the appearance of the interior walls which seemed to be made up of hundreds of small and very bright crystals. The light was not intense, but it gave the feeling that it was enveloping you and relaxing you at the same time. Even though it was a cold white, I did not feel bothered by it. The reflections on the shuttle walls created an intimate and pleasant glow that immediately relaxed the psyche and the mind. Although the technology that created these pleasant effects was different from the ones that existed in either the Grand Gallery or inside of the tunnels running from the Projection Hall, the results were very similar.

In the middle of the vehicle, on either side of the walls, a pair of three ergonomic lounge chairs were symmetrically arranged. At first glance, the chairs gave me the impression of being hard and strong; but when I sat down on one of them, the material they made softened, melting as if it were buoyant gelatin. I was then pleasantly surprised to notice that if I tapped slightly on the surface of the chair, it would remain firm, but if I pressed with a higher force, it would soften, as if melting. For example, when you sat in the chair, the material became soft and immediately conformed to the shape of the body, creating a very comfortable feeling. Any movement of the body would make that intelligent material conform to the new shape, and when you got up out of the chair, it immediately returned to its original smooth state. I said to myself that, undoubtedly, this intelligent plasticity is something that every sedentary person who might work for hours in an office would like because the material correlates very well with the physical shape of the body.

The front and back of the shuttle were each blocked by a wall of semi-transparent material, behind which I noticed several boxes placed one on top of the other, perfectly sealed and probably filled with goods. I was a little amazed to see that there was no command cabin or pilot, at least as far as I could observe. The interior was very simple, containing only six ergonomic armchairs in the central part with the rest of the space inside being used for storage. Actually, the interior space was not very big, as much due to the ellipsoidal shape of the transporter as well as to the thick walls. Before the door closed automatically, I saw the delimitation of the three areas that my guide had spoken to me about, and I estimated the wall thickness to be about

30-40 centimeters. I then saw the door sliding sideways from the inside of the wall as it pushed outward, shutting the space perfectly. Only my companion and I entered the shuttle. The two soldiers stayed on the platform. The woman communicated a few words in her native tongue, perhaps to a control center, and I immediately felt a strange feeling in my stomach as in the case of a strong acceleration, but it was easy and short-lived. I then noticed a sensation of my internal organs lifting as opposed to being pushed backwards horizontally, such as is the case when one is subject to vigorous acceleration. One explanation for this might be that the vibrational frequency had been modified to make it rise and therefore create that special sensation of ascending.

After a few seconds, everything went back to normal; and immediately after start up, the walls inside the shuttle showed bright and colorful information, including graphics systems that were all arranged in sections like large video monitors on both walls. For example, in one section which was larger, we were shown where we were and how the journey evolved. It did not, however, appear as a window on a train with landscape streaming by. The images appeared slowly, somehow synthetically contrived, and the representation of the route was punctual; but nevertheless, I realized that the velocity was disproportionate to that which was represented graphically.

Everything was represented in a map-like format. This applied to both the natural elements on the surface as well as those inside the Earth through which we were passing. I recognized the Carpathian mountain chain and the northwestern part of Romania as well as the area we were crossing beneath the surface. The image contained a dynamic view of the general landscape of the terrain on the surface; but at the same time, I was also able to view the main forms of relief and structures inside the Earth through which we were passing within the Earth's mantle. It was fascinating to observe that inter activity of images, so vivid and faithful, where information was presented not only schematically or virtually but also very realistically, with actual images of the environment on the surface of the Earth and also within it. Above these, I noticed some graphical and digital information which showed directions, curves, intensely lighted areas, and blinking colored dots, all overlapping in an admirably designed configuration. I assumed that these could be directions to other settlements and underground cities, and I also noticed that most of them were in the Apuseni Mountains. I did see, however, that two lighted areas pointed to Moldova.

Their writing was not like ours. The graphical signs that were almost continuously changing were appearing in different areas of the image but were predominantly on the upper right side. Resembling runic writing, they had something archaic in their shape, a mystery that I felt attracted to. Carefully following the route and the images from the wall projection, I noticed by the graphic indications that we were heading for an underground city located much closer to the surface and in the southern area of Transylvania. The level of depth between Tomassis and this city was very large — I would say about 1500 kilometers. Actually, our destination was so close to the surface of the Earth, at least with reference to the vivid representation of the images that we were seeing, that I was wondering if it would have been easier to descend from there to the city rather than traveling via this shuttle. This was, of course, a funny way to look at the situation because, first, our journey would not last for more than two minutes; and second, moreover, my guide told me that the city, even though it is much closer to the surface than Tomassis, is still at a depth of several dozens of kilometers.

"Apellos is a very special city with regard to its history and structure," the woman told me. "It is also very old, but still, it is different in many ways than our city. Its inhabitants are also from the Dacian people, but at a certain point in history, a hybridization with another race occurred."

While she was talking, I noticed from the pictures that we appeared to have arrived at our destination. As the shuttle stopped, all of the complex images that had been occupying a large part of the interior walls suddenly disappeared, and the door opened, sliding very quietly. A warm and pleasant light penetrated the interior of the capsule, but it was not much brighter than the inside.

THE CITY IN THE GIANT CAVITY

As we left the shuttle, I saw that we were on a suspended platform supported by a central pillar at a height of about fifteen meters above the ground. The platform was placed near a rocky wall, but it was not in contact with it as was the case in Tomassis. Below, on the left side, I noticed three separate platforms at a certain distance from each other, but they were slightly smaller.

"This is the diplomatic platform. Our arrival was announced," my companion said to me.

Indeed. A couple of meters away were two men who seemed to be waiting for us. They took a few steps toward us, stopped and bowed their heads a little as a sign of welcome. They were dressed in elegant white costumes, but the way they were tailored left me with the feeling that they were connected to a security service. The hips and the coat featured flaps, probably in place of a belt; and on the forearms I saw elbow pads while the trousers had specific stripes on the side. They wore some kind of boots on their feet with some straps at the top.

The two men were about the same height, about 1.80 meters. One of them was blond while the other had dark brown hair. They exchanged dialogue

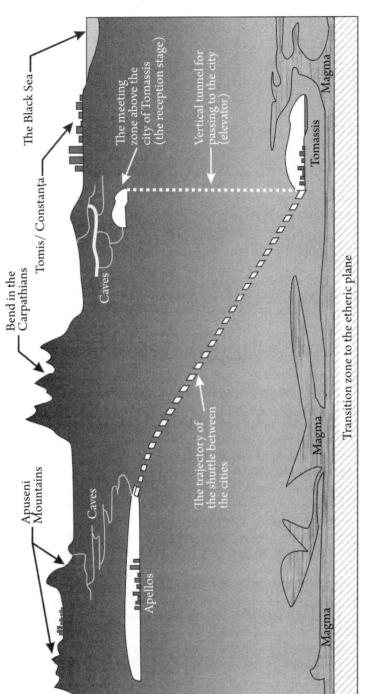

The Black Sea

Bend in the Carpathians

Tomis / Constanţa

Apuseni Mountains

Caves

Caves

Apellos

The meeting zone above the city of Tomassis (the reception stage)

Vertical tunnel for passing to the city (elevator)

Tomassis

The trajectory of the shuttle between the cities

Magma

Magma

Magma

Transition zone to the etheric plane

OVERVIEW OF THE TRAJECTORY FOLLOWED BY THE SHUTTLE

with my companion, and I noticed that they was using the same language as had the inhabitants of Tomassis.

While they were talking, I looked carefully around. Unlike Tomassis, here I had the feeling that the space was a lot more open and vast. Beneath my eyes, over a wide panorama of a few kilometers, the city stretched out, the view of which astonished me because it seemed to be taken out of science-fiction books. All buildings and constructions were made of transparent material, as if it were from crystal. The transparency, however, was not like you would see in the case of a bottle but is best described as translucent. At certain angles, I saw how the light was reflecting into the colors of the rainbow, like in a prism, creating great perspectives.

Beyond the city, I observed some hills covered by vegetation; and right underneath our platform, trees were growing that looked a lot like oaks only less tall. Instead of grass, I observed that the ground was covered with something like moss and lichen, but from what I could tell, it had a rougher consistency. Most of the city's buildings, as I could see from afar, were spherical or curved. I did not see any tall buildings, only a few small towers that were rounded at the top. I also saw pretty wide streets and very beautifully arranged tunnels and arches as well as dome-shaped buildings. The architecture of the city was totally different than that of Tomassis, and the construction material was staggering, creating the sensation of a city of the future. The light, which was also special, contributed to this. As in Tomassis, it was not emanating from a concrete source but was uniformly spread, white in color but of medium intensity, just as it is at 10 o'clock in the morning.

When the conversation of the three had ended, the blond man turned to me, addressing me very kindly in almost perfect Romanian.

"Time is too short to visit the city, but in addition to what can be seen from here, we can offer a summary of the information about us that will help for our future collaboration."

I was feeling good and accepted what he said with joy. At their strong advice, we all headed to a small pedestal on the platform that was revealed to be a command panel. I did not know its precise function, but the same man told me that this was a peripheral device that could connect to the central information of the city.

At the moment we approached this pedestal, which was like a meter high parallelepiped, it activated with different signs and information with schemes and images appearing on its surface. I had the impression that the device was a sort of selector; and indeed, with only one hand movement from a distance, the blond man was able to access a certain field. In front of us, a large holographic screen was immediately projected upwards from the pedestal. Wider than the pedestal, probably more than two meters, it was just a little smaller in height.

THE HISTORY OF APELLOS

As soon as the holographic "screen" started to play, images of that city and its inhabitants began to unfold quickly and with exceptional clarity. I realized that they were not necessarily in chronological order but that did not bother me. I was very attentive and curious to find out details about that place, even more so since the presentation was very similar to those in the Projection Hall in Bucegi.

At first, I saw the surroundings of the area: the hills that I had already seen, two small lakes, and what seemed to be a small-sized glacier in the distance. Then, all of a sudden, the images showed a sort of entrance on the mountain's ascent that was very elegantly developed. The presentation emphasized the mountain's entrance, portraying it as if it were a tourist cave, showing it from different angles and at different distances. This was the first time that I noticed the way in which the mountains were structured, like a sort of semicircle on the side, as if they were surrounding the space that we were in but at the same time curving over it. Stunned, I looked up to see the image projections; and it was then that I noticed that the holographic projections had come to a standstill or froze when I had taken my eyes off of them. As soon as I looked again at the screen, the images continued. When I looked up, however, the stream of images stopped with one image remaining available to view as if it were a frame in a roll of motion pictures that had been halted in a movie projector. It was obvious that, in a certain way, this replay was inherently connected to the direction of my gaze and was referencing just that.

Looking at the city, I did not pay particular attention to the sky as it was diffused because of the light; but now, I looked more closely at the area where we were, right next to the rocky wall of the mountains. As I noticed the wall rising overhead, I saw that it bends slightly so as to apparently block the light from above, making it appear as if the rock was immersing into something "milky". Even so, as it disappeared into the light above, I could see a certain outline of the cliffs over us as well some peaks that pierced the clouds overhead. Only then was I able to form a clear picture in my mind and understand that this place was, actually, a sort of gigantic cave that was somehow able to provide the habitat we were seeing. The ceiling of that giant cave, however, was not too high. Judging by the peaks of the cliffs that I observed above us and comparing them to the ceiling of the cave, I would approximate the height to be a maximum of seventy meters, but I realized that it varied and probably increased towards the city.

I came back to looking at the images on the screen; and as soon as I did, they started to stream once again. They were more clearly depicting the structure of that place, the mountains and their arching above, forming an immense underground cavity that was much larger than the one that I had seen in Tomassis. Although the mountain was not "growing" in height, it was somehow stretched out above the city, like a sort of bellows, with the roof continuing into the distance.

While I was looking at those images, my interest was drawn to the entrance of the cave in the mountain, something that I could not see from the platform that I was on. I then I figured out that the images that were appearing were somehow related to the interest that I was showing in one thing or another, all dependent upon what I wanted to see. From this, I realized that this was yet another type of inter activity with a direct connection to my mind, but it was even more profound and probably the result of a technology that I did not understand.

As the screen zoomed in on an image of the cave's entrance, I immediately understood that this was actually the exit from the mountain to the internal cavity in which I was then: namely, the city. I noticed that it was like a big tunnel opening, pretty tall and wide, with artificially polished edges. The intervention of the humans was also seen in the area in front of it, apparently an arrival and departure point and where I also noticed many boxes and crates deposited on one side.

Then, all of a sudden, the image showed the same entrance into the mountain, but this time it was in its original natural condition. Comparing it to the image in which it had been enhanced, I saw that it was once smaller. The edges were natural rock, and the ground at the entrance was uneven and far from being level. I immediately realized that I was seeing the history of that place, right from its beginning, even to the point where it was immersed in darkness.

The images showed two men with large beards with cuşme (the Romanian name for a head piece that the ancient Dacians wore) on their heads, each holding a lighted torch in their hand, cautiously stepping further into the opening of the cave and into the cavity in which the city of Apellos now resides. The light of the torches was weakly reflected to the upper side of the cave, showing the very solid stone structure of that very large cavity inside the Earth. Behind the two, but remaining at the entrance to the mountain, there were several other people waiting for them and carrying some large bales or bound up commodity.

From the way the images played out, I realized that those were the historical beginnings of how that area inside the planet became populated. Perhaps I was being offered to see the moment of discovery of that huge cavity so that I could have some idea of the succession of its development. Interestingly, the ones I saw that were the first to discover that cave were not "cavemen" and rather wore wearing rudimentary trousers made of thick white material, head skins with cuşme, and wide shirts that were linked to the hip with a dark belt. I assumed that these were the inhabitants of the surface, maybe even a

Rock wall

Vegetation

Rock stratum in the ceiling of the cavity

Diffused light

Creek

Buildings

Cavity arching

Rock wall

Vegetation

GENERAL OVERVIEW OF THE CITY OF APELLOS

long way before the old Dacians, and that made me think that the populating of this huge cavern inside the area had probably taken place many thousands of years ago. It was, however, a totally different story than that of Tomassis, and it seemed amazing to me that they had advanced so incredibly quickly from a technological point of view.

Out of the next series of images, I was able to understand the way in which things developed, even if I did not see too many details. At the beginning, only a few people made their way into the immense cave, but due to the fact that there was total darkness and the area nearby was extensively rocky, they left. But then, probably at a certain time afterwards, I saw another group of persons entering and utilizing a small-sized globe that was spreading a very pleasant and powerful yellowish-white light. Several similar globes were then brought into the area. They were not big — I do not think they were over one meter in diameter — but the light they provided was extraordinarily strong and constant. Soon, the entire valley and cavity was lit, revealing a landscape that was mostly rocky, arid and deserted. My initial estimation of the height of the cavity proved to be pretty correct as it was not more than 70-80 meters on the average. The space stretched out several kilometers horizontally, ascending slightly on the opposite side of the entrance to the mountain. Practically speaking, it was like a huge empty bubble with an almost ellipsoidal shape on mostly flat ground, a gigantic cavity that stretched over a large area beneath the territory of Transylvania.

Those people who brought the lighting globes were a part of another brotherhood or class of people; and, by the way they were dressed in long robes, they seemed to be priests. They were accompanied by a small group of very beautiful men and women with blond hair who, by reason of their shiny clothing and behavior, showed that they were not part of the indigenous community on the surface. My intuition told me that those beings helped and supported the inhabitants to populate and establish that community inside the Earth that is now known as Apellos. The technological advances and the way in which that place developed clearly demonstrates it.

THE LIGHT IN THE CAVITY

At first, the light emitted by those globes was a lot more powerful and had a different wavelength with its color being whitish-yellow. Now, the intensity of the light in the cavity became weaker and more pleasant; and now, maybe because of a change in its frequency, became just white light. My first impression, when I got out of the shuttle and was able to take in the perspective of the huge cavity, was that the light was "feeding" me in a certain way and inducing a very pleasant state of being within myself. Neither dry nor arid, the light seemed to be full of substance.

Unlike Tomassis, where the light comes from the natural ionization of the atmosphere, it is produced artificially in Apellos. The flowing images showed me the ingenious way in which the inhabitants of the city solved this problem. Their illuminating system is pretty much like the LED system in our technology, but instead of the ceramic material inside of LEDs, they use quartz crystals that they produce and integrate into a special composite so that the interior illumination of the cavity doesn't need auxiliary energy.

To me, this is a very ingenious idea and an extraordinary technological achievement. Those quartz crystals are produced so that pressure is placed upon them in such a way as to create an emission of weak photons that manifest as light. The rocky ceiling of the interior cavity in which Apellos resides is covered with billions of small crystals which react to the pressure caused by a gravitational difference that manifests on the giant cavity ceiling. The images suggested that there is a main gravitational attraction to the center of the planet but also a certain gravitational attraction exerted by reason of a mass of matter above the cavity. This difference in gravitational attraction acts upon the device that supports each crystal and causes a certain electrical voltage to occur within it which is absorbed by the crystals and converted into photonic emission or light.

Looking closely at the hologram in front of me, the image zoomed in; and I could see that even if a single small crystal emits only a specific frequency, due to the fact that there are billions of such small crystals in the entire underground cavity, the volume of frequencies being emitted is enormous.

As my interest in this crystal technology was very strong, I was shown the structure of the device supporting the crystals. These devices are like rounded small plates, having a diameter of about ten to fifteen millimeters and a thickness of one millimeter. They pretty much resemble the LED technology we have, with the difference being that they are made out of several successive layers of metals, each having an increasing density.

I realized that the technology is advanced because those metals were probably utilizing nanotechnology imprinted on the small plate that create electric tension through differential gravitational attraction. With a small magnet and a special converter placed over them, the converter was transforming the differential gravitational effect into an electric field, then directing it to the crystals in what amounts to a pretty complexly layered system.

The quartz crystal had a powerful magnet on top of it, thus taking the weak electric current through a vortex which, in turn, created a new variable magnetic field. The combination of a static magnetic field and a variable magnetic field was creating a permanent excitement in the quartz crystal that was generating a photonic emission; that is, light. The most interesting part of this effect is that this process is permanent and does not need another electrical source other than the one produced by the gravitational distortion.

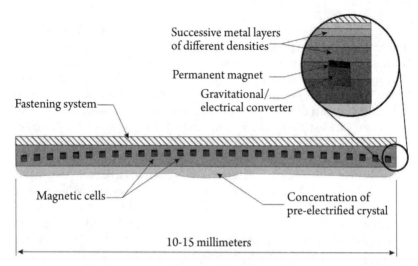

Successive metal layers of different densities

Permanent magnet

Gravitational/electrical converter

Fastening system

Magnetic cells

Concentration of pre-electrified crystal

10-15 millimeters

THE COMPLEX ARCHITECTURE BEHIND THE ADVANCED TECHNOLOGY OF FACILITATING ILLUMINATION THROUGH QUARTZ CRYSTALS

Structurally, the light emitted was calculated to cover the entire visible spectrum. Together, all of the crystals were creating an ambiance of white and balanced light that was very rich in different frequencies, flowing from the countless photonic emissions emitted by the quartz crystals. This explains the sense of well being and the sensation I had of "feeling fed" when I arrived in Apellos and came into contact with the light there. Solving this delicate aspect of living has also ensured a rich habitat for vegetation and has enabled life to thrive.

THE FIVE PLATEAUS AND THE COMPLEX SYSTEM OF CAVITIES BENEATH THE TERRITORY OF TRANSYLVANIA

It is thrilling to see the way in which a population is established and the way in which it builds a proper environment and even a destiny, especially inside the Earth. In short flashes, it was shown to me how everything had begun; how they brought bales and sorts of barrels in the first phases as well as various other objects which they stored in front of the mountain entrance to the mountain; and how they then eventually started to advance more deeply into the cave, especially after the first lighting globes arrived.

The fact that I was seeing rather large objects that the people had brought there made me think that the access opening to the cavity was pretty large itself; otherwise, they could not have managed to carry in those materials. Still, just like in Tomassis, I did not see any type of animals that might have helped them with the transport. As soon as I focused my attention to the access to the huge cave, I was shown images of the cave in sections, presenting the cavity from the right side, the bottom side and so on. From there, I saw the main corridor at the entrance which then developed into many more branches. Some of those were blocked and were rather short, but others were larger and were laid out in different levels so as if to have a "split level" effect. I did not see a continuous diagonal access path from top to bottom, but the environment had somehow been fragmented into many relatively horizontal plateaus with passage ways made in between them. As different branches of tunnels existed at each of those plateaus, one had to know the correct and primary path leading into the huge cavity below; otherwise, I observed, you would end up following the secondary branches leading into smaller caves or the path would be blocked. I cannot say, however, whether any of these smaller caves were also inhabited or not. As some of these caves were linked, I would guess that the answer is yes; but this is just a personal opinion of mine. Nothing was shown regarding it.

I counted five levels or main access plateaus to Apellos. As I looked at the sectional images that were presented to me, I was amazed to notice how complex the structure was inside the Earth, even when so close to its surface. From what I have seen, I can affirm that Apellos is in the zone of transition between the crust and the mantle area, at a relatively small distance from the surface, and that it can be accessed directly through a certain place in the Apuseni Mountains that resembles a pretty big crack in the mountain.*

In comparison, Tomassis is at the lower limit of the Earth's mantle; that is to say, at a much greater depth than Apellos. Due to that, the Dacian city is very close to the border of the transition zone to the etheric plan inside the Earth. This explains why the physical nature of matter in that place and the beings there are more refined than what you will find on the surface. Additionally, it is possible to access Apellos by walking if you know the know the correct route. Access to Tomassis cannot be accomplished in the same way but rather only by passing through certain lock chambers or spatial distortions that exist in certain well-known zones. They are either natural or were created artificially, such as is the case of the Second Tunnel through which Cezar and I entered.

I was shown the path to Apellos, at least to the first level. After one enters from the surface, there is a rather steeply declining passage to the first level. The steep descent attenuates at the second plateau and a relatively constant angle of declination is maintained to the fourth plateau, the largest of all the plateaus. I have seen that a large cave exists on that level which includes a

---

*In Romanian, the word *Apuseni* is derivative of *apus*, meaning "sunset" and the suffix *eni* which refers to a plurality as well as a group of people or objects with certain attributes that might include beliefs or other characteristics. In this regard, *Apuseni* can refer to the "people of the sunset."

THE FIVE PLATEAU SYSTEM OF THE ACCESS ROAD TO APELLOS, STARTING FROM THE SURFACE OF THE EARTH

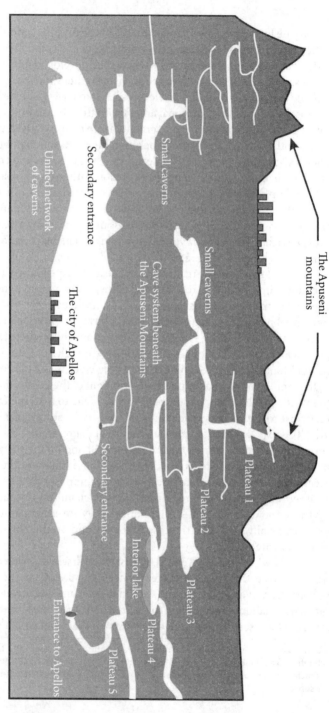

The Apuseni mountains

Small caverns

Small caverns

Secondary entrance

Unified network of caverns

Cave system beneath the Apuseni Mountains

The city of Apellos

Plateau 1

Plateau 2

Plateau 3

Secondary entrance

Interior lake

Plateau 4

Plateau 5

Entrance to Apellos

APELLOS, THE CRYSTAL CITY

pretty wide underground lake that needs to be crossed in order to get into yet another cave. It is by journeying through this last cave that you eventually reach the immense cavity wherein is the city of Apellos.

I was then shown an overview of the territory of the Apuseni mountains which suggested to me, by reason of a luminous apparition in the projection, that there was an immense cavity inside the Earth. Apellos itself had an elongated shape in the form of a kind of triangle. I could place its boundaries between the Romanian cities of Oradea, Sibiu and Alba Iulia. From the edges of this cavity, I saw it extending into other smaller caves like some "fiords," all of which made a very complex underground beneath the Apuseni Mountains.

I believe it to be important fact that both Apellos and the other "fiord-caves" extending from it are physical worlds in the same sense that our world is on the surface of the planet. Moreover, these worlds are connected culturally by reason of the access paths shown to me and just described. Based upon further explanations that I received from the blond man, I found out that they pretty often visit our world and return with many products and goods from the surface world. Access to Apellos, however, is not allowed except in cases where it is absolutely necessary.

The widest part of the inner cavity inside is oriented to the south, right beneath Roşia Montană and the adjacent town of Câmpeni. It is obviously no coincidence at all that so many problems, debates, discussions and conflicts, particularly of a so-called economic nature, were born out of the subject of extracting the gold ore from Roşia Montană. We know too well the subtleties beneath this problem, but it is neither the case nor the time for it to be presented here. These represent internationally sensitive issues involving state secrets, but the attentive reader may make some pertinent correlations.

THE TRANSPORT NETWORK

The cavity narrows very much towards Oradea, forming a kind of triangle with the wider side at the bottom. The projected images I was watching then showed me a sort of circulation "network" inside of Apellos as well as in between the different "fiords" or its branches. As the images were zoomed in on, I could see that the connections and the movement were by shuttles such as the one in which I myself had traveled from Tomassis to Apellos. I noticed, however, two other types of shuttles or capsules, one of which featured a modular transporter more that fifty meters long.

From the platform I was on, the city looked very quiet, just like Tomassis, but the underground shuttle was dynamic. Even inside the hollow of the cavity, it was quite active, but I noticed that most of the trails were relatively close to the circumference of the huge cavity, nearby the mountain's wall and with only a few vehicles penetrating radially towards the city center. Basically,

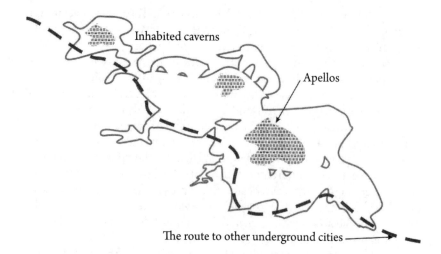

Inhabited caverns

Apellos

The route to other underground cities ⟶

THE LARGE CAVERNS AND "FIORD-CAVERNS" BENEATH
THE TERRITORY OF THE APUSENI MOUNTAINS

it was the same structural layout as in Tomassis where the shuttle tunnel follows the circumference of the mountains on the edges of the inner cavity.

I have noticed many such small and large shuttles that connect the various areas of Apellos and other outer branches of the city. Of course, I have seen the movement of such vessels penetrating zones close to the surface where there are some major stations at relatively small depths beneath the ground that serve as "reception points" through which movement and transport of goods and personnel is made with the outside. The passages between those stations and the surface were short and also secret.

Still, while I was seeing those visual sequences, I observed that the transport shuttles were taking only a small part of the goods deposited into those reception stations. Personally, I was facing a dilemma: right from the beginning of these visuals, I was asking myself how communication with the outside world took place and how the inhabitants of Apellos were arriving at the surface and travelling back. Also, I was curious as to how the transportation of goods took place; and from what I had noticed, the quantity of such was rather massive. There was no way that the shuttles could arrive to locales on the surface nor could you find many transport vehicles at the reception stations, all of which were probably two to three kilometers beneath the surface. If those from Apellos would have tried to use the caves and plateaus system that I had seen in the images, then it would had been a failure right from the start because the travelling along those passages would require immense effort and would take a lot of time. Even assuming that the route were flat, it would still take several days to ascend the almost 70 kilometers between the city and the surface of the ground. And let us not forget that the interior of the planet has countless meanders, barriers, ascents, descents, waters to cross and who knows how many other unknown elements. In such conditions, transporting goods of any kind, especially in big amounts, and depositing them into immense hangars, as I later witnessed, would be virtually impossible.

I was preoccupied by this problem, and that is exactly why I dared to ask for some information The blond man answered me with a lot of goodwill.

"Yes, this has long been a thorny problem, but it has been resolved. Here," he said, alluding to new visual sequences, "you can see our hangars on the surface where we bring various goods from your cities before transporting them to Apellos."

The screen showed images of a huge and very modern hangar in which people were bustling and using forklifts and small electric vehicles, just like in a retailer warehouse. Amazed that the activity of the underground dwellers was equally alive on the surface of the Earth, I made an enthusiastic and natural inquiry.

"But where exactly do you have those depositories or hangars? I did not expect such a big circulation of goods to exist," I said admiringly.

Smiling, the man replied to me.

"You can understand well enough that we have no permission to reveal this. Information of this sort is discussed at another level and they are beholden to higher authorities who decide such matters. Even the information that you now have access to has been previously ascertained with regard to what will be revealed to you as well as to how and when. These are important matters that cannot be treated with superficiality.

CONSIDERATIONS AND POINTS OF VIEW ON
LIFE IN THE CITIES INSIDE THE EARTH

I was well aware that such things are fully justified and fit into the logic of events.

"Due to the nature of the people on the surface and their level of understanding life, the problem of the security of our city has always been very important. Your coming here is also part of a plan, designed long ago and that happens in a step by step manner. The fact that this stage has been reached means that a real diplomatic decision was made."

His words were saying, indirectly, that future contact between our civilization and Apellos, Tomassis and perhaps other cities inside our planet was being prepared. I do realize, however, that this cannot be done so easily. Without getting into philosophical and religious details, I would mention the immense technological, social, psychological and economical shocks that Humankind would suffer after facing the reality of the existence of these civilizations inside our planet as well as the reality of the interior structure of our planet, all of which has no connection to modern scientific theory.

These two Inner Earth cities that I had accessed up to that point seemed to me like they were two enclaves of another world. I do not think it is wrong to say that, if their existence were to be known about by our surface civilization and access would be free, we would probably witness an invasion similar to the conquistadors conquering the Inca empire. From a certain point of view, things have not changed too much from four hundred years ago. The goodwill of the beings from the two cities, however, is great and they really want to help us. I now better understood the titanic efforts of Cezar, his countless journeys inside the planet and their true motivation as well as the great discretion that he has shown in this respect.

Noticing other smaller cities on the outskirts of this settlement, nestled inside smaller cavities, I asked a question.

"Did they develop independently?"

"They are like satellites of ours, but they each have their own separate status and bylaws. We communicate and help each other out, but the development is on an individual basis. The population of these cities increased massively after the conquest."

Without asking more, I understood that he was referring to the Roman conquest of Dacia, two thousand years ago. The blonde man continued his explanation to me.

"The interior of Earth is not full at all, as you say, but you can also say that it is 'rarefied,' having a lot of cavities, caves and caverns of which you know nothing about. Some of them have no association with the surface but only communicate amongst each other. Many, however, are connected through channels or other access ways to your realm. Of those, you only know a few. Caves that are used for tourism or exploring represent only the tip of the iceberg; but the cavities inside the Earth are bigger and more complex than those and exist in far greater number.

"Are they all inhabited?" I asked, opening an older curiosity.

"No. Some of them are empty even if they are capable of supporting and maintaining life. Powerful governments in your world have discovered some of them that are closer to the surface and have even built military bases there that are actually real cities in which thousands of people live. They are considered to be used as refuges in case of great calamities or cataclysms on the surface and that is why they are secret. Other cavities, although very large, are useless for the purpose of developing a society. Many of them are practically bags of gases while others have wide fresh water lakes and some have sediments, oil, or other substances. Certain powers in your world wish to exploit us by different means. Sometimes, when they get dangerously close to one of the access paths, we prevent them from doing so without them realizing what is really happening. For the time being, we cannot have any another type of contact because their intentions are almost always destructive.

"In any case, their influence inside the planet is minimal, practically meaningless," I commented. "At the same time, there are probably many other populations, cities and possibly even civilizations that I know nothing about but that you are probably already familiar with. Are there any conflicts amongst these different factions?"

Fights in the underground are pointless because they are destined to failure on both sides right from the start. There are no winners and losers. Everyone loses because the environmental conditions dictate it. It is a closed and relatively limited space, and you cannot treat it randomly. The balance is delicate and a lot of attention is required to maintain it. Powerful weapons of destruction, explosions, and as you call them, weapons of mass destruction, are out of discussion. These are, in fact, rather primitive. Even if we were to use simple rudimentary weaponry, like the type that existed in your medieval period, too many corpses would destabilize the ecosystem. Many of the cavities are not as large as Apellos, and life there needs to be carefully organized. Those of us inside the planet have understood right from the beginning that fights and conflicts are pointless. Human evolution has changed its perception and genetic information step by tiny step so that, after thousands of years, there is a fairly large difference between the beings on the surface and those inside, and this applies in almost in any field. If genetic information is healthy from the beginning, the evolution inside the planet can take place quite rapidly.

"TELEPORTATION" OF GOODS

Some things were unclear in my mind, and as I tried hard to arrange their importance, I allowed myself a comment.

"It is hard to believe that all the beings in the underground are built from the same model. I see significant differences even between yourselves and those in Tomassis; but, after all is considered, I find it to be understandable. What I do not understand, however, is if all of the communities are on the same approximate evolutionary level. Are they all peaceful and happy?"

"For those starting from the same genetic pattern, yes. They have developed based upon the same pattern. But there are also some limited communities that are different. These are beings, not necessarily human beings, who have another way of living. Some of them are not from this planet. Their worlds are dark and filled with anguish. They are isolated and their access to the big cavities, where society is considerably evolved, is blocked. They have arrived here through fate and the game of destiny, all in the context of historical circumstances which they themselves have perpetuated."

"I understand that this is the situation at minimal depths."

"The cities and civilizations inside are not only physical. Their degree of elevation increases as you go closer to the center. While we are in a cavity that is relatively close to the surface, it is natural to maintain the connection to those living there because we live in the same dimension of reality, that is, the physical dimension. It is the same for Tomassis. That is why we have rich activity and use many of your products."

I then remembered the subject which we started the discussion from and I looked at the screen that had immediately animated itself.

"Indeed. I see that you use many products from the surface."

"It is only natural. We have no plantations, agriculture, nor a complete set of elements that are necessary for survival," the man said.

"Okay, but how do you transport these products from the surface to the city?"

He passed his hand in a certain way over the projection panel, and a small cross-section of the hangar appeared on the screen. I saw a clear circle with a diameter of about three feet. Above this, I saw an arch about five meters in height that was made from a yellow-reddish color metal. A round-shaped device was attached that made the entire ensemble look like a huge shower installation. I even made an innocent remark about this in a joking manner.

"In reality, it is a high technology device that relocates the goods and the beings from there to the receiving station where they are taken by transporters," the blonde man explained to me as he smiled.

"Are we talking about teleportation?" I asked, stunned.

"No, it is not teleportation in the exact meaning that you might give to this notion. The object or being does not simply disappear and reappear in another place. It is a simpler method that does not imply the difficulties involved in teleportation. We raise the vibrational frequency of the object or the being to be transported, and then the material is 'pushed,' as if it were on rails, to its destination. The 'rails' are actually field lines, like rays of energy, between the transmitter in one location and the receiver in another. Atoms are pushed along these lines; and when they reach their destination, they are 'coagulated' by diminishing the vibrational frequency."

"Does the process take place instantaneously?"

"No. It takes some time, but it is short. Even though there is no question of speed in the classical sense of the notion, transmission takes only a few seconds due to a required sort of rebalancing of the electric and magnetic fields of the transported material. To compare it with reference to the current understanding of your science, it is as if the object travels to a parallel universe and then goes back to our universe. The technology is a bit more advanced than that of our shuttle system."

MAGNETIC CONVERTERS

From the explanations given, I understood the movement of the transport vehicles was more a problem of "local" physics, a phenomenon that in the open spaces was helped by some adjacent structural elements. The shuttles were not going on rails but were passing under some "arches" as they circulated in open spaces. In the images shown to me, I saw how they travelled at high speed both through empty spaces inside of caves and caverns but also through solid matter in between. I then understood that the travel technology used by the inhabitants of the two cities inside the Earth is not very different.

As soon as I looked at the situation from this angle, the images showed me a shuttle very similar to those from Apellos; and then, very quickly, several projections followed showing the type of converter used and the forces it generates. As I already knew about this, I realized that the transport technology used in Apellos was similar to what the woman in Tomassis had described to me, though not necessarily identical to it. I was shown how the shuttle was propelled by physical matter through the principle of changing the vibrational frequency; and then at the forefront of such a system, how gravitational attraction is converted into a magnetic field, almost identical to the "scales" type system on the cover of the shuttle that I had traveled in from Tomassis. As the vehicle was shown to me in the images, the cover was just a little different in shape to that of the one from Tomassis with one of the sides sloping and corners being slightly rounded.

The zoom on the image increased considerably so that on the surface of the converter I could see the structure of a complex network formed by the lines of the gravitational field. It intertwined with the shape of the shuttle and was rendered graphically so that I could see an interaction between it and the major network which then began to fluctuate. Then, in a very interactive way, it was shown to me how the electricity generated out of those fluctuations was taken by the system and converted to a magnetic field.

Implicit within the physical construction of the converter were some compartments with a special shiny white liquid that looked very similar to liquid oxygen, but I tend to think it was something different. As I watched how this special liquid interacted with the gravitational network lines, I concluded that it probably contributes to the conversion of gravitational energy into magnetic energy.

RETURNING HOME

After the projection of this last detail, the screen became opaque before pulling itself back into the solid pedestal upon which it rested. The blonde man turned to me and spoke.

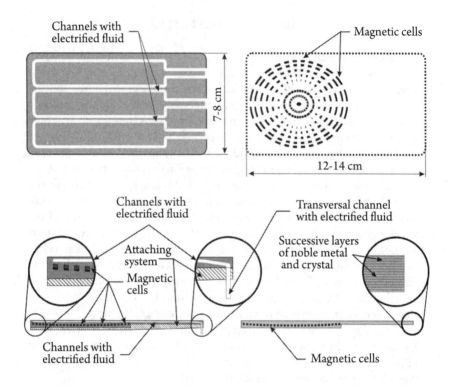

THE PRINCIPLE STRUCTURE OF THE MAGNETIC FIELD CONVERTER

"It is now time for you to return to Tomassis. Your colleague is already waiting for you."

I thanked them for their goodwill and kindness as well as for the marvelous opportunity they had provided to me of learning about the history and life of their community. I was impressed; and inside myself, I admitted that I wished to stay in Apellos as I enjoyed it very much. After saying goodbye, I entered the shuttle with my companion.

The return trip was even shorter. As I traveled, I abandoned myself comfortably into one of those chairs with their very relaxing material, thinking about everything that I had seen. Meanwhile, my female companion was searching out some information on the interactive images on the walls of the transporter.

Five minutes later, I felt a very light and short deceleration which indicated we had arrived at our destination. I stood up, and when the door opened, I walked onto the platform in Tomassis. There, I had the pleasant surprise to see Cezar, waiting for me with a slightly amused smile. Dryn was a few meters away, talking with the two military personnel. I looked at my watch and saw that the time spent in Apellos, including the travel both ways, took about forty-five minutes. My intuition was telling me that it was time to get back to the surface, and Cezar confirmed it with a knowing look. Dryn told us that the two military officers would accompany us for a while to see us out. We told him goodbye, and I thanked him especially for the care and details that he had offered. I was feeling that this wise man would play an important role in the future destiny of the cooperation that is anticipated between their civilization and the surface world.

We both ascended on a flying platform that took us up to the area of the mountain where the inter-dimensional "elevator" was. The two military people followed us on another platform. Everything was happening very fast, but I still had no impression of hurrying or hastiness. Being under the spell of all the information that I had just found out in such a very short time, I preferred not to talk, especially because Cezar seemed to be preoccupied.

I then enjoyed the short journey in the elevator and the images I saw through the transparent material that were somewhat daunting due to the very high speed. When I stepped out, I was in the reception area, but I saw more people this time. The two soldiers led us up to the section of the wall of the mountain, and when Cezar and I came directly to it, it began to vibrate, becoming translucent. Strangely, I had already felt a change of state in my whole being, as if my center of gravity had changed, and it made me very dizzy. Greeting the two from Tomassis, who bowed their heads with respect, I walked along with Cezar and beyond the reception area.

I experienced the discontinuity as naturally as possible, feeling only a shivering sensation that crossed throughout my entire body like lightning. Cezar explained to me that, in practical terms, this feeling is a result of changes in the vibrational frequency of the bioelectric field at a cellular level. While we were walking back through the tunnel, I asked if this was going to ruin the body. He explained to me that, due to the fact that the frequency differential is at a relatively close value, the body would not notice such changes in an unpleasant way, even if those were realized at a rather rapid pace. Additionally, he told me that the body "learns" such new information quickly and assimilates it through repetition. This led me to understand that it is very probable that I would feel almost no disparity during my future travels.

In the meantime, we arrived back at our original point of disembarkation in Bucegi, and I was having a bit of a hesitation as I looked at the tunnel that bifurcates, the branch that I had yet to travel on. Noticing my response, Cezar told me that branch represents a more complex travel experience than the one we took to Tomassis and Apellos.

"First assimilate what you have found out and experienced so far in the two cities. We will go through the second branch later, and you will see for yourself that here things are, in a way, more complicated."

Seeing the diffused light in the Projection Hall, I abandoned myself in the drunken magical state that it would gives me each time, even if I am only passing through it. I could not help from remarking how efficient these technological systems are which facilitate natural changes in vibrational frequency in order to allow travel to be made in a very short time.

Looking at my watch, I told myself that I was living a dream. I had originally arrived at the base at 9 A.M.; and after all of these experiences and trips, I was on my way back to the Base at 12:30. An hour and a half later, I had walked into my room and was laying down on the bed with my face upward, somewhat confused by the rapidity of everything that had happened. I was wondering if I had even departed that very morning, and now, in less than six hours, I had already arrived back but with a huge bag of information and a colossal experience.

A little tired by the multitude of emotions and energetic demands that I was not yet used to, I felt a very profound sleep coming over me. The last mental image I saw before slipping into a well-deserved rest was the splendid vision of the city of Apellos with its crystal buildings.

CHAPTER FIVE

THE GUARDIAN

The next two weeks featured considerable agitation. At certain times, the Department goes into "alert" mode, and its activity increases very much. Cezar was mostly gone, but he left me and Lieutenant Nicoară with the task of organizing a very important expedition through the tunnel to Iraq. Until then, the Middle East had proved to be the most difficult due to technological problems that could not be overcome. I will give some details when it is the right time to discuss that journey.

The expedition was going to be a joint effort, and the American crew was scheduled to arrive in two months. The organization protocols had changed significantly since the expedition to Egypt and so had the American military chiefs. As visions were not always convergent, this required moment by moment snap-judgment decision making as well and a vigilant wariness of contacts at different levels. I already had a lot of experience managing these issues, but things seemed to get more and more complicated from year to year instead of becoming more simple. Impatience, tensions, and repeated demands on the part of the U.S. put a lot of pressure on the Department, and this was felt especially after General Obadea's death.

Once the structure and logistics of the expedition were determined, things calmed down somewhat. Other services, like the Secret Services, were occupied by organizing secret diplomatic meetings at a certain level with the State Departments because some agreements were political in nature. Anticipating possible surprises, Cezar decided to take advantage of this calm period and told me one morning that we would go travelling again but this time through the second branch. As soon as he spoke, I felt a tightening in my stomach. Ever since I had passed through the second tunnel, I have felt an unmistakable but indistinct tremor, the nature of which I did not understand. On the one hand, it was like a magnet attracting me to that branch. On the other hand, a strange agitation enveloped me. But as Cezar had already experienced traveling through that bifurcation, I did not worry but happily welcomed the journey.

Of the expeditions through the three tunnels, those inside the Earth involved the least preparation. The specificity of the travel and of the contacts make everything happen quickly and precisely. It is far more difficult when visiting with governmental representatives from our world as we are required to compensate for their lack of understanding as well as hidden intentions and issues of power, arrogance and money.

I rested well that day because Cezar had told me that it would be a difficult journey and I knew that I would have to experience many adjustments in vibrational frequencies, even more than usual. Only later was I able to understand the real meaning of his words. My only surprise was that, unlike the preceding trips, he did not announce to anyone that we were coming.

"It is not necessary. Somebody is there all the time," he answered me. "I told you that we are dealing with a special situation in this case."

Following the pattern that I was quite familiar with, we were in the Projection Hall in the morning of the second day. All that was needed was for Cezar to activate the discontinuation of the first tunnel; and when he did, he beckoned me to pass with him. One of the advantages of traveling through these tunnels and paying repeated visits to the Great Hall is that the body seems to gradually assimilate the superior experience and more effectively integrate it afterwards. One never becomes bored or disinterested because your entire being is upheld and fed by a mysterious energy that seems to "activate" and offer an elevated experience or feeling during these expeditions. Through the passage of time, a specific certainty and confidence manifests which enables you to easily overcome what, during one's first experiences, was a heavy testing stone. This sense of power can be seen as a "habit" although it is more a "habit of realization" as the confidence that is acquired by correct assimilation provides efficiency and precision in one's actions. I offer these explanations because I myself was living that wonderful feeling of safety and superior understanding that such continuous practical and theoretical experience offers, especially when it is about such an esoteric subject.

Up to the time we arrived at the secret location in Bucegi and had entered the Great Gallery, we had hardly spoken. Now, we both remained silent until we arrived inside of the tunnel, right in front of the bifurcation. Passing near the area of the big cube with the frequency deviation, we entered the straight path. Stopping before the second distortion, we witnessed glittering violet that was undulating in a delightfully mysterious way.

"I have always liked this part of the tunnel," Cezar said with an enigmatic smile.

We both walked beyond the distortion with a motion that was suggestive of a slow down in the flow of time. For a moment, I felt a genuine resistance to our forward movement, but that was immediately followed by a feeling of release as if I had suddenly become lighter. The tingles I felt during the crossing lasted longer than those in the Tomassis branch, but they disappeared after a few yards. After passing through the distortion, the tunnel seemed to be identical with the part before the distortion, but I soon noticed that it started to widen like a funnel, becoming more and more illuminated. This was a remarkably novel experience which was reinforced even more by the perception of a sea breeze and the unmistakable smell of a beach. I was amazed and impatient to solve this intriguing mystery. After all, I had just entered into the mountain and now I was about to get to the seashore.

The tunnel made a wide curve to the left and I observed its grandiose expansiveness that was in the shape of a giant megaphone. I could even hear the first sounds of sea gulls screeching and the calm sound of the waves. Rushing ahead of Cezar, I followed the curve to the left of the tunnel. I stopped suddenly, finding my feet in a yellow sand facing the sight of a small island with rich green vegetation. Even though I am accustomed to stunning experiences, I was still amazed because I did not understand where the tunnel had disappeared to. Looking up, around and behind me, the tunnel was there; but, when I looked ahead, I could not see the edges of the "funnel" which seemed to dissipate into the air. Even the color of the sky seemed to intermingle with the color of the borders of the funnel, becoming thinner and thinner as I looked upward until simply getting lost in the air. It seemed that I was looking at an extraordinary well done painting or I was just emerging out of a television screen in a reality that I did not know how to define.

"Sometimes a short relaxation would do no harm," joked Cezar as he came close to me. "I am thinking of bringing a lounge chair; maybe an umbrella, too."

We both laughed, but the truth is that I did not understanding a thing. Staring at that almost unreal and unnatural landscape, I could not explain it in any way. The beach was deserted and dry with dry wood and algae. The sand spread far into the inside of the island, about thirty meters from the very clear and calm ocean. The air was pretty cold and very refreshing, but the vegetation that started from the beach seemed to be luxuriant. I saw palm trees and even big ferns. The island appeared to be uninhabited and, at first glance, we recognized that it had a relatively round shape with a diameter of several hundred meters. I could see, for example, the bend of the island to the opposite side, all beyond the green jungle just ahead of me.

I still did not understanding anything. I looked upward to the very clear sky with only a few white solitary clouds, and I saw the bright sun at its zenith. We had entered the Projection Hall a little before nine o'clock in the morning, and to get here we only needed about five minutes. I made a gesture of giving up, renouncing any possible solutions because nothing seemed to connect. First, the temperature of the air was inconsistent with the type of vegetation; and then there was the position of the sun at the zenith on a little patch of an island in the middle of the ocean to which was added an immense funnel that became lost, coming out of the water and emerging into the air until it became indistinguishable.

After joking for a while over my stupefaction, Cezar spoke to me as he looked across the wide ocean.

"Just imagine how surprised we were when we arrived here for the first time. We were expecting a totally different view and, in any case, a presence.

Everything you see right here is the same as what we saw ten years ago. No change at all. The same beach, the same vegetation, as if time stood still. Back then, I did not know what to do. The team was made up of four people, and we had equipment with us as I had no information about what to expect. The console had shown there was a blockage beyond the distortion."

"So, this is our whole trip?!" I exclaimed, amused. "After all, where are we? At least tell me that we are still on Earth."

Cezar closed his eyes and clasped his hands at his neck, leaving the breeze strong enough to cool his face. Smiling slightly, he replied, "Yes, of course we are on Earth, but nevertheless, one cannot determine one's position here by using any kind of instrument. Nothing works and everything is in a mess. It would have been impossible to figure out what had happened if the Guardian had not arrived. You will see him soon as he always arrives a certain while after a team comes here. You will, however, find him waiting for you on the beach if you happen to come by yourself. This is indeed a mystery, but keep in mind that you cannot consider such a being to be like the others that you are already familiar with."

"All right; but where does this man come from? And what is it about this island?"

I was already feeling some discomfort at the thought of having neither a reference point nor any sort of inspiration up to this point. Cezar continued to gaze in a dreamlike way toward the horizon. Without turning to face me, he answered.

"It's an anomaly. I do not know that I can describe it any better. What I'm telling you was explained by the Guardian himself. This branch of the tunnel was descending inside the planet, right to its center; but at some point, something unpredictable happened that was never anticipated by the original builders and the space-time structure was altered in this area of the Earth. It was a terrible cataclysm, and the tunnel came into the category of so-called 'collateral effects.' The vibrational frequencies changed, but those inside did not want to completely break the connection in this direction. They considered it too old and important to be cancelled completely, so they generated this intermediate "outpost" as a bridge between the physical plane and the etheric plane. At this moment, we are no longer in the physical plane; so, you have no position to measure. If you still miss it, you can look for the tunnel where you can find some physical traces, albeit altered from the distortion."

I remained stupefied. For the first time, I was finding out that I was in another plane of existence than the physical one. Out of reflex, I thought of modern scientific theory and mentioned this to Cezar.

"I know that this is only mere 'magic' to scientists, even a blasphemy from the point of view of their principles. With all of these, however, here we are, definitely not in a place on Earth where you could be found."

He made a short pause, reflecting upon what he had to tell me. Knowing him as I did, it meant that the information to come was important.

"You have to understand that the physical plane represents only a small part of the unthinkable vastness of Creation," he said. "In a way, you could say that it is a particular aspect of the etheric plane because these two planes are somewhat intertwined, not unlike Siamese Twins. General representations show us that the etheric body is covering the physical body, but it is, in fact, also inside it. Meridians and subtle energy paths, which are not seen but which are known by esoteric traditions, are proof of this. Actually, we might just as well say that the etheric plane is the one that encompasses the physical plane and not the other way round. That's why we meet the etheric plane in the 'interior' of the planet, but it also envelops the planet from the exterior. Basically, there is a very close connection between the etheric and the physical planes because their vibrational frequencies are relatively close."

"I do not really understand how the physical plane can appear out of the etheric plane," I said, confused. "They have different vibrational frequencies."

"By a kind of condensation of the etheric vibrational frequency," answered Cezar, "which then decreases to the frequency specific to physical matter. The etheric plane is like a 'foam' of vast water."

"That's all"? I asked, amazed by what he had said. "Is the physical plane just like an etheric foam?"

"Yes. The physical plane is small compared to the etheric plane and has a narrow frequency of vibration. By comparison, the etheric plane has a wider range of waves, starting from an etheric aspect very close to the physical plane, almost ectoplasmic, and up to elevated etheric frequencies, close to those of the astral plane, such as some cities in the center of the Earth.

Thinking of the recent experiences I had, I said, "That would explain our repeated and relatively easy crossings between these two planes," I said. "It's almost like a conversion from one frequency to another."

"That's true," said Cezar. "A simple example is that, at zero degrees (Celsius), water turns into ice, but those pieces of ice float through the liquid water that surrounds them and supports them. That's like the etheric and the physical plane. The vibrational frequency of the water has fallen and the water has 'contracted' or 'condensed' into ice. By analogy, the ice manifests as residing in the physical plane, but at the same time, the ice continues to be 'wrapped' and penetrated by the surrounding water that did not freeze. Similarly, the physical plane is surrounded by the etheric plane and also penetrated by it because, as the ice seems to be 'something' other than water, it is still water when it is heated and melts when you increase its frequency of vibration. This also explains why there is a relative correlation between what you see in the physical plane and what you encounter in the etheric plane."

171

I carefully looked around once again and could say that, generally speaking, everything seemed normal in terms of "substance." If I put aside some of the oddities I have already mentioned, I could say that we did not see too much difference between the physical plane we came from and the etheric plane in which we now were, at least according to Cezar's description.

Cezar then continued his explanation.

"Strictly speaking, the alteration of space has brought us to somewhere in the Arctic Circle, a little further north of Iceland. This zone somehow represents a tradition for accessing the Inner Earth except that those who have lived this experience and wrote about it have not totally understood what they were dealing with nor have they described it correctly. This is the same endless problem and false controversy with regard to getting 'inside' the Earth through 'the opening at the North Pole'."

I was familiar with this problem because I have read and seen different representations, depictions and even known photographs of the so-called 'cavity' leading to the center of the Earth. I have also read the reports of my American colleagues about the decades of investigation in the Arctic. Obviously, there was no opening in the ground and no curvature in the physical plane leading to the center of the Earth nor was the water of the ocean leaking out anywhere. There are, of course, an entire series of anomalies in this region that have been reported on over time, including the bizarre behavior of devices used for guidance and control, but no open path to the interior of the planet has been described and represented in the books, articles nor even classified materials of the Navy which tolerate the idea in their computer data base as they have no plausible variations of how to explain the phenomena.

"Everyone wonders what this opening to the interior of the planet is, what shape it has, how great it is and where it is. Many believe that in order to visit the inside of the Earth at the poles, there must be a huge hole in the Earth's crust and that one must follow the curvature of the crust in order to arrive there, but in fact, things are different and I have already explained this to you. The endless controversies only arise due to ignorance, and this begins with the way in which different 'positions' are interpreted on Earth, but these are just conventions."

"Still, you know that such interpretations are tempting because the experiences we have are very vivid and close to our normal life," I said, based upon the readings we had already taken.

"Yes, but they come from misunderstanding the problem. For example, you're standing at the base, and if we're going to interpret in a mechanical and somewhat infantile way, when you get to Australia in the Southern Hemisphere, your head should be down. But, if you actually travel there, you see that it's not like that; but rather, you remain the same way you were when you were sitting in the base training area."

I was a little confused and agitated by Cezar's approach because these "physics problems" were, in my opinion, in the category of the puerile category, being suitable for the first year of high school.

"I know the eternal story with the question of 'Why do we not get off Earth when we walk through the circumference and why we are not head down when we get to the opposite side?' Everyone knows that there is gravity and we have little chance of getting off the surface of the planet. Also, everyone knows that the radius of curvature of the Earth is so great in relation to our size and the speed at which we move that the surface always appears to be flat; and so, we will always be with our head 'up'."

"Not everyone knows this," Cezar answered patiently. "But even if they knew it, it would only be a partial vision of the problem. The notion of 'up' or 'down' is conventional. If you were looking at the planet from the cosmic space, up and down would not make any sense."

"What do you mean by 'partial vision'? I asked, looking at him in wonder.

He bent to the ground and began to draw with his finger in the sand.

"The fact that the force of gravity acts and does not allow the body to detach from the surface of the planet, regardless of the angle it makes with it, is a general consensus explanation at a macrocosmic level. But, if you look at what happens at the microcosmic level, in the cells for example, the situation is no longer simple. The magnetic field lines will influence each atom and molecule in your body as you modify your position on the surface of the Earth, and that influence will be reflected differently in the organization and structure of your cells. At different points on the surface of the planet, the direction of the magnetic field is different, so the influence on the cells of our body is also different. However, we do not realize this because the process is slow, and the structural changes are not very big. Accordingly, it appears nothing has happened; but in reality, there have been some magnetic changes in the body."

"All right. So what about it?" I asked impatiently.

"The problem is similar to what happens at the poles when someone gets inside the planet, and this is what I am actually trying to explain. And here the process in slow. If you are in such a zone, you are no longer solely under the influence of the magnetic field on the surface but rather become subject to an interference pattern which is really an admixture of two different magnetic fields, one sourcing from the interior of the planet and the other connected to the surface. To give another perspective on things, it is like you are on the surface of a Mobius strip that becomes twisted, but you are actually remaining on the same surface.

Looking carefully at the drawing that Cezar had made in the sand, I said, "What I do understand is that when you pass into the interior of the planet, you are no longer in the physical plane."

"Yes; then you gradually pass to the etheric plane. When you enter the zone passing into the Inner Earth, the magnetic field initially has a higher intensity in that area at or near the surface and its direction is almost perpendicular to the surface of the Earth. We could say that gravitational attraction and magnetic field lines almost overlap. Advancing toward the poles, the magnetic field of the Earth decreases, but for those whose consciousness is open, a gradual entrance into the etheric plane is produced, allowing one to continue their way to the interior of the Earth.

"There is a conical zone in which the magnetic field is smaller, but there are also other forces that appear, including those related to the rotation of the Earth. At the poles of the Earth, the magnetic field of the planet significantly decreases and this decrease forms the 'cone' that I was telling you about. You enter the inside of the planet at the base of this cone that is located inside the polar circle and it has a weaker magnetic field. There, the orientation of the magnetic field lines facilitates the process of passing to the 'inside' of the Earth, for if the intensity of the magnetic field decreases when you initially descend inside the cone, it then increases by the fact that you, apparently, are continuing to descend, but you are actually approaching the central source."

For the first time, I was truly understanding the passing to the "inside" of the Earth via the poles.

"But isn't this influence of the magnetic field exactly what determines my passage into the planet?" I asked, to get a better understanding.

"Sure. Once you cross the Earth's magnetic field in the Arctic Circle, there is a certain alignment with the gravitational pull, and the energy released by the atoms' response to this process causes them to rotate rapidly. It's a phenomenon related to quantum mechanics. Amidst an accumulation of factors, the energy of your cells increases as they are excited; therefore, we can say that their vibrational frequency increases. After this 'shower' of energy, your cells will 'want' to retain their excitement, and thus 'choose' to go towards the growth of the magnetic field while retaining some particularities of the orientation towards the gravitational attraction. This 'choice' is equivalent to the slow entry into the etheric plane, and this in turn makes it possible to penetrate gradually to the center of the planet. Of course, this process occurs only to those who are trained and have a certain level of understanding. It also does not happen at any time or anywhere but is correlated with what we might call 'universal necessity' as well as with the will of the wise in those inner worlds."

So absorbed in Cezar's explanations, I almost forgot where I was. I then asked him a question.

"In this case, why is it that everybody who is succeeding at this is talking about getting inside the planet?"

"They then pass to the etheric plane, but their cells no longer align with the magnetic field at the physical surface of the planet but rather with the magnetic and gravitational field lines from the etheric plane of the Earth. Then, there is an 'inversion' with the surface that is produced that creates the sensation that they are 'inside' when, actually, they continued to go forward."

"How can this be? Do I have the same surface but with two different planes of manifestation?"

I was stunned because I could not understand how was it possible to pass from the influence of the terrestrial magnetic field influence to the gravitational field in the etheric plane.

"The vibrational frequency of the etheric plane is relatively close to the vibrational frequency of the physical plane and that is why the two planes, many times, seem to be glued together, meaning that they are close. This is

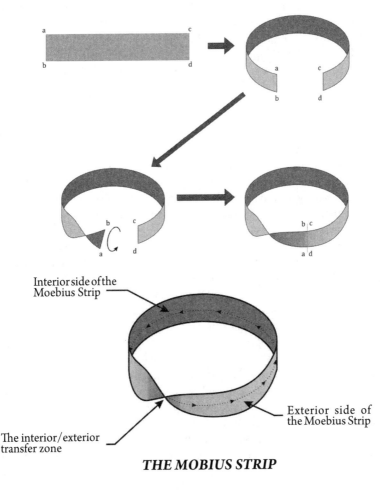

Interior side of the Moebius Strip

Exterior side of the Moebius Strip

The interior/exterior transfer zone

THE MOBIUS STRIP

the reason why it is pretty easy to pass from one to the other if you are in the right place under the right energetic conditions.

Only then did I begin to better understand that passing from the physical to the etheric plane, or the other way around, is like an inversion or reversal of the surface of a Mobius strip. Apparently, we do not feel it, but it exists. For example, when we fly by a plane from Bucharest to Canberra, we do not feel that something inverts within the cells of our body when crossing the different magnetic field with different directions, even if we are moving from one side of the Earth to the opposite one.

"The same thing happens in the case of accessing the planet at the poles. Beyond the zone of the Arctic Circle, we feel almost nothing, but gradually, we see areas and views appear that should not be there," explained Cezar. "We are at first confused, then impatient; and in the end, panic can appear. Still, curiosity and amazement often win out because the things that you then see are really extraordinary. The entire experience is stunning and you see what a wonderful opportunity it has been for you to live those moments offered to you. Inside your mind, the idea gets formed that one has travelled to the 'inside' of the Earth, but this derives mostly because the surface where we live is thought of as the 'exterior.' Fundamentally, if we say that we are entering 'inside the Earth,' we are not wrong, but the way in which the notion of 'interior' and 'exterior' is conceived in three-dimensional geometry is out-of-date. Also, the way in which one gets 'inside the Earth' is typically conceived and represented in a completely wrong fashion."

Cezar sketched a new drawing in the sand and continued explaining.

"The passing zone is favorable at the poles because the rotation of the atoms around their own axis is increased, unlike the situation around the Equator where the apparent mass is bigger. It is like the gyroscopic effect: if you weigh a spinning top, it will be lighter when it is rotating than when it stands. The difference is infinitesimal at the atomic and cellular level, but it accumulates at the level of a physical body. Considering a specific model or example, we can say that the vibrational frequency of the spinning top increases when it rotates. At the poles, a similar phenomenon to the gyroscopic occurs. All the atoms in your body will be under this gyro-magnetic influence — they 'rotate' faster and have greater energy. The vibrational frequency rises and then you get into the etheric plane, even though you are maintaining the same direction of movement and apparently remaining on the same surface. But the 'inversion' or reversal that I told you about is produced, and the mind will interpret that it arrived 'inside' in the same way that it interprets that one's head is 'down' when in Australia."

As he spoke, my gaze was drawn over his shoulder to a being approaching us on the beach. Although it was still far away, I was quite perplexed because it seemed gigantic to me. Feeling a certain shivering thrill, I let Cezar know.

"Yes, the Guardian. He never rushes things and arrives exactly when the discussion comes to an end. Watch carefully and you will see that he does not stop but walks continuously at the same pace. Neither stopping nor slowing down, he will be here exactly when we are ready for him."

"We could go meet him," I suggested.

"You can try, as we did, but you will see that it is useless," Cezar answered. "Nothing changes; the distance remains the same. It is confusing, but if you consider that the rules of the physical plane do not apply here, the phenomenon becomes somehow explainable. You can barely understand the world that the Guardian comes from, and that is exactly why it is so hard to get there. You have no mental point of reference and there is almost no correspondence or agreement between what you know and with what you are with in this environment. It is a very elevated level of existence compared to our world."

For a few moments, we both looked in his direction. I was practically hypnotized by his imposing stature and at the same time by the imperturbable calm with which he stepped, always focused and looking downward, but I strove to be attentive to what Cezar was saying to me.

"The Earth is like a Mobius strip. Its exterior surface continues with its interior surface because they are not actually separated, but a lot of people do not think this way. They think that a line of separation exists and that if you stand above it or below it to any degree, then you are on the opposite side. Hence, one concludes that they are 'inside'. Actually, it is a trick of the mind because they are just comparable situations. I was telling you that, based on this idea, and if we strictly judge things by it, if I am standing up at the North Pole, I should be upside down at the South Pole. But, if instead of this vision, it is understood that the cells of the human body always arrange themselves along the magnetic and gravitational field lines, then these things can be better understood."

"Indeed. This is a quantum phenomenon, but I can't distinguish these changes. I cannot figure them out."

"That is right. We do not perceive them in real time unless they are major and produce an inversion like the one that we talked about, such as when you pass into another plane and get 'inside' the planet. But even then, what we see is actually what the senses perceive as new in the environment in which we now are, not necessarily an internal change in the cellular structure."

Maybe we do not have the adequate receptors for this, or perhaps our sensitivity to these energetic changes is weak," I said.

"Yes, these could be possible explanations," Cezar admitted, "but some animals feel these changes quite strongly. Migratory birds are one example, but it applies to other terrestrial animals as well. Although you do not figure out when and how the cells of the body energetically rearrange when you fly by plane to Australia, these animals are capable of detecting even the very fine

MOEBIUS STRIP REPRESENTATION

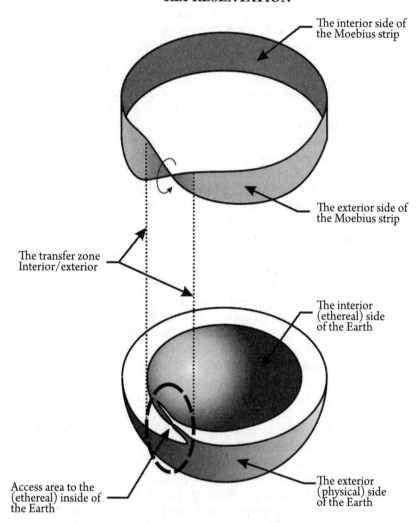

The interior side of the Moebius strip

The exterior side of the Moebius strip

The transfer zone Interior/exterior

The interior (ethereal) side of the Earth

The exterior (physical) side of the Earth

Access area to the (ethereal) inside of the Earth

SECTION OF THE ETHEREAL CAVITY OF THE EARTH

ANALOGY BETWEEN THE MOEBIUS STRIP AND ACCESSING THE INNER EARTH

changes in the magnetic and gravitational field lines. We only perceive the geometric change. The quantum factor that produces a vibrational change is more subtle, appearing only as an effect."

The conversation captured me again, and I forgot the Guardian's approach for the time being.

"This thing with the cellular rearranging or disruption sounds rather abstract," I said, "especially because the person does not feel anything."

"It depends upon from which angle you look at the problem. If you consider it only from a human perspective, then the cells remain the same; there is no difference because the being feels nothing or almost nothing and concludes that nothing happened. But, if you look at it from the perspective of energy, then every electron, proton, atom, molecule or cell — absolutely everything — leaps to a higher level of energy because there are gyrations that excite the atoms which then move on to another level of existence. At one point, this transformation becomes major, and the transition to another plane is like when you penetrate the Earth. This, however, is precipitated by certain conditions in the magnetic field and their orientation by reason of the gravitational pull."

"Okay; but the rest? A journey to another point on the planet should also cause cellular changes because, as you say, the magnetic field lines have different directions."

"That's right, but these changes are comparatively much smaller because the energy is also much less. If the experience is repeated, however, changes in the magnetic field, even small ones, disrupt biological organisms by influencing their metabolism. The specific set of psycho-mental attributes and other human characteristics are different from one region to another, and this is primarily due to the subtle influence of the magnetic field which impresses itself upon life. Science is just in the beginning stages with these researches and studies and is not too willing to give it much importance. The magnetic field, of course, is not the only factor of influence, but it is a determinant."

"If we leave aside cultural differences and customs, we see that there is a specific set of general ideas and behavioral characteristics in society."

"Yes, because the intensity of the terrestrial magnetic field is unchanged globally, at least over fairly long intervals. But where more serious magnetic field fluctuations exist, the changes are also obvious. There are also magnetic fluctuations that are often sudden and unpredictable, but the interesting thing is the fact that we can't say the same about the fluctuations of the electric field. That remains constant at the surface level of the Earth. A correlation between the two manifestations should exist, but it does not appear. You would say that the laws of electromagnetism are not respected even if, globally, things seem to be all right. Still, the details should make one think."

I then found the right moment to relate that aspect to the phenomena in the center of the planet.

"If science is not clear about how the terrestrial magnetic field is born, then how would you expect it to explain its fluctuations? The idea of a 'dynamo' in the middle of the Earth that would produce, they say, this magnetic field, is only a theory and it explains almost anything, not to mention the phenomenon of getting into the 'interior' of the planet and into the subtle planes. Only after I learned about the singularity in the center of the planet did I better understand what's going on. Otherwise, you cannot reliably explain a whole series of phenomena through the simplistic explanation of the 'dynamo'."

"That's right. If there is a dynamo, then it should provide a constant magnetic field around the planet, but it fluctuates unpredictably and nobody knows why. But, the electric field of the Earth doesn't fluctuate in unison with the magnetic field. Even if it is said that the electric field maintains a continual uniformity on the surface, certain fluctuations should still be measured electrically when a magnetic fluctuation occurs, but they do not appear. These issues are not taken into account."

"Probably because of deeply rooted fixed ideas," I said. "I consider myself pretty open-minded from this point of view, but I still have had trouble getting used to this new perspective on the interior of the planet. I think people are so indoctrinated and accustomed to the idea that the Earth is a solid sphere that you have to dig into in order to get inside of it that they can't think in any other way."

"Yes. To them, and especially to some scientists, aspects like changes in frequency, subtle planes, or the idea of a central black hole represent only the utopian product of the imagination. Just because they have not seen all of this and have not experienced it does not mean that it does not exist. At present, we have an aggregate of erroneous or obsolete scientific ideas and principles that have only an immediate and somewhat local applicability but which are considered to be universally valid."

"It is hard to get out of this circle of dogma and principles", I accentuated, relying on my own personal experience.

"It is hard for people to understand the 'interior' of the planet because they only want to judge the problem exclusively at the level of the physical plane and from a three-dimensional orientation. This point of view takes into account an axis system with three dimensions in which something is considered to be exterior and something else is interior. In reality, the 'interior' of the Earth, and especially the zone in its center, is 'something else' because it is in the subtle plane. You do not realize that you get in there, as I told you, not by walking on the same surface nor do you see downward 'curvature'. But, once you arrive inside, you can see from a distance a certain concavity which is not like the one in an inner (gigantic) cavity."

"Yes, it is true. Most people struggle to understand how there can be an empty interior of the Earth. The interior exists in the etheric plane, but the connection between exterior and interior; namely, between the surface and its interior side, is not as it is typically explained. I mean, you don't arrive with your head upside down, walking on the bending of the crust of the Earth. This is not happening because you are actually passing into another plane. Think about it. When you pass from the physical to the etheric, what would you relate to so as to figure out that you are standing up or not? You no longer have a reference point because you changed the perception of the environment. You passed from the physical plan to the etheric. The exterior surface and the internal are bound through this 'inversion', like a Mobius strip, and you do not even figure out that you got to the inside of the Earth this way until you start to see distinct signs of another world. By then, you are already in the subtle plane."

The imposing figure of the Guardian was getting closer and closer, and I realized that it was probably time for him to arrive next to us. I don't know if I really had anything more to talk about to Cezar, but I felt that the being came to us precisely at the right time that it should have. Due to its exceptional presence, I was a little timid at first. He was, I think, over three meters high, and I had my head bent a bit so that I could better see him. I still had not yet escaped the sense of the unreal caused by the subtle nature of the etheric plane in which we were. Having already extended myself beyond the limits of the physical plane, I saw myself as if in a movie with giants.

Still, that imposing presence proved to move with incredible delicacy and his smile was full of kindness and wisdom. The apparent height and size gave an overwhelming impression, but when you looked into his gentle eyes of very deep blue, you wouldn't want to do anything but embrace him with an open heart and to abandon yourself under his protection. The clothes were very simple: pretty wide blue pants and a white shirt with a big opening at the neck that was tied at the belly with a narrow belt. I would say that the material of which they were made of was like a linen cloth but it was more fine than it. The footwear resembled dark brown sandals. His presence brought an extraordinary calm; and without wanting to, I then thought that this would be an excellent therapy for those who are stressed and agitated.

"We can go now," he said, looking at us with a wonderful smile.

His voice was warm and compassionate. Even though I was hearing it very well, I did not see him moving his lips. I figured out that the communication here was mainly telepathic. Although this was awkward at the beginning, I soon found it agreeable, being very simple and convenient. We followed him back to where he had come from, about a hundred meters to a small bay, in the mouth of which was a very simple boat make out of wood. It was not tied to anything, floating on the water right near the shore without being influenced by the movement of the waves. The Guardian made a gesture, and we climbed in the boat. The Guardian then joined us. To my surprise, I noticed that when he climbed into the boat, it did not get any heavier nor did it move more than when we climbed into it. I was waiting for a powerful list or tilt after he got on board, but the weight of the Guardian did not seem to be any heavier than ours, even if he was about twice our size.

With calm gestures that were always focused, he sat at the end of the boat. I was expecting to see some oars, but instead of these, the Guardian bent over and lifted a long spear-like piece of wood that he sank into the water, pushing the boat out into the open water. I was wondering how successful he would be in doing this because the lance was not longer than three meters, but I saw that, even though we were out of the bay, the water remained at about the same depth. It was probably an area of shallow waters, as in the tropics, even though we were, theoretically, in the area of the Arctic Circle.

While I was thinking about all of this, I saw a strange fog quickly rise up around us which did not exist when I was looking out to the shore. In a few seconds, the fog became so dense that I could not even see the Guardian. Suddenly, I felt a shock as if the boat had hit something hard. I thought we had hit some rocks and that water would soon enter the boat; but in fact, in a way that I could not explain, we had just hit up against the shore. Nothing seemed to make sense, but I remained lucid and remembered that, in the subtle realms and under such very special conditions, such as being in the presence of the Guardian, reality suffers major distortions that cannot be logically understood by our three-dimensionally referenced minds.

I stepped silently out of the boat and onto the sand, following the Guardian who had begun to climb a narrow walking path, bordered by rich vegetation. The fog began to diffuse more and more, and when we arrived to the top of that path, after walking about fifty meters, it was totally gone and the view left me breathless.

In the valley below, I saw a small-sized but very well ordered city. The way in which the shapes of the buildings, streets, and the central square were placed gave me the impression that the city was extremely well organized and meticulously planned. Beyond this town, far away and somehow on an upper level, I saw the glare of a second city. It was stunning, resembling Apellos to a certain degree but obviously in another category of vibrational frequency. The buildings were taller and more daring in their architectural style, but the material from which they were built was also like crystal but more transparent and more glittering than what I had seen in Apellos.

While looking to assimilate what I was seeing, I noticed how the Guardian and Cezar were looking at each other, and even though I could not hear anything, I realized that they were having a telepathic conversation. Unlike as occurs in the physical plane, conversations in the etheric and subtle planes are almost always telepathic with a voice heard inside the mind where images are also projected.

At the moment I observed the telepathic dialog between Cezar and the Guardian, I simultaneously heard the voice of the latter.

"What you see far away is the entrance to Shambhala. It is difficult to get there. It was even hard for Cezar."

I was awaiting other explanations, but the Guardian, just like Dryn, seemed not to waste too many words. I quickly understood that he was speaking only if it was absolutely needed and when he was asked.

"Where are we actually?" I asked anxiously.

"Near the center of the Earth. Even though we are not going to Shambhala today, our visit still has a meaning. You will not be able to go later, however, because it is necessary for some time to pass before your consciousness can understand what is there."

I admit that I felt a bit discouraged, but I still had the prospect that it was something to look forward to.

"Are we just looking?" I asked.

The Guardian nodded.

"Many more events will be connected between now and then, but the way in which it will happen will become clearer later on. You need to be patient and careful."

It was funny. I felt that I had a thousand questions that I wished to ask; but still, I was able to get focused enough to ask even one. I just asked what first came to my mind, a hidden thought that I had since we were on the beach, after exiting from the tunnel.

"Are you the Guardian of Shambhala?" I asked?

He looked at me with an immense kindness and understanding for the somewhat infantile way in which I posed the question. After a few moments, I heard his warm and gentle voice inside my mind.

"I am one of them. People still believe that all of this is legend."

This is indeed true, but I was most interested in what I was seeing on the horizon: Shambhala. Being at a certain height, I could even see a little beyond the great wall surrounding that magnificent city. The buildings were tall, semi-circular, and shining like a diamond. Even though the distance was far and I could not observe the beings in the city, it gave me an impression of intense activity. Above the buildings, I was seeing diverse flying objects and the reflection of the lights indicated pulsating life. Without knowing how, I understood the fact that the city was immense and that it represents a sort of center that is exactly the way it appears in countless written narrations on its existence, accounts that are taken in jest by the ignorant and arrogant scientific community.

Actually, the reality is unsettling. The magnificent and benefic radiation that this realm emanates to the inhabitants is fascinating, and the mere fact that I was watching it from a distance flooded my soul with joy. At the same time, I understood why stories about Shambhala seem implausible when they are told to others, for it is very difficult to express what you see so that your words are as close as possible to the truth. There is a big difference between the specific vibrational frequency of the realm of Shambhala and that of our world. Accordingly, and to the best of their ability, humanity interprets the narrations on Shambhala to be like fairy tales or perhaps even something akin to ghost stories. This, however, is nothing other than a product of ignorance that makes us all lose because it blocks or slows down the possibility of getting there. Unfortunately, the scientific paradigm of today is not at all to our advantage because Shambhala is not a physical realm nor does it significantly radiate into our world for the time being.

The voice of the Guardian woke me out of my reverie.

"It is time to go back now."

As I looked at him with a deep state of detachment, I had the sensation that he was making certain efforts to express himself in the context of my logical system of understanding things. I nodded my head, and we turned to start walking down to the bottom of the hill where the boat was expecting us. Once again, we emerged into that mysterious fog for a short while, and when we got out of it, I discovered that we had returned to the small bay on the island.

The Guardian said good-bye with a slight bow of his head, and he disappeared into the fog. I remained for a few moments afterwards, looking into the place where the boat had disappeared.

"He told me that you will have the opportunity to go deeper with the experience you had today," said Cezar.

I did not believe that a simple visit could impress me so strongly. I was looking for other reasons for how I was reacting. In my mind, I thought perhaps it might be from either the rather extreme passage between the different planes, the fog, the presence of the giant, or maybe even by reason of the fast speed by which things had happened; but down deep inside, I knew that all was due to the indelible impact that the vision of Shambhala had left upon me. I confessed these feelings to Cezar as we headed to the cone-like opening of the "sectioned" tunnel.

"Consider for a moment that you feel this way just by reason of having taken a glimpse at the entrance to Shambhala. For that matter, however, you still have not seen Shambhala but just the entrance to it."

Although I wished to express my exuberance, I did not comment. Still under the spell of that semi-trance state, we quickly passed back through the tunnel to the Projection Hall. Less than two hours had passed from the moment of our departure. In the final analysis, such expeditions prove to be very efficient. As the access was pretty fast and easy, I could now better explain the big number of excursions that Cezar had taken in recent years. The mystery remained, however, as to why Cezar did not return for several months during some of those excursions. He did not say much about it, and I have no permission to reveal other details at this time.

We returned to the base where Lieutenant Nicoară let us know that two American officers had arrived in order to prepare the expedition through the tunnel to Iraq.

INSIDE THE EARTH

CHAPTER SIX

THE MAGIC PORTAL IN YOSEMITE

Organizing the expedition through the tunnel to Iraq was starting to have unpleasant surprises. We knew about and expected the arrival of Major Cross, but it was not until we returned to the base that we discovered the fact that he was accompanied by another person, apparently a high dignitary of the American government. Samuel Cross was a good friend of Cezar's and the fact that he had not announced anything about this character could only have one explanation: he was taken by surprise himself, not expecting the arrival of the unknown American official.

Our suspicion was confirmed because, on the same day we returned to the base, Cezar was phoned by the Major. After having a short talk for a few minutes, Cezar announced to me that it was necessary to have a meeting with them in Bucharest. The Major told him that he faced a fait accompli that he had to comply with.

"He is a Venerable Master," Cezar told me (referring to a highly placed Freemason), "but what else would you expect? He has special authority, but it is not clear yet what he wants. Samuel doesn't know anything."

Finding my heart beating strongly, I have never liked surprises of this kind as they usually mean constraints of some sort. We both left that afternoon for Bucharest and arrived at the Marriott Lounge at about six in the evening. Even though I was perfectly aware of the nature of these activities and meetings, as well as the specificity of the Department's work and the secrecy it involves, I sometimes still experience a vague sensation as if all of this is a dream, as if I might surprise myself some day by thinking that what I am living through is actually real.

This very rapid succession of planes, dimensions, frequencies, realities, worlds, and different lands, beings and situations, sometimes contradictory, can lead to certain slip-ups if you are not anchored as you should be with regard to what you know and what you want to do. For example, a simple combination of events such as those I experienced during the previous day was enough to induce at least the seeds of doubts about the surrounding reality. Early that morning, I had entered the Bucegi mountains; and from there we passed through a spatial distortion and arrived in the etheric plane. We then met a giant that was over three meters tall who led us to the center of the planet where I was able to view the fabled land of Shambhala from far away.

Then, after returning to the base, we were now in Bucharest at the Marriott hotel at a reserved table waiting for the American Major and a governmental dignitary who was accompanying him, apparently a Venerable Master.

For some reason, I thought that it was my "duty" to be somehow "worried" because my mind was dictating to me that all of these experiences I had were not plausible. Looking at my watch, I noticed that these events happened in an elapsed time of about nine hours; and that's what gave me the vague impression that I might be dreaming. As I watched Cezar calmly drinking his lemonade, I returned to my regular state of mind, at least to the point where I was not as overwhelmed. Telling him briefly of my fears and the way that I saw the situation, he looked confused for a few seconds but then started to laugh, exhibiting a very good mood. In the nearly twenty years since I have met Cezar, I think that I could count on my fingers how many times I have seen him laughing. This was one of those occasions, and it was auspicious for me because it "woke me up" from the relative panic into which I had entered. I then understood how important it is to always remain focused and mindful with regard to who I am and what I do at every moment. Analysis, evaluation and assimilation of one's experiences can be attended to after the fact, during moments of break and relaxation. As Cezar began to explain how this worked, we were interrupted because the two Americans had arrived.

I had known Major Cross for several years because we had to collaborate in order to organize some important Romanian-American gatherings at the base. There were multiple exchanges of information with him which included telephone discussions and two spur of the moment encounters, and the impression I had of him was positive. A firmly established officer, I think he was a little over forty years old, and I knew that his duty was much greater and more important than his military rank. I never brought the subject up; but due to various references he alluded to, I have realized that he has access to certain classified information and domains that are not even under government control but just the military. Cross was well known at the Pentagon, and General Roddey had supported him for promotion, probably due to his young, open and powerful spirit. Back then, Chris Roddey was still the head of the American faction that collaborated with our department, and a very tight friendship existed between him and General Obadea, often reflecting itself positively with regard to the very delicate aspects surrounding the location in Bucegi. After the death of the General, Roddey probably wanted to reinforce his position that had been somewhat damaged by this unfortunate event; so he promoted Cross as his protege. It was our luck that the Major had some important qualities: he was an honest and intelligent individual that you could rely on. Maintaining a certain balance with political, administrative, and intelligence factors regarding "the problem of Department Zero" has always been a delicate spot and has depended upon, among other things, the nature of those empowered to collaborate with us. The relative instability that followed in the wake of General Obadea's death was quickly brought into balance by the combined efforts of Cezar and General Roddey which halted certain tendencies to undermine the collaboration protocols that had long since been put in place. Those of us who were here from the beginning knew very well that this collaboration was equitable for both sides, despite the various kinds of interventions and pressures that existed.

Nevertheless, some decisions and influences simply cannot be avoided. They are far above the province of any political decisions. Apparently, no one knows where such power and influence comes from, but we have already had certain experiences in this area. It is very hard to avoid such interventions which burst onto the scene like a bolt of lightning. In such cases, neither one's rank nor assigned duties matter; only the relationships and influences that you have. Typically, decisions of this nature are handed down indirectly through intermediaries without anyone knowing who issued them. The cases in which such individuals come personally to discuss such matters are extremely rare, and this always signifies that the problem is very serious and important. Personally, I knew of three such cases: the original visit of Signor Massini, the one in 2010 when we received a visit from of a high representative of the Council on Foreign Relations, and now we were preparing for the third, an important discussion with another Venerable Master that I knew nothing else about except that he has opened all the gates of power. This did not sound good at all, but as it turned out, the problem was actually much simpler.

After Major Cross introduced everyone, we all sat at the table but only after our personnel had security checked it. There were five people guarding us: two posted at the balcony railing on the next floor, one at the entrance and two in the hall. We could have chosen one of our regular places: one of the houses that the Department has at its disposal; but Cezar preferred to insist on this place, regularly used for business meetings, in order to give another shape to the discussion in the event that there was an attempt to impose pressures or make demands. This would not have been as easy had we met in the silence and the solemnity of a conspiratorial safe house.

The Venerable One was aged. I think he was more than seventy years old, but he possessed a special commanding appearance. Despite his age, neither his dress nor behavior revealed him to be old-fashioned or conservative. He was impeccably dressed and I could see famous fashion brands on his clothes and accessories from the highest level; and the way he expressed himself showed that he was, doubtlessly, a very intelligent man and a dandy. There is, however, in spite of these characteristics and features, always something about these beings, a sort of "seal" on their face and soul, that can best be described as "hardness, suffering, and hidden torture."

I will not present the discussion that took place right here because it involved many more technical aspects that I am not allowed to present; but I will say, however, that the Venerable One "asked" less than we expected, at least in the beginning. He wanted us to give up our rights to study and research a matter of international concern: any artifact we might recover from our forthcoming expedition through the Third Tunnel. Right from the start, this was considered to be a tunnel with problems. Although the request was not too serious, something still did not fit the general scenario because it was hard to believe that a Venerable Master of this level would travel all this distance just to assure our acceptance of an apparently simple matter that could have been negotiated through intermediaries. The interests therefore must have been much deeper and longer term, but they could not yet be easily recognized because we did not yet have any information. The unpleasant side of such meetings is that you are not quite allowed to say no. It is an unwritten rule, but one of the most powerful of the protocols established in the collaboration between the Americans and ourselves regarding the location in Bucegi. A refusal from Department Zero would be like a Phyrric victory because it can trigger, through the unbelievably complex and formidable connections of the Organization, much worse consequences than if the initial terms would have been negotiated. Rash action in this way risks a break down of everything built this far. That is why the balance has to be maintained through well-chosen diplomacy and inspired negotiations.

One cannot certainly not ask for anything, as there are some well established limits in this regard, but such demands and meetings generally act like a "red phone-call" to a president: you cannot ignore it. What can be done, however, is to try certain renegotiations along the way to obtain certain compensations, but you cannot end the meeting by a refusal. There is an entire chain of dependencies that was created from the very beginning involving enormous funds, ultra-advanced technology and political and command interests, all of which are manipulated by the invisible forces of the Organization, that could change the ratio of influences if the game is not played intelligently. It is like a difficult hand of poker. You do not know for sure if it is bluff, but you don't have the courage to risk a bet because you do not have powerful cards either.

The meeting went well and without tension. After all, there was no reason to refuse the Venerable One because he had only asked for something akin to an exclusive license to exploit something we had not even discovered. This did not bother us too much because our interests were not directly touched, but the personal presence of the Venerable Master remained, and what he truly wanted remained hidden. An entire year of research and counter-intelligence was needed to finally discover what was underneath his apparent business. I will not go into details, but I will say that it had a personal aspect about it that had to do with the family of the Venerable One.

After we left the hotel, I went to the villa of Elinor, and Cezar went with the Major. The next day, as we drove back to the base, Cezar gave me a short briefing on his private discussion with Samuel Cross.

"For some time now, they have been operating a department they founded which was based upon our own model. Cross was put in charge of the command and he asked my opinion about certain aspects. He then said something that interests us directly. Actually, he made an invitation."

I looked at Cezar curiously at this point because I had no idea what he was referring to. For a moment, I thought it was about other specialist courses, such as I had participated in with remote viewing, and I asked him if it was about that.

"No, it is a special invitation for you and me," Cezar answered smiling. "A special place and a delicate situation. He said that, for now, they don't have people prepared to correctly understand and document what it is that is there and he wants to appeal to our experience."

It was indeed something special. Cezar then briefly told me what the Major had told him.

"They discovered a special place in Yosemite Park in California. Actually, the Counter-Intelligence Service of the Navy has known about it for a long time. The problem is that it is placed on the territory of an Indian reservation and it is a somewhat restricted area. Their information seems to say that the shamans there have a place of passage to the interior of the Earth, but it cannot be used in any regular sort of way because it requires a certain type of ritual. Even if they were to have the Army intervene, they still couldn't use that special entrance. Apparently, they cannot control the phenomena, and this disturbs them. Nobody understands what it is there and they have thought to ask us to share our experience."

We were going to go with Major Cross after we finished all the other aspects of collaboration related to the expedition through the Third Tunnel. Indeed — in two days we were on a plane to Madrid, and from there we were taken to the Rota Naval Base, near the ocean. As the major had some issues to deal with there, we had some down time while waiting for our travel to America. I spent a day on the ocean shore, relaxing myself and putting my thoughts and information in order.

From there, the three of us flew by a military plane to Norfolk, Virginia where we remained for a day. Then, we flew by Command plane to Las Vegas. From there, we were taken by car a relatively short distance (four hours) to Yosemite Park. In front of us was another car with four military personnel. The Major's justification for this was that it was indeed a special operation, and the place where we were moving through was out-of-the-way. This was indeed true, as after we had walked on the main road for a while, we turned to a secondary road that ascended up into the hills.

We reached an area like a small plateau, fenced to the left by a fairly tall wooden fence that seemed to be electrified. Beyond the fence was a wide valley where a very beautiful and intensely colored forest of late autumn was growing. To the right, off in the distance, I could see mountains with snowy peaks on the background of a perfectly clear sky. I walked under a large and old wooden archway, on top of which was written the name of the reservation and the name of the Indian village. Basically, this was a village that preserved American culture, but I remarked from the very beginning that there was something different about the general atmosphere there. The place gave me the feeling that it is an exclusive and even secret area. I asked the Major if the area is open to visitors.

"This place is not secret, but it is out-of-the-way," he answered me. "It is an area for those of their people who are especially interested in mysticism or shamanism. They have here an extraordinary secret, but we cannot have access to it. As they have told us, it is like a kind of gateway to the interior of the Earth. It's a tradition kept in great secrecy."

"And you've left this secret alone?" Cezar asked, smiling.

"Initially, it was intended to move the settlement to somewhere else in order to have military control over the area and of that specific point, but we realized that it would have been nothing more than a gratuitous maneuver because it would have proven to be useless. Something would be missing, and we would not be able to use their knowledge. Besides that, they have many governmental agreements, papers and contracts since the time of the Civil War that would complicate things."

"Has this generated any unpleasant effects? Do they hide what they know?" I asked.

"No. They are calm. It is a problem of maintaining a tradition. From what we have figured out, we cannot use their knowledge as long we are not managing the process. They do not want to reveal it, and I also believe that they are not ready to know it either," Cross sincerely admitted.

When a group of men appeared on the road, we stopped on the right side, a small distance from the archway at the entrance. The Major told us that our visit had been arranged, but he asked us to remain inside the car for the moment. He got out of the car and greeted these people. One could see that they knew each other and shared a good relationship. They were medium-sized men, and I could easily figure out from their features and clothing that they had many characteristics of the American Indian race. The four military men also got out of the other car, but they kept a certain distance from the group and maintained a relaxed attitude.

Taking advantage of the lull in the action, Cezar shared some additional information with me that the Major had told him.

"The problem with this place is not that it would represent a threat, but rather, it is a powerful space-time distortion. For the community here, it is sacred and only they know how to access it, so no matter who it is, whether it is the Pentagon, us or somebody else, it is the same thing: we don't have the key to get in. While this has disturbed officials on our side, they have decided not to push things but rather to maintain amiable relationships for purposes of collaboration."

"It seems weird to me that they have not yet let anyone go through that gate," I said. "Why would they let us in precisely at this time?"

"There have been a few persons that went beyond; and it is from them that things became clearer as to what it is about. The Indians told them that it is a realm inside the planet, but they didn't wanted to tell them any more. They respect the directives of those inside who are much more advanced, but even if they are somehow forced to tell the secret, it would not have any practical use for others. It is the same situation in the case of the Great Gallery or access to the subtle planes: selection through resonance."

"All right; but how can they get in there?"

"I don't know. We'll see if we are allowed to enter. It appears that the gate was discovered before the Civil War; and from that time, it was protected from generation to generation as a big secret."

Cezar stopped because the Major had come to the car and told us that the locals had agreed to our visit.

"They already knew you were coming," said the Major, a bit unsure. "I don't understand how this is possible because we only just announced this to them right now and in our presence. We were going to explain who you were, but they already knew."

We all went down the gravel road, passing some pretty big wooden cabins that were nearby. Some had the American flag placed before them and others had their doors open. In front of them were small groups of people having discussions. I was surprised to see that not all were of Indian origin, but some of them were definitely Native Americans. While the community did not seem to be too evolved, the people appeared both intelligent and dignified.

Beyond the cabins, I saw houses made out of mountain stones that had two columns in front like those in Greek temples, only smaller. That made me think a little because I could not recognize any connection to ancient Greek civilization nor understand what its purpose or influence would be in this part of the world.

We then came to a more imposing building, probably a sort of town hall, that also had the American flag flying, but next to it was another flag with unfamiliar markings. Above, on the upper part of the roof, I could see a big placard between the branches indicating this was Yosemite Park. On the same placard, I also saw an Indian specific blazon: a big raven feather with the peaks of three mountains underneath. I will not, however, offer many more details regarding this as the location is still out-of-the-way and very important. Those who live there are very much concerned about their silent status of non-involvement. Additionally, there is a commitment to U.S. military forces which I must respect.

As we walked along the road and it turned slightly to the left, one of the group who seemed to be a leader of theirs approached Cezar and myself. Without any introduction, he told us that we would be going through a portal to the center of the Earth, and that it had been announced that they will receive our visit. We looked at Major Cross who gave us a gesture that he knew none of this. The man, whose name was Watuk, spoke to us.

"Very few people have come to see this place. It is our heritage and we keep it in great secrecy. There are, however, certain conditions to fulfill, and Mezina* will tell us what has been decided by those living in the inside."

Watuk was a dignified descendant of his predecessors: not too tall, but surprisingly agile at about fifty years old, he had long hair and a smiling but serious face that showed great firmness or resolution. I do not think that he was a shaman, but he had an important role in the Elder Council of that community. He talked with determination, pointing to a small path leading to a more isolated place where we saw three wooden cabins. We headed to the one on the right which had already caught my attention. The space surrounding it was clean and beautifully arranged with walkways and a lot of greenery, all of which was very well maintained. The cabin was old, but I remarked that it was somehow built over another building that was even older than it. I figured out that this was done in order to protect the original edifice, but I did not understand why it would have been necessary to resort to such an unusual method in order to preserve it.

When we arrived at the entrance, the Major addressed Cezar.

"From this point on, only you are to go. We will be waiting; and I have already spoken to Watuk. They have strict rules in this regard. It is a sacred place and there are certain conditions to fulfill."

The Indian opened the door and made room for us to enter. From the moment in which we stepped into that cabin, I had the distinct impression that I had jumped two hundred years back in time. The initial wooden construction was so old that it squeaked from all joints when the door opened. The wood had not rotted, but it was as if it was "tired" by the passing of time. I paused after a few steps from the entrance in order to familiarize myself with the semi-darkness and to better observe the details. I could then hear Watuk's voice once again.

---

* *Translator's note: Mezina* is a word that can be translated as "the youngest daughter and sister in a family."

"This building has remained exactly as it was since it was built in 1776. The land on which you now are is old Indian territory. Our ancestors inhabited this land, and some of us come directly from their genetic line."

The cabin was over twenty meters long, and the width was about seven meters. The ground inside was dry and rocky, obviously in contrast with the fertile soil that surrounded the outside of the structure. On one side, I saw some very old rusty tools and also two logs. Everything was left intact and without any intervention, exactly how it was in the year of its construction. On my right, I saw a very dry shrub and some thistles on the ground that had been left exactly as is without having been subjected to any interference from the outside environment. Everything there seemed to have "stopped dead" at that past time, a time when something very special had happened.

After allowing us time to adapt to the atmosphere, Watuk spoke.

"There are two conditions. First — you have to go to a certain place in this room and be there at certain moment. The second condition is that you cannot pass beyond unless there is a feminine component. Mezina fulfills this role for the men who go inside."

We looked at him inquisitively because we were both men.

"You will go one by one," Watuk said.

"Who knows the precise moment in which we have to be in that special place?" Cezar asked.

"Mezina. She is the intermediary and she knows what to do."

As he spoke, a girl of about twenty years old appeared at the door and approached, taking only a few steps toward us. She wore traditional Indian clothing with a long skirt to the ground, a leather blouse with fringes, and she had moccasins on her feet. She was not tall, and her beauty was not in the Western style but rather came from a force emanating from her inner being. The cheekbones protruded slightly and were characteristic of features specific to Native Americans. Her perfect long black hair was tied in two braided ties at the back, leaving a long bang.

Coming before us, the girl bowed respectfully and then looked at Wutak.

"She is the one who will accompany you on your journey," he said. "She has traveled on this road many times and knows of the realm inside the planet. You now need to decide who is the first (of you) to go."

I suddenly became agitated because I did not understand at all what was going on. There was nothing in the entire cabin that would suggest where or how we might depart on our journey. After I made an impassioned look at Cezar, he said that he would go first.

Coming close to his person, the girl looked at him intensely for a few moments. She then smiled slightly and said something in an unknown language which was probably their local language.

"Mezina says that she is compatible with you," said Wutak, translating her words for Cezar. "She says that it is a joy to meet a traveler who knows the wise men of the world. This is good; otherwise, the portal wouldn't open."

I gasped, hoping no one noticed. The girl then came next to me and looked at me directly. She had very beautiful almond-shaped black eyes, but I had the impression that even though she was looking at me, her look seemed to extend beyond the physical realm. Unlike the case with Cezar, she looked at me much longer, about a half minute. I was starting to feel hopeless when she suddenly spoke again.

"There is compatibility in your case, too," Wutak said.

I breathed a sigh of relief, as if a boulder was taken off my back. I then noticed an increased respect from Wutak towards Cezar and myself, and I suspected that it was related to the "verdict" given by the one that was called Mezina. Later, I found out from Major Cross that, up to that point, only one other person had been found who was compatible to travel inside the Earth together with Mezina. This was a psychic who was collaborating with the Pentagon. Their problem was that they could only come up with a limited number of "candidates" to be checked and only at certain time intervals at certain times of the year. Our opportunity was during one of those periods, and the Major was impressed by the fact that we were accepted. Cezar explained that it is very possible that this was due to the fact that he had traveled to the inside of the planet many times before, and this had somehow embedded a specific energetic impression into his being. As for myself, I had the chance to be embedded with the energy of the magical zone inside the Earth when I was in the presence of the guardian of Shambhala. Even though I knew that this was not the complete explanation, it still had meaning. In reality, what counts is the level of consciousness and purity of being at an emotional and mental level.

As is the case with our Secret Services back home, there were also backstage fights at the Pentagon regarding their collaboration with Department Zero. The problem that seems to very much irritate ceratin important officials is that they cannot have control over such phenomena or locations in the way they are accustomed to all over the world. Even if they convinced themselves to be resolute over such matters, their anxiety remained, and like a derailed train, this could cause certain effects that could be felt in certain details of the collaboration. Major Cross told us that it is not an easy job to resolve such tensions or outbursts, and we understood this very well because we have also faced many similar situations.

Happy to have fulfilled the compatibility requirement necessary to pass through the portal, I became anxious for the actual journey. As Wutak and the girl went to the area behind the cabin, we followed them closely. I noticed that there was an area of moist soil as if someone had been digging recently.

As we stepped to the area where the hard-packed soil conjoined the moist soil, we stopped. As the girl took Cezar by the hand, they both walked into the middle of the loose ground. Wutak gestured to me to remain near him. Withdrawing her hand from Cezar, Mezina turned to us and made a sign with her right hand. Wutak then pulled a long wooden dagger from underneath his coat as he bent over and left it on the ground. Viewing it up close, it appeared to be very old with all sorts of symbols and inscriptions having been carved into it. The handle was cracked to the point where it was almost split into two pieces. I admit that I was a little disappointed and not too impressed, telling myself that I was a witness to a shamanic ceremony and thinking about how easy and simple it had been for me to pass through the tunnel to the inside the planet in Bucegi. But I then realized that this was simply another form of access to the civilizations inside the planet, all of it being based upon a certain shamanic ritual required to activate the energy needed to open the portal.

I did not have too much time to think about what was going on because the girl recited a short incantation with equal tonality that was more like an extended sound and less like a word or line of words. I soon realized, however, that she had mastered the exact tonality needed to activate the subtle latent power of the magical dagger. Then, immediately behind her and Cezar, I saw the air "undulating" and becoming semi-transparent in part, like a square screen with sides of about two meters. As Mezina turned towards the distortion, I could not see clearly what was behind this square area, but she took Cezar by the hand and they both walked through the screen, instantaneously disappearing.

Even though I was used to such phenomena, having experienced it many times, I admit that I still felt a certain wrench. I felt somehow unsure, not regarding such phenomena itself, but with regard to the methodology of accessing that phenomena. Seeing no scientific or stable support, I was bothered by the idea that there was no corridor, tunnel, nor any devices but only a very old wooden dagger that had also disappeared at the same time the two had passed through the portal. I was somewhat uncomfortable with the thought that I was facing elements considered to be magical and that I could not fully comprehend. Even though I understood almost nothing about the technical details by which I was able to travel through the tunnels in the Projection Hall, my experiences there were based on incredibly advanced technologies, and to me, that somehow made me more confident.

Feeling pretty embarrassed and at the same time a little worried, I stood next to Wutak, not saying a word. Like a block of rock, the Indian remained immobile, standing with a fixed glare at the screen as it slowly undulated, having a somewhat pearly color. I did not dare to ask a thing as I suspected that he was somehow mentally, and perhaps emotionally, plugged into the whole process. In fact, everything that was happening there had no connection to our ordinary reality in the outside world, including science and the laws of physics. I reflected on the fact that these absolutely simple beings, without pretensions or great aspirations and being full of modesty and dignity, have had access to an extraordinary world inside our planet and have enjoyed its benefits for hundreds of years; and now they were going to allow us, who consider ourselves to be more "evolved", to enter that realm. Once more, I was realizing that, in order to have knowledge, you do not necessarily have to have either money or technology. And to the contrary, if these are not used correctly, this can keep you away from any true knowledge.

I think, however, that the phenomenal simplicity of the entire process was what inhibited me the most. By simply observing, you almost cannot believe what you see and you wonder if it is not a hoax or you're not going mad. There is such a big difference between what we are accustomed to seeing and what is actually happening that the tendency of the mind is to refuse and reject everything, even though it is obvious and occurring right before our eyes. We are tempted by prejudice to consider those people who can actually give us real initiation and knowledge as primitive or even retarded. We do this out of arrogance and hubris because we cannot admit that other people sometimes have more efficient and easier methods of perceiving reality than ourselves. We are used to believing that we have already discovered all that can be discovered; that we possess the "great secrets" of nature, and what we don't know or don't understand cannot be true but is to be despised and satirized. In fact, however, modern or "official science" is corrupt in most of its aspects.

While I was musing over these thoughts, Mezina suddenly emerged through the undulating pearly screen in front of me as the dagger materialized exactly in the position in which it had been placed on the ground by Wutak. By my approximation, the girl had not been absent for more than a minute. She came to the demarcation line, took my hand, and we walked together onto that moist soil. Everything was happening without a word; precisely, in well-established stages. As I came near the screen, I hesitated and restrained myself slightly. Mezina perceived this immediately because she stopped and looked inquisitively at me.

"Do you agree to pass beyond?" she asked, looking deeply into my eyes.

I nodded affirmatively, looking at the screen. Closing my eyes and holding her hand, we walked through that "screen." I immediately felt that I was being immersed into a high speed of particle flow and began to relive the sensation of "lift travel" that I had experienced in the elevator when I was in Tomassis, but now the speed was even higher. I saw successive layers of the interior running by me at a dizzying pace in front of me: rocks, lava, holes, water, and crystals. I was a bit dizzy, yet in a pleasant way, with neither the sensation of nausea nor other discomfort.

Suddenly, I opened my eyes and saw that Mezina was already a few meters in front of me, looking ahead. Looking down, I saw that I was standing in an area bounded by a circle having a radius of about three meters, precisely contoured into the rock of the mountain. In a dizzying speed in front of me, I saw rocks, lava, holes, water, and crystals. I was a little dizzy, yet in a pleasant way without feeling nausea or other discomfort.

To my utter astonishment, I saw the dagger to my left with its tip inside the circle as opposed to the outside where it had been prior to our passing though the portal. I realized then that the dagger, being a magic element of the process, undoubtedly represented the "key" to the entire energetic activation phenomenon of the portal.

I then directed my attention to the place where I actually was and began to feel that I had arrived into a virtual paradise that was giving me an intense sensation of wellness and joy throughout my entire body. I had felt something similar in Tomassis as well, but the sensation here was more refined and it appeared immediately upon becoming aware of the place.

I saw that I was actually in a huge hallway that opened into a semi-circular terrace with an extraordinary view. To either side, I saw four big tunnel openings dug into the rock of the mountain, each having a circular opening of about four meters in diameter. They were dug directly into the rock of the mountain and two of them featured a sort of columned terrace that served as an opening into the mountain. The hall in which I found myself was like a terrace that had been dug into the mountain that opened widely. Its arch was held up by some pillars, also carved from the mountain, which rose from the base and then curved into a cupola above. Absolutely everything there was made out of the rock of that mountain. I did not see any displaceable, separate, or moving part nor anything else that was made of other material. Everything that could be seen was carved into the mountain as if the entire space had been "hollowed out" of the mountain.

Looking in front of where I was, I realized that we were somewhere at a high altitude because I could see vast green vegetation beneath the terrace and a rich forest spreading to other mountains that were seen in the distance on the horizon.

On the floor of the room were large stone tiles forming a fan-shaped pattern that extended vertically onto the back wall of the mountain. Although it was noticeable that the tiles were polished and showed a different finish than the rest of the rock surface, some of them were somewhat deteriorated or damaged on the edges, a sign that they must have been there for a very long time. The burden of time could also be seen in the columns, which probably looked quite splendid when they were created, but now they were worn down by the thousands or tens of thousands of years that had passed and diminished their original brilliance and finish. Some had cracks while

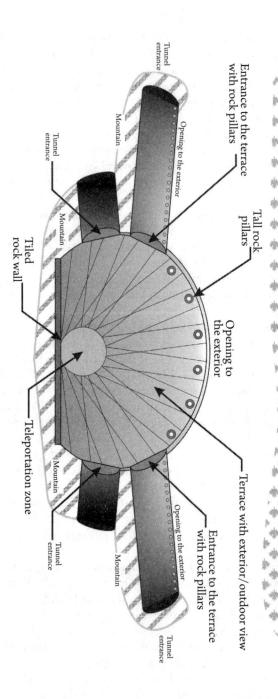

SEMI-CIRCULAR TERRACE IN THE MOUNTAIN

Tunnel entrance

Entrance to the terrace with rock pillars

Mountain

Opening to the exterior

Tall rock pillars

Tunnel entrance

Opening to the exterior

Mountain

Tiled rock wall

Teleportation zone

Terrace with exterior/outdoor view

Entrance to the terrace with rock pillars

Mountain

Opening to the exterior

Tunnel entrance

Mountain

Tunnel entrance

Vast Forest

200

the symbols on the others seemed to be shimmering, especially where we saw traces of moisture. Despite the imperfections, the columns retained an imposing presence and nobility which created a sense of sacredness.

The tiles had been dug out and placed so as to serve as a boundary between them and the mountain rocks. Where they merged into the rock wall, each tile presented a pattern formed only by lines and dots. On the tiles that continued vertically on the wall of the mountain, I saw symbols on the ends of each tile made up of combinations of lines and dots, and simply viewing them gave me a creepy feeling in my body. This was followed by a vivid emotion enveloping me, even though I did not understand anything that those signs represented. Their impact on my subconscious, however, was very strong.

THE PATTERN AND SYMBOLS ON THE VERTICAL STONE TILES

In front of me, beside the imposing pillars on the edge of the hall, Cezar was viewing the landscape. I noticed that Mezina was looking at me and she discreetly gestured for me to go to the pillars, near Cezar. I proceeded, carefully walking on those very old rock tiles. Near the circumference of the hall, to the exterior, I saw two big corridors with terraces, one on the left side and one on the right side, both continuing as tunnels into the mountain. Their walls were not finished on the inside, but you could see carvings that were far from crude and definitely not barbaric. The ground floors of the corridors were like a rock mosaic, but right down the center, each had a perfectly straight line made out of rock tiles. The two tunnels extended beyond the pillars at the entrance for about twenty meters before completely emerging into the darkness of the mountain.

Standing next to Cezar, I watched him daydreaming, gazing at the canvas of nature beneath us. After slowly approaching to share his view, I was both

THE LUSH LANDSCAPE STRETCHING BENEATH THE TERRACE

surprised and amazed at the vast view of archaic beauty and lushness as it filled my soul with calm joy. About 50-60 meters below us, a valley full of luxuriant vegetation extended to the horizon, with two massive mountains on either side. Reminding me of an oasis from the Sahara, the landscape was captivating because it not only offered a superb view but also a calming of the spirit with an uplifting sensation of gratitude and enchantment.

Not too thick, the vegetation was luxuriant and diverse; and it was somehow creating within me the sensation of some long-gone era. The trees were sort of like hybridized palms amidst moderate undergrowth with very beautiful flowers at the ends. This layout gave the entire landscape a distinct air, making it vivid and enchanting.

In the middle of that vast forest, I saw a road, not too wide, extending into the mountains before getting lost in the rich vegetation. While that seemed to be the main access road through the palm forest, there were narrower pathways on either side.

THE TYPE OF TREES THAT PREDOMINATE IN THE FOREST

LIZARD SPECIES, LIKE THE MONITOR

It was in this location that I saw, for the first time, animals inside the Earth. This species was a sort of lizard, reminiscent of the monitor lizard but more active in its movements. On its back, there was a crest like an iguana. I also saw insects, (flying) mites and birds. Life seemed to be very rich there and everything seemed to express a deep sensation of peace and security. This made me feel very quiet, and the thought came into my mind that if I had the opportunity, I would like to stay in such a place for a long time.

Somewhere in front of us and just a little to the right, we saw some kind of pavilion on one of the cliffs. It was like a small house made of wood with stone stairs descending to the ground that led to a cobbled and narrow path that became lost in the forest. The edifice was completely white with wonderful green vegetation twisting about it, giving an air of relaxation and meditation to the whole scenario. I think that was the exact purpose of the beautiful structures which appeared on other cliffs in the distance: to serve as a place of meditation to facilitate the rest of the body, mind and soul in an atmosphere full of peace and balance.

I then looked at the clear sky, and for the first time, I saw "the sun" inside the Earth. It had a slightly smaller size than what we see as our sun in the sky and had a white-bluish color. The sky was clear, but its blue was not as intense and a little more faded than what we see on the surface world. I also saw some white clouds, but they were not as precise in shape as those in our sky and were more diffused, suggestive of small areas of fog. The sun was giving off a gentle and very pleasant light that was emanating maybe sixty to seventy percent of the light intensity that we are used to on the surface.

While we were watching that sun and sky, we suddenly felt another presence behind us. We turned around and, indeed, in front of the left

HOUSE-LIKE STRUCTURE ON THE CLIFF

tunnel inside the mountain, I saw Mezina, respectfully bowing in front of a tall man. I heard her talking with him, but I did not understand what they were talking about.

The man then approached us. He was about two meters tall, had long black hair, black eyes, and slightly olive skin. He was dressed very much like Dryn, with a sort of white frock, elegantly tide at the middle with a golden belt. I must admit that his appearance was impressive, as much through the extraordinary charisma that he emanated as through the nobility of his walking. His behavior was majestic, and his gestures exhibited a perfect control and balance of being.

Coming next to us, he saluted with a slight bow of the head. He then spoke to us, and just as in the case of the Guardian, I was hearing his voice in my mind, and it was in the Romanian language. It was clear and very pleasant. From time to time, images appeared in mind that were being telepathically transmitted by that man in order reinforce and clarify what he was saying.

"This portal is very old, a lot older than the last great cataclysm on the Earth's surface. Some of the wise men came here and built this communication network."

Simultaneously, he transmitted certain images of human beings entering that valley and the sequences through which they created the terrace with the four tunnels. It was then that I realized that these were beings from Ancient Atlantis but from an era long before the total disappearance of that legendary continent.

"We have arranged for you to come here because it is, in a certain way, a part of a necessary succession of events."

It was like hearing the identical words of the Guardian being repeated. In my mind, I clearly saw a specific place in southern Argentina and a person I knew to be a shaman. The tall man then gave us another transmission.

"He is waiting for you in that exact place, two weeks from now. It is an important meeting and a new journey to the inside of the Earth."

I was a little confused because I did not really understand the purpose of these trips and experiences. The man then looked at me directly and telepathed to me that the explanations for these different experiences and ways of penetrating the Earth that we have access to will manifest later. There is a collective purpose rather than individual or separate purposes at work. He showed me that, in the future, this knowledge we are acquiring will be like a seed for changing the mentality of other people about the interior of the planet.

The man then told us that we had to go back because there is a window of time that has to be respected. I was slightly disappointed because I was hoping that we would get a chance to at least explore some of these tunnels and also visit the populated cities beyond the forest. For example, on the horizon and a very great distance away, I could see a certain glow between the mountains that appeared to be white buildings, but they were so far away and the image was blending with the color of the sky and the whitish fog that I am not sure it was actually a city.

Respecting what was asked of us, we headed for the transfer or teleportation circle. When we got there, Mezina beckoned me to enter that circle. She then lifted the dagger from the ground, oriented it in a certain way and then intonated the same sound as she had when we originally came. Almost immediately afterwards, I felt like a whirlwind had powerfully sucked me up and had delivered me back in the way that I had come. Suddenly, I became aware of the fact that I was on the moist soil I had departed from and that Wutak was watching me. He beckoned me to come near to him while Mezina went back through the portal and returned shortly thereafter with Cezar.

The girl gave the magical wooden object to Wutak who covered it with the leather piece that he had and put it inside the interior pocket of his coat. We all headed for the exit where the others were waiting for us. Saying goodbye to the Indians on amicable terms, we left the reservation, sharing our adventures with the Major on the way back. This included the story about the man indicating we would meet the shaman from Argentina, but we did not mention the location, and as Major Cross was diplomatic, he did not ask any more about it. At a certain level of rank and with proper preparation and understanding, superior officers perceive such things correctly and with elegance. Afterwards, in a private talk that Cezar had with the Major, I think that they also exchanged information of another sort. That, at least, was what I could deduce from what I was told.

Three days after those events, I was again in my room at Alpha Base, contentedly thinking about the wonderful experiences that I had lived. I was feeling that something in my being had matured and that I had acquired a deep intuitive understanding which gave even more profound meaning to these events.

Impatiently, I was awaiting for our departure to Argentina and the meeting with the mysterious shaman.

CHAPTER SEVEN

THE CENTER OF THE PLANET AND THE SUBLIME WORLD OF SHAMBHALA

The experience in Yosemite impressed me, particularly by its apparent simplicity; but at the same time, through the unconventional methods used which are usually interpreted through the term *magic*. These represented a mystery to me, and it is my opinion that the native Indians were equally in the dark with regard to the true meaning of the phenomena that happened there. Obviously, it was an initiatory process; accessible only to the shamans from their community, but it was also a practical and very efficient method that represents a real challenge to explain in terms of science. I will try, however, to offer a correlative explanation, combining certain elements that are obviously magical with some aspects that have a scientific meaning. For example, the girl offers a unique and precisely identified frequency with regard to the emission of that sound. The magic dagger probably serves as an intermediary factor with sound being a trigger to create a specific energetic resonance.

What is really challenging to a rational being who experiences such a phenomenon is that, even though one does not understand the process involved or the various factors associated with it, events are still happening and they are bewildering to the degree that they are not referenced to one's regular knowledge and perception. Even Cezar was bemused by the adventure in Yosemite, telling me that he was particularly interested by the presence of that wise man who came and transmitted that information, which served as a very strong suggestion, about going to Argentina. As a matter of fact, we immediately identified the place shown in Argentina after returning to our country; then waited impatiently for the day of departure after all other arrangements for the journey were made.

The trip to Buenos Aires was routine but long and tiring. After spending the night in the capital, we took the plane to El Calafate in the province of Santa Cruz. As we would be going to a deserted mountainous locale, we decided to rent a jeep from the airport because we thought that a powerful vehicle would be more useful. At the first company that we consulted, they had no available jeeps. On the second day, they had two but neither had a GPS. This was not a problem, however, because we could use a mobile phone GPS.

Twenty minutes after taking our baggage from the airport, we were already on our way to the point indicated by the wise man inside the Earth, in a region that we located in the Cerro Pinaculo Mountains. I can give the precise location here because I do not consider that we are revealing any great secrets in doing so, especially because this point does not represent the exact "gate" to get inside. It is found at a small distance from that point; and according to the wise man, locating the precise entrance requires meeting the shaman. Cezar said that providing the location would not shed any more light for enthusiastic seekers as, even though the spot is close to the area of the portal, it could prove to be a source of frustration for them. Moreover, potential daredevils would only see in that desolated zone an almost arid plateau, a dusty road with an abandoned station, and beyond, some green fields of vegetation in a circular shape. Despite my protests, Cezar remained inflexible with regard to revealing the location. I am now inclined to say that he was right about it being practically impossible to identify the portal without guidance, especially because it is situated in a hollow in the mountain that is like a narrow cavern. That is why the wise man gave us the contact details for the shaman from Argentina.

At a certain point, we had to get off of the main road whereupon the landscape became even more arid. It was like we were travelling through Martian valleys and hills with rocks, reddish soil, mountains and a desert. Here in the heart of Patagonia, I could not help but notice the special vibration of the area as well as a mysterious characteristic that was like a force that was not at all interested in the agitation and the tribulations of the world but rather in purity and evolution.

We were the only ones in this remote area as the GPS eventually indicated that we had to get off the rarely travelled secondary road we had been following in order to ascend a relatively smooth slope that was full of rocks and stones. Besides the lichen and some small shrubs I saw amidst the boulders, there was no sign of life. I didn't even wanted to think what an engine breakdown or the loss of the GPS signal would have involved. To our advantage, however, was the fact that our jobs required us to use cell phones with global coverage via satellite and this enabled us to find the exact point where we could meet the shaman.

I did not see him until the last possible moment, only after we turned around the edge of one of the more rocky hills, just before the tall mountains. He was just simply standing still, erect, waiting in the direction we were approaching, the only one possible in that mountainous terrain. I do not know how he could possibly have arrived in that deserted wilderness. He did appear, however, exactly as I had seen him in the mental image that was projected to me by the wise man inside the Earth, right down to the most specific details. He was wearing a backpack that was not too full over a carelessly unbuttoned jacket with a checked shirt underneath. His pants were green and shabby, and his footwear consisted of scuffed boots. As we approached in the car, I intuitively grasped the lack of interest of the shaman with regard to his dress. He was tall, thin, about 60 years old, and the long hair that reached down the middle of his back streamed into white and dark strands. There were several small objects in his hair: several rings, a feather, and even a tiny little eagle carved in wood. I saw red and white lines on his fingers, and on the forehead, he had a long and wide indigo line.

He seemed to be waiting for us, but his look and attention were somehow diverted. Stopping a few meters away, we got out of the car and got closer to him. The man did nothing, did not move, and made no gesture. Very intently, he watched us with penetrating black eyes that made his deeply creased sun-burned face look even more severe. Cezar addressed him with a few welcoming words in English and then asked him precisely what we needed to do next. The shaman was not saying a thing but just looked at us. He was not hostile but neither was he brimming with amiability. There were some embarrassing moments until I addressed him in Spanish, once again explaining what was obvious to each of us: that we are the ones that he was waiting for. After listening carefully, he made a short gesture of approval; and without a word, he beckoned us to follow him.

Without hurrying, we began our ascent on a steep slope, passing by the boulders and rocks with even steps. It was not necessary to worry about the vehicle because the desolation of the area was complete. As I walked in silence, I again asked myself how the shaman had arrived at the meeting point. We had travelled about fifty kilometers from the airport to reach it, and a long part of the journey was through the arid desert and on an abandoned secondary road. As I did not see any other car, I assume that the shaman did not drive there. I wondered if was driven by someone who had then left.

The entire experience seemed pretty strange to me; but at the same time, challenging. Starting from the way in which this connection was brought to our attention until the actual meeting with this strange character, who appeared as if he was from another world, everything seemed to be taken from a Tim Burton film, except for the fact that it was very real.

We continued walking through rocks and stones, descending and ascending through the hills until the ascent became rather steep and consisted only of rocks. To a certain extent, walking through this arid and rocky emptiness reminded me of my experience with Repa Sundhi in Tibet as we travelled to the entrance of the cave where I met the goddess Machandi. The only difference here was that the landscape was more red and the mountains less tall.

After making our way around a bigger rock, a man and woman suddenly appeared in front of us, standing and seemingly waiting for us. They were about ten meters in front of us, at an opening in the mountain rock. If you looked at the entrance from the angle from which I could see as I was climbing, you would have said that there was nothing there, but as my position changed, I saw that the opening in the mountain appeared wider, but it did not particularly attract special attention. From the images that the wise man had sent us, I neither recognized the area, the opening in the mountain, nor the two people in front of us; but I was suspecting that we were only given the information that was necessary to facilitate the beginning of our travel in order to meet our guides.

The man and the woman were less tall than the shaman, but they seemed to have an older ancestral connection than him. The clothes that they wore were of good quality, and their long shawls evoked in me a similar identification with the clothing of the people in Peru or Bolivia save for the fact they were not wearing comparable hats. By my estimation, the woman was about forty years old and the man forty-five. Their faces were serene with traces of smiles. Stopping a few meters away from them, we saluted them in Spanish. They bowed; and unlike the shaman, the man simply told us that they were waiting for us. He also spoke Spanish but with a certain accent. They then beckoned us to follow them, but the shaman stayed put. Even though we had our mobile phone GPS and knew the coordinates of where we had left our vehicle, I was hoping that he would once again wait for us. Walking behind the two, we entered a small cave on a mountain slope. It was obvious that this was not a travelled path, but even if it was, its location in the mountain and the way in which it was somehow hidden from sight made it difficult to be identified.

When we entered, I had the certain impression that I was descending on an inclined plane, and this gave me a sensation of slight dizziness even though the ground ahead was level. The corridor we had entered was not too long, about five to six meters; and afterwards, it opened into a normal cave. As soon as we walked into the small space of that cave, my sensation of dizziness and descending disappeared. The cave was pretty narrow, not too tall, and extended a small distance into the inside the mountain.

I then had one of the most interesting experiences I had ever had up to that moment when, after we had moved a few steps into the mountain, it seemed that Cezar and I were passing together through different sections of space and time. At first, I thought that it was only my distorted impression, however, I became convinced of the reality very quickly. Even after the first few steps, I saw moisture appearing on the walls and also tiny water springs that were pouring down along them. I was apparently still in the same mountain cavity, but something had somehow changed; and this all happened without myself being able to figure out how. I was only seeing the effects.

As I moved further into the cavern, huge crystals appeared on all sides, some being up to one meter high. They spurted out in all directions and some formed bundles, like a bouquet of flowers. I had the feeling that there were similar halls of crystals in this cavity we had entered and that the landscape would somehow change unexpectedly as we would enter each one. I figured out that, due to the spatial distortion we were passing through, we were walking very huge distances and that we were also experiencing an alteration of our consciousness. It was clear that this little cave was a crossing point, an access portal to the subtle dimensions of the Earth's interior, and that the way of travel through the physical plane to the subtle one was really astounding. With every step that I made, I had the feeling that we were going through enormous distances and that the surrounding reality changed according to the "area" I was passing through.

As I advanced further towards what I thought was the bottom of the cave, going behind the two guides, I suddenly felt a strong wave of heat, indicating to me that we were probably passing through a zone with melted magma. I felt like I was in a sort of trance; but at the same time, I was perfectly lucid and aware of what was happening.

After that heat sensation, I saw another zone with crystals and then moisture again, even more highlighted than the first time. Suddenly, I had the impression that I had passed through a door, even though I saw nothing of the sort. All of a sudden, the passage in which we were was perfectly dry and we had come to its end. There, I saw, dug into the rock, a rectangle with a small arch above it through which the man and woman passed, disappearing from our sight. Without a worry, I passed first, immediately followed by Cezar.

Suddenly, I found myself inside a house. It was as if I had just emerged from a storeroom inside the house. I saw the man closing the door behind me, and I noticed, somehow strangely, his hand pressing the door handle at a much slower pace than would be expected. At the moment when the door completely closed, however, I was startled, as if I had emerged out of that trance-like state and was returning to a normal condition. My impression was that I was now completely integrated into the reality of the subtle plane in which I had just entered without having anymore connection to the physical plane. It was like a clear delineation had been made so that I now had a precise knowledge of the reality around me. Later, after talking to Cezar about our experience and analyzing its various stages, I understood that my assessments and judgments about what I was seeing were based exclusively upon associations that I was familiar with from the physical plane. The long train of conceptions and ideas that were imprinted in my mind with regard to the laws and specifics of physical matter created a kind of slowing down of perception as we penetrated into the etheric plane, and it accentuated as we advanced to higher frequencies such as the astral. Closing the door behind us meant a clear breaking of the connection with the physical plane.

I then oriented my attention to the place in which I now was. It was a large room with many windows and very beautifully carved wooden chairs. I then realized that the way in which I was perceiving what was surrounding me there was completely different than my previous experiences in which things appeared only in one reference frame. Here, they were somehow nuanced. For example, those chairs might have looked old at first glance, even if they were elegant, but when you looked at them more closely, the perspective on them changed in a fine way, making them appear as modern objects, tastefully and highly refined. It seemed to be more of a matter of detail: the closer you looked at an object, the more exceptional it became or the more perfected it appeared to be.

The room was harmonious and very pleasant. In the middle, there was a table that seemed to be made out of glass because it was transparent, and I saw a container with some fruits and a vase with flowers in it. The strange way in which I was perceiving things extended because, while I knew there was a bookcase on one wall of the room, I could not actually see it there. In physical terms, I would have said that it was invisible, but Cezar explained to me afterwards that I was not able to see certain elements because my consciousness and senses were not yet properly adjusted to the frequencies specific to the plane which we were in, thus causing certain uncoordinated perceptions between what I was seeing and what I knew to be. Still, even figuring out all of those relative oddities, I was not bothered by them at all as I considered them to be normal somehow.

I began to realize that in that advanced reality within the Earth, knowledge was manifested in a superior way. For example, on the right side of the room there were two large and elegant wall-mounted windows that did not have glass, but I could tell, nevertheless, there was a barrier there. While I could see what was outside, I knew that someone on the outside could not see inside.

In front of me was an exit door from this "house," and to the left, I saw another door to what we could call a kitchen. I did, however, not see any of the appliances or utensils that we are used to, such as a stove, oven or other items, but within the field of my consciousness, I understood that this was the place where the creatures of that house prepared their food.

Through the opening of the door, I could see many fruits and a sort of device which I knew everything about in spite of the fact that I cannot explain how or why. Somehow, I knew that the device was used to directly extract the pure subtle energy of each fruit, just the way we extract juice with special appliances. I then heard the voice of the man who was accompanying us, but I was only hearing it in my mind. He was clearly speaking a language that I did not know, but I understood very well what he wanted to say.

"We have indeed reached a higher stage evolution where we extract the energetic essence of the fruit which we then consume."

He then entered that room that I associated with a kitchen and came back with that device which resembled one of our juicers. It had a sort of tall vertical body and a sort of sphere into which the essence was probably extracted. Picking up a fruit off of the table which seemed to be an apple, although bigger and thicker, he placed it in the appliance. He then made a movement with his hand, putting it over the sphere, whereupon I heard a faint tingling sound, and I perceived a penetrating odor similar to a strong tea consisting of apple and cinnamon. The man then detached a small pot-like container from the device and showed me its contents: a small amount of a substance that appeared to be semi-liquid.

"This is what we consume from fruits," the man told us. "It is a very pure and energizing element."

He showed us how he kept the food: in a sort of apparatus that I saw in a niche at the back of the room; but even though I knew there was some sort of device there, I could not see it with any clarity, its appearance reminding me of a blurred or faded bubble. Although I did not understand anything, it seemed to me that the man knew what I could and could not see as his explanations were insightful.

"For the time being, you can't distinguish it (the device) because your mind has nothing to associate it with, but it serves the function of maintaining the food in an optimal condition. We eat only vegetables that are neither dehydrated, dried, nor preserved at a low-temperature."

Saying this, he took another fruit, similar to an avocado, then took off an item from a shelf that I initially thought to be a string and passed it over the fruit. It turned out that the "string" was actually the mouth or opening of an "energetic bag" designed to preserve the product in its present condition without its energy being in any way lost, compromised or altered from a qualitative point of view. It was only after the fruit came into that "bag" that I could see an outline around the food manifesting as a very fine field of energy. The man then put the food in that appliance which now, after the explanations I was given, appeared to me in a slightly clearer form.

Within the left side of that big room, there were stairs leading to a floor which I felt was an area with rooms for those living there to rest and sleep. The lower chamber had a door to a corridor that led to several small rooms that were like storage stalls where various objects were placed. Generally, the functionality of the house was roughly the same as what we know in our world save for small differences that are specific to the subtle plane in which it exists. The technology, of course, is more advanced. For example, they also had a sort of window blind that could be dropped, dimming the light; but when that was done, the blinds "stick" to the surface of the window, even though the window apparently contains no glass to adhere to. The man explained (telepathically) that they have light all the time, and this is why they must resort to this method for periods of rest or sleep as it enables the house to become dark.

We then went outside through what we could call a *door*. In reality, however, there was nothing there. The space was defined for a door although it was not rectangular and the upper side was curved like a small arch. From inside the house, I was seeing everything that was on the street outside, but after getting out and looking behind myself, I saw that the space designated for the door was opaque and had a dark indigo color. I stopped and put my head through that door and immediately saw the inside of the living room. Then, I took my head out and had the opaque surface in front of me, and I could not see inside. I played around like this a couple of times, coming in and out of the house again with my entire body. It was most likely a protective energy screen, programmed to have that specific effect. The screen was not only visual, it was also temperature-sensitive. As we entered the house, we noticed that it was warmer, and when we went out into the street, the temperature was lower. In other words, the energy-saving and protective screen technology that they use for windows and doors secures the family's personal environment.

After clarifying these matters to my satisfaction, I came back to the others who were impatiently expecting me and somehow amused. We started to walk down a street that had a slight slope, seeing only a few people. It was explained to us that it was early "morning" to them and most of the inhabitants in the city were in the resting cycle and sleeping.

The streets were paved with polished stone, similar to what I had seen in Tomassis. We walked to the end of the street and then on to two smaller streets until we came to a large square with a very beautiful fountain in its center. The water was bursting forth vertically into different shapes, but the interesting fact was that it was appearing only from what could best be termed the "top half," the bottom half of the spouting water being invisible. It was as if the water only materialized at the half-way point before forming into the beautiful shapes that it would then make.

The people that I was seeing on the street were neither tall nor exuberant, but I could see a refinement and kindness of their soul from the way they looked and from their happy faces. Their features were Amerindian but in a very refined form.

"The fact that we live under the light of this sun has, over time, facilitated certain structural changes in us, at all levels," the man explained. "In comparison to the sun on the surface, it is a completely different influence."

Cezar then asked him about their origin.

"We have been here for thousands of years, even before what you know as the Mayan civilization. Our ancestors are those who founded the Olmec and Toltec civilizations on the surface. A part of them remained there while others came here."

The man explained to us that this was not the only city with descendants of this lineage. Those we know in more recent times as Mayans and Incas also had ancestors who lived inside the planet, although in different areas.

"But, our city is very old and, in time, it evolved towards the center of the planet, where we are now. Here is the heart that supports everything, and here are the very tall people that some on the surface have heard of. You know very well what this is about," the man said, turning to Cezar. "We have taken on the task of showing you this way of access. In the future, it will have be shown to have a certain importance for Mankind."

Understanding that the man was referring to the world of Shambhala, I felt a profound emotion because I suddenly remembered what I had experienced in the presence of the Guardian and what I saw when he showed us the extraordinary brilliance of Shambhala and the feeling of spiritual elevation that had accompanied it. I strongly wished to see that wonderful world again, and now I was receiving the confirmation that I was now at the right place at the right time.

In perfect synchronicity, we went from the square to a main street that opened up to a view of the horizon where I could then see and recognize the magnificent beauty of the world of Shambhala. Far away, beyond a gulf that I associated with a lake, I saw the glittering of the white walls and imposing buildings of that fairy-like land. The mere fact of seeing these things gave me a feeling of dignity and extraordinary force that was subtly infused into my being, creating a state of sacredness and nostalgia that reaches out into infinity.

What I felt was a very profound force of knowledge, an unwavering weight of spiritual authority that reaches beyond any context of slippage or imbalance. I slowly bowed my head in a sincere act of humility and gratitude for the deep wisdom that is spread by the beings in this wonderful land.

Looking beyond to the horizon, I could see the slight curving of the Earth, but it was very far away and appeared more as a blurred vision that was lost in the dense blue of the sky. My intuition about the remote city was then confirmed to me by our guide as he made a wide gesture with his hand, pointing to those walls and spoke.

"There is one of the entrances to Shambhala. We'll come back a little later to admire the view."

I was vexed to see that the man was using the same name that we also use for the superior world inside the Earth, but he explained to me that the spiritual tradition of Mankind is responsible for preserving this name as a memory from ancestral times when things were different on the surface of the Earth. The name has been transmitted over eons up to the present day.

We spent a while admiring the splendid vision that stood before our eyes, after which the man invited us to go further onto the other streets of the city. I felt a very pleasant warm wind that was touching my skin and creating an extraordinary sensation of wellness throughout my being.

At first, the city created the impression of being ancient, but this only amounted to a first impression because, as my attention became focused, things seemed to change as I could now see a modern and even technologically advanced aspect. None of the buildings exceeded

GENERAL VIEW OVER SHAMBHALA FROM THE CITY OF UTKLAHA

one story in height, and the houses were adjacent to each other without any yards. Behind the houses and the main square sprawled lush forests. Nature seemed to blend very well with the activity and presence of the people.

After a detour, we arrived again in the central square where I saw some people this time. Their clothing was simple but refined. I saw that most of the men wore a sort of robe, long to the heels, split down the sides, and with pants underneath. The women wore a long dress that was tied at the waist with an elegant belt. The dress was tailored with feminine aspects and beautiful folds on the sides. Their footwear were sort of small boots that resembled galoshes except that they were a lot more elegant and had a strap on the side. Even though the footwear seemed soft, I noticed than when it hit the tiles, the bottom (of the shoe) would harden, but when biological matter, like soil or grass, was stepped on, it would mould according to that shape.

I admired the refinement of their clothing, and even though it was simple, it was very elegant and designed with good taste. For a while, I studied our two guides; and especially so because they represented a very nice couple. The woman was captivating through the harmony of her form and a commanding appearance, and this was doubled by reason of a great kindness emanating from her that manifested through her large eyes which were a mixture of gray and hazel. Her dark brown hair was long and curly, and she wore a round-shaped medallion without a wire at her neck. Seeing that I was interested in the symbol engraved on it, she explained that it represented a sort of coat of arms of her family's ancestry. She explained to me that the medallion adhered to her skin without being held by anything due to the resonance created between its specific vibration and the feelings in her heart. Considering that I was in the lofty atmosphere of the etheric plane, such phenomena seemed perfectly explicable to me as it was more energetic in nature and less material.

Their garments were not representative of what others wore. When we arrived at the fountain in the square, I saw people wearing tight clothing. I figured out that those people were preoccupied by a certain activity that we would equate to sports in our world. A short distance in front of us, one of the men was moving pretty fast toward the sea, probably to swim or to engage in a similar activity.

Watching with greater attention, I noticed that we were actually on the edge of the city which stretched far to our right. From where we were located, the village seemed to lie on a peninsula that extended deep into the sea, and on the horizon, we saw the realm of Shambhala with its walls and other buildings beyond it. Looking to the right, toward the city, I noticed several high-rise buildings that had a special architectural line, though not necessarily futuristic. I realized then that the closer they were to the city center, the higher were the buildings.

I then turned my gaze to the sky and watched it more carefully. Their sun was exactly overhead at its zenith and was not changing its position. Even if it was not easy, I could look at it without being blinded because the intensity of its light is about two-thirds of our sun. Its size was also smaller, about half of the diameter of the solar disc that we see in our sky. The light was gentle and the air warm, like it would be during May or June. Since we arrived here, however, I noticed that the air had less oxygen than we have on our surface world, but its lack was totally compensated for by the subtle energy it contained. Our guide explained to us that this was due to the special radiation of the sun inside our Earth that is actually the etheric manifestation of the black hole in the center.

The sky was not blue as we see it on the surface but more like a combination of blue, white and grey, making it appear somewhat diffused. The light itself seemed to be "milky" as if it were comforting each shape on the skyline by putting into a protective covering. I also saw clouds in the sky that were appearing in clearer shapes than those of the sky in Tomassis.

The man told us that we were on a peninsula that extended into the ocean. I was surprised to hear this term, but he confirmed that it is an immense ocean and that other areas of the planet's interior still have large expanses of water, lakes and even seas. I already had experienced this in Tomassis where I saw that great sea or what was at least a large lake. In addition, I knew about the suspicions of scientists and their measurements attesting to the existence of an inner ocean, so I could easily understand this, however, the term "ocean" seemed amazing to me at that time, especially because the waves that I saw were very small. The man explained that this is due to the special configuration of the land in this region of the peninsula which forms a gulf, thus protecting the shore from bigger waves.

I am inclined to believe that the water of this ocean is sweet, even though I cannot say this with certainty. Generally speaking, I figured out that you are allowed to ask what they want you to know, and if you want to also ask other questions afterwards, something seems to stop you. The situation was somewhat similar in which a group visits a museum and listens to the explanations of the guide. You can ask two or three questions, but after that, you are beholden to the direction of the guide and the agenda that he is there to serve. Therefore, I did not ask anything about the water in the ocean, but I felt a certain internal knowledge, specific to that plane in which we were and where things happen differently than at the surface; and somehow, I knew that the water was still different than the ocean water on the surface, thinking it to be sweet and salty at the same time. I also knew that the specific energetic quality of the water was caused by the action of the sun in their sky, just the way the air has a special energetic charge in it.

In the meantime, we walked down that street and arrived at the ocean beach that was covered with clean white sand. Several small and sparse cliffs were pleasantly contrasting with the gentle glare of the sand. At the end of the stone-paved road, beyond which was the sand of the beach, there were several shrubs surrounding the area.

I gazed wildly beyond the bay at the splendor of those buildings and the white walls that meant the entrance area into the realm of Shambhala. Being a little closer to that land and having a completely free and clear perspective without the obstruction of other buildings, I was able to better see some of the features of that sublime realm. The buildings were tall, bright and transparent, seeming to be made of diamond. They were imposing, with bold shapes and spiral features being dominant. This time, however, I could see with greater clarity that behind those majestic buildings were other constructions, but it was as if they were hidden in some kind of halo through which I could not distinguish too well. I asked the guide what that the halo is and what it was hiding.

"The halo is unique to your perception," the man answered me. "It represents the limit to which your consciousness can understand what it sees. Beyond this limit, it can no longer perceive the vibrational frequency of what is there and that is why it appears occulted or hidden to you. I, however, clearly see that reality and so does your friend."

I knew that Cezar had been to Shambhala many times in the past, but he never opened up on this subject, and I felt it was a barrier that must be respected and so I did not insist on asking him about it. I felt a great joy for him, and I was hoping that now, as my experience became richer, I would find out more from him, aspiring to go to that realm myself.

The man continued with his explanations.

"Still, even among the inhabitants of our city, there are few who have the capacity of seeing "beyond the halo." The majority see it just the way you are perceiving it now. People only see the entrance areas of these buildings that you are looking at now, and they cross the gulf often to go there to receive teachings and spiritual training. It is like an apprenticeship zone because it only signifies the entrance zone to the realm of Shambhala. In order to effectively get to Shambhala, you need to be in the region that you see far away, covered by a 'halo.'"

Even though I understood the principle of what he had said, I still remained attached to certain conceptions and tendencies that are inoculated into the existence of the physical plane. For example, I wanted to know what precisely would happen if someone were to go to the peripheral zone of Shambhala; and from there, continue on their way to the halo in order arrive inside that fabled destination.

Looking slightly amused, he appreciated the innocence of me asking that question and he answered me.

"Even if someone were to do that, one would find oneself on the mountain or in the forest. You cannot know something that you are not yet ready to know. This is the reason why many of our peers go to that apprentice zone of Shambhala, like a spiritual school, through which they evolve and refine their consciousness. Later, they become capable of accessing the consciousness plane of Shambhala and enter the territory."

Still, it was not too clear if other beings from other zones and cities inside the Earth were also coming to this region. It seemed to me that the commuting required would be too complicated.

"Perhaps it is easy for people here to have access," I asked, "but for others inside or even at the surface, it seems that they would have a difficult time accessing these learning sessions. I imagine there are no collective excursions."

"You judge such things in the spirit of physical laws, but here things are totally different, especially regarding this realm that many of you on the surface consider to be legendary or mythical. You see it with your own eyes. It is as real as possible, even if you do not have access to anything other than a small part of it. What many people cannot understand, however, is the fact that Shambhala is not located somewhere precisely. It is indeed an independent stand-alone world, but it has branches in different places so that those who are prepared can enter into this realm whether they are from the other side of the internal cavity of the Earth or from other cities or worlds, including the surface of the planet."

"And how do they do it?" I asked, very interested.

"Through certain dimensional gates, like the one through which you also came here, to Utklaha."

I remained thoughtful, telling myself that anyone could have stumbled upon such an inter-dimensional gate. The man immediately picked up my mental inference and he corrected me.

"Apparently, you could say so; but in reality, things are totally different. The access is very strictly controlled, and it is not a mechanical or automatic process as you might think. For example, in order to have access, it is not enough to know that there is an opening to the world of Shambhala in some particular place. Even if you get to the place where you know a gate exists, you still cannot pass unless you know certain rules of its cyclicity or of its specific position. Besides that, there are also guardians of such special places."

All of a sudden, the memories of my recent travel and the meeting with the Guardian encompassed me.

"Are you such a guardian?" I asked our guide sincerely.

"I received this task from the wise men. I keep an eye on the passing from the surface to the world of Shambhala through the gate by which you came. They announce to me who should come here and who should not. It is a task that I have assumed with my family."

"Was it imposed? Is it like a job or something else, like a service?' I asked, curious to know how things are there.

"It is neither a job nor a sport nor an occasional habit. It is a natural attitude, something that develops naturally according to one's degree of understanding. No one is imposing anything to someone else here."

I then thought of our condition on the surface world and the manipulation, lies and oppression existing almost everywhere in all sorts of shapes and sizes and compared it to the silence, calm, and wisdom ruling here inside the Earth, near Shambhala. Who would want go back to "prison"? But still, things have a purpose of their own and there is a certain order of things that has to be respected.

Before I could go further with my philosophy, the man beckoned me with his hand, making an invitation to continue our way back to the city. With the streets still relatively empty, we walked like this for a few minutes with our guide a bit ahead and his wife always on my left, but a bit behind. I perceived her wonderful, sweet and dignified presence; and at the same time, a delicacy that emphasized her strong personality. She brought gentleness, affection, femininity, and harmony into our group and I could feel it clearly.

We approached the mountainous part of the city, and on the left side of the beach and the bay, the man pointed to the horizon. Looking carefully, I was able to notice, even if rather blurred, the ample internal curvature of the Earth, but only on a relatively small scale. Even so, the feeling was overwhelming. I saw everything as a gigantic blue-tinted structure, even though it seemed to be aerated due to the great distance to it.

"Only from this angle can you see the inner curvature of the Earth and only if it is clear and without clouds. It cannot be seen from other areas due to the light and radius, but if you look right here, the light falls in a certain way and you can understand that you are inside the planet."

I could only vaguely see the curvature on the horizon when I looked to the realm of Shambhala near the beach, but from here, you could see it so much better and from a greater height, even though it was a great distance away. Theoretically, the curvature should be observable from any point or city inside the gigantic cavity in the center of the planet, but in practice, there is no difference to the way in which we see it at the surface: the line of the horizon is closed before the eye clearly perceives the curvature. On the surface, it is downwards and we cannot see it. Inside, it is upwards, but the nature of the light and the distance makes it fade away almost completely.

When you are inside the Earth in the immense subtle or ethereal cavity in its center, a very special feeling arises, a certain experience that cannot be mistaken or compromised. The most appropriate depiction of that emotion is that you feel protected. Apparently, someone on the surface world might harbor the consideration that, once one gets inside the planet, they would feel either constrained, limited, or sealed to the degree they cannot see the stars or the sky and cannot have the sensation of open air. With regard to this, there is no such problem for the inhabitants of the center of the Earth because, as our guide explained to me, their spiritual level allows them to understand

and to feel to a certain measure that the Universe is in themselves. From this point of view, they do not have to see the stars in the sky to know or to feel that they exist in the immensity of cosmic space. In a way, it is like the issue of happiness: you cannot find true happiness in the exterior world no matter how much you search for it, but only when you go inside your being do you get to its springs. A hermit, surrounded by the rock of the mountain where he cannot see the stars in the sky, never suffers because of remaining motionless for years in his cave. Neither does he suffer from claustrophobia or from not having enough space. His very rich inner spiritual experience brings him much more knowledge and sensation than all the stars in the sky.

Being there, in the cavity of the center of the Earth, I felt a sensation of protection, wellness and safety. I was not scared and now better understood the psychology of the inhabitants inside the planet who feel very free and content. They live in a total symbiosis with nature, without intervening with it such as occurs on the surface; and from what I could figure out, violence does not exist.

The man turned to us, making a gesture to move on. We turned to the square and then saw more people on the streets as well as vehicles, the first I had seen. They were anti-gravitational and resembled small uncovered or open capsules, moving through the air at about one meter in height without any noise other than the swish of their passing through the air. Apparently, I could say that the person sitting down inside was driving the vehicle, but in fact, I did not see any steering wheel or joysticks. Instead, what I noticed was like a sort of computerized board, but I cannot be sure on this detail because I did not get closer to the vehicle.

The guide then showed us other vehicles in the sky that were a lot bigger and were flying at a great height. They had a tubular and cylindrical shape and were probably used to transport goods and people. Along with the intensification of the aerial activity, the atmosphere in the city took on more of a technical air, and, at the time, it induced a state of spiritual exaltation. The big cylindrical vehicles in the sky had different routes at different heights and some of them were heading right to Shambhala. I also saw other smaller flying vehicles amongst them of different shapes. All of those shuttles were flying rectilinear, but at different elevations. This intensification of aerial activity, combined with seeing the bright majestic buildings of Shambhala, created in me a very strong feeling what would be thought of as futuristic. Still, almost the only sounds that I heard were natural ones and sometimes, on the rare occasions when we spoke, our voices, because most of the conversations were telepathic. The flora and fauna assured the general sonorous background sound. I was hearing and seeing insects flying, the water of the ocean swishing, the murmur of the trees, and the squeal of some birds that resemble pterodactyls from ages passed, but these were of smaller sizes.

While I was looking at that pretty intense aerial activity, I saw an immense vertical vortex starting to appear. It resembled the vortex of a tornado in certain aspects, but the foot of the "funnel" was erect. Around the funnel, along its length, there were several rings. The vortex was huge and darker in color than the rest of the clouds, creating a mysterious but terrible power.

I saw the foot of the funnel come near the ground, but it did not touch it. Then, almost immediately, I saw three shuttles, one very big and two smaller ones, accompany it, coming from above through the opening of the funnel and then moving out into the atmosphere of the city. They had the shape of a lens and the big one was like a double lens. The shuttles headed to the right and towards the center of the city which was quite a big distance from where we were.

Astounded, I watched this phenomena as I heard our guide talking as he pointed to the vortex.

"There is what you on the surface say is the geographic South Pole. The vortex represents the passing zone; and it opens up at precise moments when certain magnetic fields are aligning themselves. We know precisely when these important moments occur."

At the beginning, I was surprised to hear his voice which was gentle and warm but strong. I perfectly understood what he said to me, but I was hearing the sounds of a language that I did not know. I recognized it is Mayan, but it was probably a derivative or evolved version of it. Recovering from the initial surprise, I focused myself once again on the problem of the vortex. I thought that the countless mysteries and weird stuff that has occurred in Antarctica, among which is the memorable experience of Admiral Byrd, are not at all coincidental and can now be confirmed.

"In other words, are we just about under the South Pole now?" I asked, almost not believing.

"Yes," he answered, "on an approximate vertical line."

"This means that anyone passing through there arrives through the vortex to here?"

Cezar intervened.

"Only if they allow it. You know, we discussed this before."

"That is correct," said our guide. "The vortex opens only at certain moments and just in certain conditions. It is not a constant phenomenon."

"Indeed," I responded. "I have already discussed the problem with Cezar and it could be applicable in this case. On the surface, vertically, when someone in the physical plane passes through that point, they do not feel anything special if the subtle connection is not made. But, if you are in a more elevated state of consciousness, and if the wise men of Shambhala allow your access, then slowly, small step by small step, you get in, even though you did not even notice it at the beginning. But, after a while, you see how the landscape starts to change. The snow gradually disappears and vegetation appears in its place. You can see even animals. Then, at that point, you are already inside the Earth."

The man then spoke to me.

"There are two possibilities: either we are the ones allowing the access or asking for it, as it was in your case; or he or she is already a pretty evolved spiritually being that can 'catch' the necessary state to get into our world. At the same time, it is their right and their merit."

"Is this also valid for entering the realm of Shambhala?" I asked.

"Of course. It is just that there are some successive stages. The world of Shambhala is 'stratified' with a hierarchy of different levels, like rings. If you envision a ring-like structure, you get only to the ring that corresponds to your consciousness at a particular moment."

I was astounded, and at the same time, a bit discouraged. I was not even allowed access beyond the first wall, it representing the entrance to Shambhala, or the first ring, never mind further access to the center which, as I understood from our guide, represents the Supreme Wisdom.

"You need to understand that these rings are like energetic barriers that you cannot overcome unless you have the necessary preparation," the man specified, probably noticing that my understanding was not exactly correct but inclined to the same type of physical interpretation as in the surface world that made me think of the rings as concentric walls.

"You get deeper according to your level of consciousness," the man also specified. "There have been some civilizations in your world that have applied the same ring structure as a physical construction, but its profound significance is subtle in nature and refers to the barriers corresponding to the level of consciousness."

From here, the discussion extended to the level of knowledge and technology possessed by the diverse community inside the Earth as well as the planes of consciousness that they have access to. This, however, presented a problem to me that had been bothering me for a while, and I thought it was proper to bring it up as this point.

I knew from my discussions with Dr. Xien and Cezar that, as you go to the center of the planet, the vibrational frequency rises and the planes of manifestation culminate with the causal plane in the center of the planet. Logically, the realm of Shambhala is an exponent of the highest frequencies and that is exactly why I saw it right in the center of the Earth. Still, I was not succeeding to explain to myself how this is possible since Utklaha exists only in the etheric plane, even if it does possess a high frequency. In my opinion, there was not sufficient space with which to measure a certain proportionality of manifestation in order to explain the jump from the etheric to the causal. We were in the etheric plane, and I was seeing Shambhala over the gulf, the symbol of life and spiritual illumination. To me, it seemed "too close" and that's why, while we were ambling to the house of the man and woman, I asked Cezar a question, in a bit of a whisper.

"We are in the center of the planet and we are still talking about the etheric plane? Where do the astral, mental and causal planes of the planet compress?"

Cezar seemed to make an effort to understand what I actually meant. After a few seconds, he spoke up and answered me but with a bit of admonishment in his voice.

"You are thinking too mechanically about things. Penetrating the subtle planes as you move further into the center of the Earth cannot be treated strictly with reference to dimensional measures, such as in kilometers. You see the entrance to Shambhala from here, where the frequency is a lot higher, and apparently, you are only a stone's throw away from this realm, in the etheric plan. Logic tells you that Shambhala should also be in the etheric plane, or at least at an entrance to the astral plane, because it is very close and there is not enough space, proportionally speaking, to account for passage to the superior planes: the astral, mental, and causal. In reality, however, this is a problem of manifesting quality: namely the vibrational frequency, and not a matter of quantity (dimension). You are thinking quantitatively when, actually, the problem is referring to a qualitative point of view. You do not measure the distance between the ethereal and causal in terms of meters."

His explanation clarified once more how important it is that, when we think about the subtle and spiritual aspects, we do not let our minds be fixated only upon the laws of the physical plane and the attitudes and prejudices that accompany such.

In the meanwhile, we were heading to the house of the family, and we arrived there in a short period of time. As we walked, the man had the time to tell us that the cities inside the Earth exist at different depths and each one, including those in the central cavity, have their own personality, knowledge, tradition, and level of consciousness. Even if these are connected and they communicate, each structures its existence on its origin and individuality.

As we all entered the house and entered into the big room, I was drawn to the bookcase, near one of the walls. I continued to know that the bookcase was there, but I was not seeing anything on the wall there. Seeing that my attention was fixed on this, the woman came closer to the wall and made a gentle gesture with her hand, like a fan, whereupon an apparition gave itself away and allowed me to see that bookcase. The space that the shelves occupied was not big, and the books had a special format. Curious, I got closer and took out one of these books, none of which resembled what we are used to. The pages or leafs were much thicker and the books here generally had the appearance of a carrying case with CDs (compact digital discs).

Each "leaf" represented a domain or a history covering a long period of time. For example, when I examined such a book "sheet," it covered the history of Mankind for nearly a thousand years. The sheets were actually "states of knowledge" that were accessed or "dipped into" by simply touching the hand of the leaf. I told myself that what I was seeing here was even more technologically advanced than the archives from the occult chamber in Egypt, to which I have had access to during my travel through the First Tunnel. It was no longer about holographic projections nor about watching images. Everything was perceived by a direct interaction between that book and one's consciousness. You knew and you understood the informational content on the page. I rapidly figured out that this also involves an extraordinary efficient process of inter activity. I could enter in the informational content and select what I wished to know. This could be applied in a general way or in a detailed manner, all depending upon what interested me.

I discovered all this in just few seconds of manipulating one of the books in the bookcase. It was a much advanced and somewhat "empathic" knowledge that allowed for easier assimilation of information. I felt there were books about medicine, history, culture, science, construction, and many other areas.

The first book that I took off the shelf was on medicine, and by merely keeping it in my hand, I knew what that treatise was on: mainly, bones and the skeleton. I felt this was general information. If I wanted to know something in detail or to look for precise data, the information would become much more detailed; and this way, the study could begin. I put the book back and I took another that was on the human culture and civilization of the entire planet. When I opened it, I immediately understood the way in which the information was structured, and it was almost like a verbal process. If I was choosing a year, there was synthesized knowledge of what happened in different parts of the world at that time period, such as in China, Europe, America and in other areas. It was like a global history, an overview of the historical course of Mankind. I noticed that this history did not present just the important events that took place only on the surface of the planet but also the ones occurring in the cities and communities existing inside of it, as they also have their own history and evolution. Insisting upon this aspect, I was curious to find out more about Utklaha. That "leaf" covered a period of hundreds of years of history, starting with the year 1100 A.D., and it gave me information about events in the Orient, Spain, and Britain; but I rapidly focused on the history of the city in the center of the planet and understood that the inhabitants of this city were at that point already experimenting with antigravity technology in their shuttles. This eventually evolved into the technology that I saw in Utklaha. While the soldiers and knights of the Early Middle Ages had been occupied with wars and the Crusades specific to our history, those inside the Earth had already applied levitation and had already realized the first longer travels with their shuttles, contacting other superior beings in the process.

I was curious to find out what had happened before this, and I returned the book and picked another which documented a history from an older period. When I touched that leaf, I was acquiring the knowledge of that book, but at the same time, I also saw correlating images. The leafs had "writing" on them that were actually some signs with a bit of relief. When they were touched by the fingers, the information seemed to "flow" into the consciousness where it was also "seen" by it. I was effectively living the information that I was receiving, seeing the correlating images with it; and at the same time, I was perfectly aware of the ambience of the chamber that I was in and also of what I was doing at the time. In a very pleasant and interesting way, my consciousness was accessing multidimensional levels and it made possible a special knowledge to which I could have access in a very special way.

Interested to find out how Utklaha appeared, I then knew and saw at the same time that, about 2300 years ago, there was only a simple village or hamlet in the area in which I was, placed in the middle of the forest. Almost everything around was only forest. I also understood that the first ones who lived there were from the Olmecs and Toltecs. These were the witch doctors and wise men of them who had access to esoteric knowledge and to the portals that allowed them to get inside and to establish the first houses, being practically the first settlement in that region. Then, little by little, others arrived here and became citizens of their civilization. At a certain point, I saw a massive increase in population, but the city was already evolved by then. When I was "reading" this way, it was not as if I was reading line by line from a regular publication. The history that I was finding out was pretty dynamic and I think that I was actually covering it from one century to another so that I then had a global perception over an extended period of time. I figured out the subtle dexterity of how to "read" this way, but it being the first time that I did it and with no further time available, I could not investigate anything in detail. I could have accomplished this, however, because I noticed that there was "writing" on these leafs; and if I looked more carefully — it was a little pointed and in relief format — I saw that it became finer and finer with the information becoming more and more thorough.

I then perceived a telepathic transmission from the man saying that the time of our departure was coming. I closed the book, put it back on the shelf, and the woman also made a gesture by hand as that apparition or "film projection" that covered the book case disappeared from sight. I the saw a girl coming from the upper floor, descending down the stairs. The woman introduced her as their daughter. She was seventeen years old and she was indeed beautiful, combining more features from her mother than from her father: the same long and curly hair, the same color of the eyes, and the same dignified and delicate air that the woman had. Her body was very harmonious and well proportioned, emanating the energy specific to her age. As far as I could tell, she had inherited from her father the structure of her nose and mouth, for here the physical features were similar.

We were introduced as coming out of the "outer curve" which I thought sounded interesting because it was the first time that I heard the way that they relate to our world. Greeting us, the girl looked at us with some curiosity, then went on and left the house, heading for the square.

I then knew that we had returned to the surface. The man came near to the door in the wall through which we had arrived, and he opened it because it was the only door in the house that was normal and like the doors in our world. It was completely dark beyond it, and this at first caused my heart to beat strongly. The man then made a sign as he entered into the darkness, followed by Cezar and then me. The woman came after me, and I heard her closing the door.

In the moment during which we walked in that darkness, the surrounding environment lightened up. I saw the corridor that was a few meters long, like a niche, and then the cave as we went backwards through all of the various stages that we had passed through when we came. These different stages or zones were characterized either by moisture, heat, or crystals. When we arrived in the high temperature zone, just like upon our arrival, I entered a trance-like state in which I maintained lucidity, but everything around me seemed to be moving in slow-motion.

At a certain point, after having the false sensation of ascending, even though I was on level ground, I arrived at the front of the cave exit. Cezar and our guide were outside, and a bit further, in about the same place where we had left him, the shaman was waiting. The woman arrived behind me. The visit to the center of the Earth had not lasted long, but it was full of information and wonderful moments.

The two guides slightly bowed their heads to us, a sign of goodbye, and then reentered the cave, disappearing from our sight. The shaman led us to our vehicle, but he refused to let us give him a lift to the city, so we returned to El Calafate and the hotel where we had booked a room. Still feeling like I was in a trance, I wished only to sleep and I did so until the next morning.

I noticed that after every return from a journey inside the Earth, I felt somewhat like an outsider to the surface world for some time. I was talking less and sleeping more, but after two or three days, everything was back to normal. Cezar told me that those sensations would disappear after several trips because my body would gradually adapt to the vibrational characteristics of the interior of our planet. Although the long flight home prolonged my condition, everything went back to normal after I arrived at the Base.

It took me a month to sort out my notes and sketches about the trips I had made inside the Earth and also to establish with Cezar what I am permitted to say. While I was dealing with all of this, I also took care of the last details of organizing a very important expedition to Iraq.

The travels that I made to the inside of the planet brought about a major transformation of my knowledge and understanding of the world. They have paved the road to amazing experiences and revelations that have given me long searched for answers. All we have to do is give up on dogmatic thinking and follow the intuition from our heart.

EPILOGUE

While the book you have just read required a relatively short amount of time to read, quite literally thousands of man hours have gone into the translation, editing and production process, not all of it by myself. I bring this up because, as the editor and publisher of the English edition of Radu Cinamar's various works, I feel it is incumbent upon me to give some context with regard to the information presented in this book.

I have now been a publisher and author for over a quarter of a century. Never in that time have I ever met with so much difficulty in bringing a work to fruition. It is not that my other publications have been easy, as some required years of research and adroit mental gymnastics to complete. *Inside the Earth — The Second Tunnel*, however, wins the prize with regard to being the most challenging. These difficulties extended across a very wide panorama of factors ranging from the translation process to the finer contractual details. There were also other business priorities and personal factors that contributed to the slow launch of this unique and rather remarkable work, but these aspects were minimal compared to the raw inertia that had to be overcome to get the actual translation done. For example, after the original Romanian book was published, it took me eight months to get an actual copy of it in my hand and at least another six months to receive the digital files and work out the details of the contract. The translation, however, proceeded from the time I received the original book. This process was extremely cumbersome for a variety of reasons; and perhaps it would have gone like clock work if my familiar Romanian translator was not having a baby. It is not important, however, to bore you with details but only to inform you that I was opposed by various factors which, in the final analysis, can best be identified as psychic resistance. In other words, it was as if various forces did not want this book to come into print.

If I were to share details of what happened, you would readily counter with logical solutions that should have been employed. In such instances, your ideas would be correct. In practice, however, logical procedures and strategies produced inadequate responses or solutions. The good news, however, is that all of these difficulties have been overcome. I do not expect such ridiculous problems in the future and that applies to the translation process as well. It is as if a barrier has been crossed, and a not insignificant barrier.

I do think, however, it is advisable to add more context, not only in regard to the difficulties encountered in publishing this book, but also with respect to the phenomena and circumstances that it presents.

Although many Romanians are well-educated, speak English and share many Western customs, there is a huge chasm between their culture and that of America. When we bring in the esoteric factors, there is an even greater chasm. While I am referring to the issues which both Cezar and Radu bring up in this entire series of books, there are also other esoteric factors that they do not mention. Ever since Dr. David Anderson brought me to Romania in 2008, I have sought to bridge this chasm as best I could in order to share the live spiritual legacy of an ancient and mysterious land which has been overlooked, obfuscated and even vilified.

The main point here is that if a book is this hard to produce, it is an indication that there is something worthwhile inside; and perhaps more to the point, such trials and tribulation are indicative of what is known as initiation in the esoteric world. Whether you liked or resonated with this book or not, you have been introduced to an entirely new world as well as a new way to think about it. This is the gift of Radu Cinamar.

With regard to my personnel correspondence with Radu, he went silent in 2011. This was after a message when he told me to expect a visit from his mysterious friend, Elinor. That meeting never happened; but the reason for it was that I was personally not ready. That will change in the near future.

I did finally hear from Radu this year, in June of 2018. He answered personal questions I had about Elinor in a letter written a year before. Radu also wanted to know why the book had not come out yet and if I had a problem with the content (I did not, save the ordeal involved in getting it translated). Additionally, he apologized for his long hiatus in communicating as well as the fact that he would be mostly inaccessible for the near future. What he did offer me, however, proved insightful (regarding a personal matter).

As for the future, Radu plans to write at least another six books or so; and while such a proposition is always subject to change, his Romanian publisher told me that he expects Radu's next book to be published in the Romanian language in early 2019. It will be released about the same time this English edition of Inside the Earth hits the shelves in America.

Whether you believe the information herein or not, Radu has presented an incredible paradigm that can be either ignored, rejected, or appreciated and used as a template by which to seek out your own evolution. It is my opinion that if we are to be either so clever or lucky to engineer our lives in such a manner that we might have similar experiences to Radu, we had best do a lot of personal work on ourselves. In the meantime, I will respond as rapidly as possible to any new work that is presented by Radu Cinamar.

Peter Moon
Long Island
November 3, 2018

THE TRANSYLVANIAN SERIES

TRANSYLVANIAN SUNRISE is the story of an unprecedented archeological discovery beneath the Romanian Sphinx in the Bucegi Mountains. Radu Cinamar visits this secret site where he witnessed a holographic Hall of Records left by an advanced civilization and three mysterious tunnels leading deep into the bowels of the Inner Earth. *Transylvanian Sunrise* chronicles the political intrigue surrounding the discovery of these artifacts which represents the dawn of a new era for Mankind.
288 pages, ISBN 978-0-9678162-5-8..............................**$22.00**

TRANSYLVANIAN MOONRISE corroborates Radu's story with newspaper articles as he is sought out by a mysterious Tibetan Lama who takes Radu on a mystical journey to Tibet where he receives a secret initiation and a sacred manuscript from the blue goddess Machandi. This is an initiation of the highest order that will take you far beyond your ordinary imagination in order to describe events that have molded the past and will influence the future in the decades ahead.
288 pages, ISBN 978-0-9678162-8-9...................................**$22.00**

MYSTERY OF EGYPT features an expedition to explore the First Tunnel in the holographic chamber: the one to Egypt. Ancient artifacts are discovered which tell the history of the Earth in holographic form, the most controversial of which include remarkable adventure that includes explorations in time to the First Century A.D. This book also includes updates from Cezar since their last meeting.
240 pages, ISBN 978-1-937859-08-4...................................**$22.00**

THE SECRET PARCHMENT — FIVE TIBETAN INITIATION TECHNIQUES presents invaluable techniques for spiritual advancement that came to Radu Cinamar in the form of an ancient manuscript whose presence in the world ignited a series of quantum events, extending from Jupiter's moon Europa and reaching all the way to Antarctica, Mount McKinley and Transylvania. An ancient Romanian legend comes alive as a passage way of solid gold tunnels, extending miles in the Transylvanian underground is revealed to facilitate super-consciousness as well as lead to the nexus of Inner Earth where "All the Worlds Unite."
288 pages, ISBN 978-0-9678162-5-8...**$22.00**

THE WHITE BAT — THE ALCHEMY OF WRITING
Told in a personal narrative, Peter Moon relates how he was being drawn to Transylvania via the dream of a white bat, long before he became involved with Montauk, only discover that there are actual white bats in Transylvania that are unknown to science. This book synthesizes the dream process with the creative process and teaches you to do the same.
288 pages, ISBN 978-1-937859-15-2...................................**$22.00**

THE STORY BEHIND THE STORY

(How Radu Cinamar's Works Came to be Published)

Radu Cinamar's books include some of the most uplifting tales imaginable, more often than not leaving the reader with a desire to experience what the author has put forth. His most recent book, *Inside the Earth — The Second Tunnel*, teaches us that a significant ascendancy in consciousness is required to even begin to penetrate these fantastic realms. The potential that his work represents makes his books some of the most positive in the entire history of literature.

It is important to note, however, that it was only after the *The Montauk Project: Experiments in Time* was published in the Romanian language that Radu Cinamar sought to have his original manuscript (*Transylvanian Sunrise* in English) published.

The way this came to pass was when Sorin Hurmuz was working as an editor at a major Romanian publishing house and his boss asked him to review *The Montauk Project* in order to see if it was suitable for publishing in Romanian. Although Sorin advised him to do so, the publisher declined and Sorin responded by opening his own publishing house, Daksha, in order to publish *The Montauk Project*. It was only as a result of this that Radu saw the Romanian version and approached the publisher via the internet. A deal to publish the original manuscript was soon arranged.

It should not be too much of a surprise that the publication of *The Montauk Project* would be the catalyst for these remarkably positive books, the reason being that the Montauk Project itself represents the antithesis of what is presented in Radu's work. It is therefore only natural that a book exposing it would be the key to bringing the incredible stories of his experiences out of the woodwork

The Montauk Project has been a very powerful instrument in waking up the world with regard to its heritage as well as the potential for the future. In celebration of the 25th anniversary of its original publication, we have released a Silver Anniversary Edition. In addition to this, there is a major media series in the works that we hope will debut in the next few years. We are also sad to comment that the release of the new edition coincides with the death of the primary author of *The Montauk Project*, Preston Nichols, who passed away on October 5, 2018. A tribute to the memory of Preston has been put up youTube. In the meantime, research into the nature of time will continue.

The Montauk Project
EXPERIMENTS IN TIME

SILVER ANNIVERSARY EDITION

A BRAND NEW VERSION

The Montauk Project was originally released in 1992, causing an uproar and shocking the scientific, academic, and journalistic communities, all of whom were very slow to catch on to the secret world that lurks beyond the superficial veneer of American civilization.

A colloquial name for secret experiments that took place at Montauk Point's Camp Hero, the Montauk Project represented the apex of extensive research carried on after World War II; and, in particular, as a result of the phenomena encountered during the Philadelphia Experiment of 1943 when the United States Navy attempted to achieve radar invisibility.

ISBN 978-1-937859-21-3 $22.00

The Montauk Project attempted to study why and how human beings, when exposed to high powered electromagnetic waves, suffered mental disorientation, physical dissolution or even death. A further ramification of this phenomena is that such electromagnetic waves rescrambled components of the material universe itself. According to reports, this research not only included successful attempts to manipulate matter and energy but also time itself.

It has now been over twenty-five years since *The Montauk Project* originally appeared in print. In this *Silver Anniversary Edition*, you will not only read the original text, accompanied by commentary which includes details that could not be published at the original time of publication, but also an extensive summary of a twenty-five year investigation of the Montauk Project which culminated in actual scientific proof of time travel capabilities.

ORDER TODAY FROM SKY BOOKS

THE ASTONISHING SEQUEL

MONTAUK REVISITED: ADVENTURES IN SYNCHRONICITY pursues the mysteries of time brought to light in The Montauk Project and unmasks the occult forces behind the science and technology used in the Montauk Project. An ornate tapestry is revealed which interweaves the mysterious associations of the Cameron clan with the genesis of American rocketry and the magick of Aleister Crowley and Jack Parsons. Montauk Revisited carries forward with the Montauk investigation and unleashes a host of incredible characters and new information.
249 PAGES, ILLUSTRATIONS, PHOTOS AND DIAGRAMS.......................$19.95

THE ULTIMATE PROOF

PYRAMIDS OF MONTAUK: EXPLORATIONS IN CONSCIOUSNESS awakens the consciousness of humanity to its ancient history and origins through the discovery of pyramids at Montauk and their placement on sacred Native American ground leading to an unprecedented investigation of the mystery schools of Earth and their connection to Egypt, Atlantis, Mars and the star Sirius. An astonishing sequel to the Montauk Project and Montauk Revisited, this chapter of the legend propels us far beyond the adventures of the first two books and stirs the quest for future reality and the end of time as we know it.
256 PAGES, ILLUSTRATIONS, PHOTOS AND DIAGRAMS.......................$19.95

THE BLACK SUN

THE BLACK SUN: MONTAUK'S NAZI-TIBETAN CONNECTION explores the intriguing connection between the Montauk Project and the Nazi-Tibetan alliance. This includes the connection to advanced technology at Brookhaven Labs at Yaphank which also boasted the largest contingent of Nazis outside of Germany. Photos are included of the mysterious Vril flying craft build before and during World War II. All of this leads to the Third Reich's quest for holy relics and a penetrating look in the secret meaning behind the Egyptian and Tibetan "Books of the Dead."
256 pages, ILLUSTRATIONS, PHOTOS AND DIAGRAMS.......................$24.95

Spandau Mystery

A historical novel by Peter Moon which reveals how the mysterious deaths of General George Patton and Deputy Fuhrer Rudolph Hess were intertwined through the Nazi's secret flying saucer technology, as the Germans, directed by Tibetan elders, sought to harness the Vril, an energy so powerful that it can change the very nature of the elements themselves. *350 pages*..........................*$22.00*

The Montauk Pulse

If you would like to receive updates on the continued adventures of Peter Moon and associated subjects such as the discoveries of Radu Cinamar and updates on time control scientist, Dr. David Anderson, you should subscribe to the Montauk Pulse newsletter which will also feature updates on these subjects and other key developments, including the Montauk Project itself. The Montauk Pulse has remained in print and has been issued quarterly since 1993. The Pulse directly contributes to the efforts of the authors in writing more books and chronicling the effort to understand time and all of its components. Past support has been crucial to what has developed thus far. To subscribe, send $20.00 to Sky Books, PO Box 769, Westbury, NY 11590. If order is from outside the U.S., please add $12.00 for shipping. You can also subscribe via PayPal to *skybooks@yahoo.com* or visiting *www.skybooksusa.com*.

The Time Travel Education Center

The Time Travel Education Center was created in 2015 in order to educate the public on the simple math and science behind the concept of time travel (with free videos) and also to keep people informed on related aspects to this very avant-garde and rarified subject. You can find out more about the Time Travel Education Center and become either a paid subscriber or a free member by going to *timetraveleducationcenter.com*.

Sky Books

For more information on these or additional titles or to purchase books (also, see order form at back of book), please visit:

www.skybooksusa.com

Sky Books   ORDER FORM

We wait for ALL checks to clear before shipping. This includes Priority Mail orders. If you want to speed delivery time, please send a U.S. Money Order or use MasterCard or Visa. Those orders will be shipped right away. Complete this order form and send with payment or credit card information to:
Sky Books, Box 769, Westbury, New York 11590-0104

Name	
Address	
City	
State / Country	**Zip**
Daytime Phone (In case we have a question) ( )	

☐ This is my first order ☐ I have ordered before ☐ This is a new address

Method of Payment: ☐ Visa ☐ MasterCard ☐ Money Order ☐ Check

—   —   —

Expiration Date   **Signature**

TITLE	QTY	PRICE
The Montauk Pulse (1 year - no shipping US orders)...$20.00		
Montauk Project SILVER ANNIVERSARY EDITION...$22.00		
Note: There is no additonal shipping for the Montauk Pulse if you are in the United States. **Subtotal**		
For delivery in NY add 8.625% tax		
U.S. Shipping: $5.00 for 1st book plus $1.00 for 2nd, etc.		
Foreign shipping: $20 for 3 books		
Total		

Thank you for your order. We appreciate your business.